Mastering Azure Serverless Computing

A practical guide to building and deploying enterprise-grade serverless applications using Azure Functions

Lorenzo Barbieri
Massimo Bonanni

BIRMINGHAM - MUMBAI

Mastering Azure Serverless Computing

Commissioning Editor: Vijin Boricha
Acquisition Editor: Meeta Rajani
Content Development Editor: Ronn Kurien
Senior Editor: Richard Brookes-Bland
Technical Editor: Komal Karne
Copy Editor: Safis Editing
Project Coordinator: Vaidehi Sawant
Proofreader: Safis Editing
Indexer: Pratik Shirodkar
Production Designer: Nilesh Mohite

First published: November 2019

Production reference: 1211119

Published by Packt Publishing Ltd.
Livery Place
35 Livery Street
Birmingham
B3 2PB, UK.

ISBN 978-1-78995-122-6

www.packt.com

To my wife, Catia, and my son, Gioele, for their support and encouragement.
To all my extended family for their love and dedication.

– Lorenzo Barbieri

To my wife, Floriana, for her patience and support (honey, I love you).
To all my family, which has always believed in me.

– Massimo Bonanni

Packt.com

Subscribe to our online digital library for full access to over 7,000 books and videos, as well as industry leading tools to help you plan your personal development and advance your career. For more information, please visit our website.

Why subscribe?

- Spend less time learning and more time coding with practical eBooks and Videos from over 4,000 industry professionals

- Improve your learning with Skill Plans built especially for you

- Get a free eBook or video every month

- Fully searchable for easy access to vital information

- Copy and paste, print, and bookmark content

Did you know that Packt offers eBook versions of every book published, with PDF and ePub files available? You can upgrade to the eBook version at www.packt.com and as a print book customer, you are entitled to a discount on the eBook copy. Get in touch with us at customercare@packtpub.com for more details.

At www.packt.com, you can also read a collection of free technical articles, sign up for a range of free newsletters, and receive exclusive discounts and offers on Packt books and eBooks.

Contributors

About the authors

Lorenzo Barbieri specializes in cloud-native applications and application modernization on Azure and Office 365, Windows and cross-platform applications, Visual Studio, and DevOps, and likes to talk with people and communities about technology, food, and funny things.

He is a speaker, a trainer, and a public speaking coach. He has helped many students, developers, and other professionals, as well as many of his colleagues, to improve their stage presence with a view to delivering exceptional presentations.

Lorenzo works for Microsoft, in the One Commercial Partner Technical Organization, helping partners, developers, communities, and customers across Western Europe, supporting software development on Microsoft and OSS technologies.

I would like to thank Massimo for his hard work and support. I would also like to thank all the people from Packt that worked with us on the book, who were always professional and a source of encouragement. Last but not least, I would like to thank my patient wife, Catia, and my son, Gioele, for their love and support.

Massimo Bonanni specializes in cloud application development and, in particular, in Azure compute technologies. Over the last 3 years, he has worked with important Italian and European customers to implement distributed applications using Service Fabric and microservices architecture.

Massimo is an Azure technical trainer in Microsoft and his goal is to help customers utilize their Azure skills to achieve more and leverage the power of Azure in their solutions. He is also a technical speaker at national and international conferences, a Microsoft Certified Trainer, a former MVP (for 6 years in Visual Studio and Development Technologies and Windows Development), an Intel Software Innovator, and an Intel Black Belt.

I would like to thank Lorenzo for thinking of me when he began writing this book and assisting me with my first writing experience. I would also like to thank all the people from Packt that worked with us on this book, who were always professional and provided encouragement. Last, but certainly not least, I would like to thank my patient wife, Floriana, for her love and support (honey, I love you).

About the reviewer

Mikhail Veselov is a professional software developer with over 14 years' experience in .NET stack technologies, and this is the second book he has reviewed. His work with cloud-based applications began in 2011, since when he has completed a variety of projects. He holds two degrees—in math and computer science—from Saint Petersburg State University, Russia. He is also a big fan of the bass guitar and origami. You can ask him any questions at `vmatm@ya.ru`.

I want to thank all my teachers and those individuals who have helped me during my career, especially the Saint Petersburg Computer Science Center. My personal thanks go to my family, who have supported me throughout my life, and to all my friends all over the world.

Packt is searching for authors like you

If you're interested in becoming an author for Packt, please visit `authors.packtpub.com` and apply today. We have worked with thousands of developers and tech professionals, just like you, to help them share their insight with the global tech community. You can make a general application, apply for a specific hot topic that we are recruiting an author for, or submit your own idea.

Table of Contents

Section 2: Azure Functions 2.0 Deployment and Automation

Section 3: Serverless Orchestration, API Management, and Event Processing

Preface

Application development has evolved from traditional monolithic app development to using serverless options and microservices. Building highly scalable applications using a serverless approach and Azure technologies is a challenge for most organizations. *Mastering Azure Serverless Computing* covers all Azure serverless technologies, as well as both the technical and business aspects of using serverless inside Azure, showing how and when to use every technology in an effective way.

Who this book is for

This book is intended for people who already know serverless technologies but who require a more detailed understanding.

This book begins with a look at various tools that you can use to develop, test, and deploy solutions based on Azure Functions. You will learn how you can extend the Azure Functions runtime to support your custom triggers and bindings. You will also learn what programming languages Azure Functions supports, and how you can use the language extensibility to create support for your favorite language. With a strong foundation in Azure Functions 2.0, you will learn how to deploy and configure an Azure function and understand how you can test (using the dependency injection pattern inside your Azure Functions) and monitor a complete solution. You will also see how API Management and Event Grid can be used in a serverless manner. Toward the end of the book, you will get to grips with technical and cost-related best practices. The book will also show you how to use, and when to avoid, serverless in solutions that are under our control or that should incorporate parts from different sources.

By the end of the book, you will be working seamlessly with Azure Functions.

What this book covers

Chapter 1, *Developing and Running Azure Functions*, shows you what kinds of tools can be used to develop, test, and deploy a solution based on Azure Functions.

Chapter 2, *Customizing Your Azure Functions*, explains how you can implement your custom triggers and bindings to adapt Azure Functions to your requirements.

Chapter 3, *Programming Languages Supported in Azure Functions*, covers what programming languages are supported by the Azure Function runtime and how you can support your favorite programming language.

Chapter 4, *Deploying and Configuring Your Azure Functions*, explains how to deploy your Azure Functions on Azure and how you can configure them.

Chapter 5, *Leverage the Power of DevOps with Azure Functions*, explains how you can leverage the power of Azure DevOps on your Azure Functions, and how to implement a CI/CD approach in serverless technologies.

Chapter 6, *Testing and Monitoring*, shows how you can test your Azure Functions using dependency injection and how you can monitor them in a production environment.

Chapter 7, *Serverless and Containers*, explains how you can leverage the power of containerization to host Azure Functions to have high scalability on your solutions.

Chapter 8, *Orchestration as a Code – Durable Functions*, explains what Durable Functions is and how you can use it to implement a workflow using a programming language.

Chapter 9, *Orchestration as Design – Logic Apps*, covers what Logic Apps is and how you can use it to implement a workflow using a design approach.

Chapter 10, *Empowering Your Serverless API with API Management*, explains what API Management is and why it is important in a serverless world.

Chapter 11, *High-Scale Serverless Event Processing with Event Grid*, explains what Event Grid is and why it is important to implement an event-driven architecture.

Chapter 12, *Best Practices and Use Cases for Azure Serverless Computing*, differs from the other chapters in that it builds upon the technologies that you have learned and explores some best practices and use cases for Azure serverless computing.

To get the most out of this book

In this book, we assume that the reader already knows the fundamentals of serverless and serverless technologies in Azure and that they also have knowledge of C#.

Download the example code files

You can download the example code files for this book from your account at www.packt.com. If you purchased this book elsewhere, you can visit www.packtpub.com/support and register to have the files emailed directly to you.

You can download the code files by following these steps:

1. Log in or register at www.packt.com.
2. Select the **Support** tab.
3. Click on **Code Downloads**.
4. Enter the name of the book in the **Search** box and follow the onscreen instructions.

Once the file is downloaded, please make sure that you unzip or extract the folder using the latest version of:

- WinRAR/7-Zip for Windows
- Zipeg/iZip/UnRarX for Mac
- 7-Zip/PeaZip for Linux

The code bundle for the book is also hosted on GitHub at https://github.com/PacktPublishing/Mastering-Azure-Serverless-Computing. In case there's an update to the code, it will be updated on the existing GitHub repository.

We also have other code bundles from our rich catalog of books and videos available at https://github.com/PacktPublishing/. Check them out!

Download the color images

We also provide a PDF file that has color images of the screenshots/diagrams used in this book. You can download it here: https://static.packt-cdn.com/downloads/9781789951226_ColorImages.pdf.

Conventions used

There are a number of text conventions used throughout this book.

`CodeInText`: Indicates code words in text, database table names, folder names, filenames, file extensions, pathnames, dummy URLs, user input, and Twitter handles. Here is an example: "An Azure Function written in C# is a static method decorate by a `FunctionName` attribute."

A block of code is set as follows:

```
public static class SimpleExample
{
    [FunctionName("QueueTrigger")]
    public static void Run(
        [QueueTrigger("inputQueue")] string inItem,
        [Queue("outputQueue")] out string outItem,
        ILogger log)
    {
        log.LogInformation($"C# function processed: {inItem}");
    }
}
```

When we wish to draw your attention to a particular part of a code block, the relevant lines or items are set in bold:

```
public static class SimpleExample
{
    [FunctionName("QueueTrigger")]
    public static void Run(
        [QueueTrigger("inputQueue")] string inItem,
        [Queue("outputQueue")] out string outItem,
        ILogger log)
    {
        log.LogInformation($"C# function processed: {inItem}");
    }
}
```

Any command-line input or output is written as follows:

```
c:>npm install -g azure-functions-core-tools
```

Bold: Indicates a new term, an important word, or words that you see on screen. For example, words in menus or dialog boxes appear in the text like this. Here is an example: "Simply choose the menu **File** | **New** | **Project**."

Warnings or important notes appear like this.

Tips and tricks appear like this.

Get in touch

Feedback from our readers is always welcome.

General feedback: If you have questions about any aspect of this book, mention the book title in the subject of your message and email us at customercare@packtpub.com.

Errata: Although we have taken every care to ensure the accuracy of our content, mistakes do happen. If you have found a mistake in this book, we would be grateful if you would report this to us. Please visit www.packtpub.com/support/errata, selecting your book, clicking on the Errata Submission Form link, and entering the details.

Piracy: If you come across any illegal copies of our works in any form on the internet, we would be grateful if you would provide us with the location address or website name. Please contact us at copyright@packt.com with a link to the material.

If you are interested in becoming an author: If there is a topic that you have expertise in, and you are interested in either writing or contributing to a book, please visit authors.packtpub.com.

Reviews

Please leave a review. Once you have read and used this book, why not leave a review on the site that you purchased it from? Potential readers can then see and use your unbiased opinion to make purchase decisions, we at Packt can understand what you think about our products, and our authors can see your feedback on their book. Thank you!

For more information about Packt, please visit packt.com.

Section 1: Azure Functions 2.0 Fundamentals

This section shows the reader how to create an Azure Function, how it works, how to customize it, and how to use languages other than C#.

It comprises the following chapters:

- Chapter 1, *Developing and Running Azure Functions*
- Chapter 2, *Customizing Your Azure Functions*
- Chapter 3, *Programming Languages Supported in Azure Functions*

1
Developing and Running Azure Functions

Azure Functions is one of the serverless technologies offered by Azure. It allows you to run code on-demand in response to a variety of events.

In this chapter, we will provide a brief explanation of what Azure Functions is and how it works. We will also introduce all the tools you can use to create, develop, and test a solution based on Azure Functions. The first tool we will look at is Azure Functions Core Tools, which is the most important tool you can use when you start to develop your Azure Functions solution because with it you can create, test, and deploy your Azure Functions. In this chapter, you will also learn how Visual Studio and Visual Studio Code can help you to improve your developer experience and how you can use other tools to support the documentation and testing phases.

This chapter will cover the following topics:

- Introduction to Azure Functions
- Azure Functions Core Tools and the Azure Functions runtime
- Creating Azure Functions in Visual Studio and Visual Studio Code
- Using the OpenAPI specification to document the API
- Using ngrok to expose a local Azure Function on the internet
- Debugging an Azure Function both locally and remotely

Technical requirements

If you want to start to develop solutions with Azure Functions, you have to know one of the languages Azure Functions supports (at this moment in time, C#, JavaScript, Java, and Python). If you do, you'll easily be able to follow this book.

The Microsoft entry point for the Azure Functions documentation is located at `https://azure.microsoft.com/en-us/services/functions/`. Starting from there, you can find technical documentation, whitepapers, and samples, and you can navigate to the GitHub repositories for the different tools you'll encounter in this book.

Finally, you can find the source code for this book at `https://github.com/PacktPublishing/Mastering-Azure-Serverless-Computing/tree/master/Chapter01`.

Introduction to Azure Functions

The Azure Functions platform allows you to run a piece of code (basically a simple function) in response to a wide variety of events; for example, you can run code when a client makes an HTTP request or when someone puts a message into a queue.

There are two fundamental concepts to understand when approaching the world of Azure Functions—triggers and bindings:

- Triggers are what cause a function to run; they define what kind of event the function responds to. A trigger tells you how a function is called, and a function must have exactly one trigger. Triggers have associated data, which is often provided as the payload of the function, and you can use the data contained in the payload to better understand the nature of the event that wakes up your function.
- Bindings are the way functions can exchange data with other cloud services such as Storage, Queue, or Cosmos DB. Bindings are defined in a declarative way: this means that you declare what kind of binding you need (for example, you might want to manage data with a Cosmos DB instance or write data into Azure Table storage) and the Azure Functions runtime provides the actual instance to the function to manage the data.

An Azure Function can have multiple bindings, and every binding can manage data input or output (or both—binding data can be received by the function or sent by the function to the connected services). A trigger can have only the input data (a trigger only receives data from the connected services and cannot send data to the services).

In version 1.x of the Azure Functions runtime, triggers and bindings were included in the runtime itself, while in version 2.x, triggers and bindings must be added as extensions, using NuGet packages. This means that you can reference only triggers and bindings you actually need and don't need to have all the supported triggers and bindings available for Azure Functions. Furthermore, the extension approach used by version 2.x allows you to create your own triggers and bindings. The advantage of being able to implement your own triggers and bindings is to delegate to the runtime the creation and the life cycle of the instances used by the function. In essence, the runtime acts as a dependency resolver for the instances required for the function. In runtime version 2.x, the only triggers available without adding extensions as NuGet packages are `HttpTrigger` and `TimeTrigger`; they are included in the Azure Functions SDK.

At the time of writing this book, the languages supported by Azure Functions (in version 2.x) are C#, F#, JavaScript, Java, Python (in preview), and PowerShell. The following table shows all the languages supported by the related frameworks:

Language	Framework
C#	.NET Core 2.x
JavaScript	Node.js 8 and 10
F#	.NET Core 2.x/3.x
Java	Java 8
Python	Python 3.6
TypeScript	Supported through transpiling to JavaScript
PowerShell	PowerShell Core 6 (preview)

The Azure Functions runtime is also designed to support language extensibility; that is, it's possible to create your own language worker process to manage your own programming language. The JavaScript and Java languages are built with this extensibility.

As for version 1.x of Azure Functions, a function app is a container of your functions. In version 2.x of the Azure Functions runtime, unlike what happened in version 1.x, a function app can host functions written in a single programming language.

An Azure Function written in C# is a static method decored by the `FunctionName` attribute:

```
public static class SimpleExample
{
    [FunctionName("QueueTrigger")]
     public static void Run(
         [QueueTrigger("inputQueue")] string inItem,
         [Queue("outputQueue")] out string outItem,
```

```
        ILogger log)
    {
        log.LogInformation($"C# function processed: {inItem}");
    }
}
```

FunctionName allows you to set the name of the function that is the function entry point. The function name must be unique in your project (that is, the function name must be unique in a function app). It starts with a letter and only contains letters, numbers, _, and -, and is up to 127 characters in length. You can call the method what you like—the Azure Functions runtime doesn't care about the name of the method but only the name of the function defined in the FunctionName attribute. The project template often creates a method called Run but you can change it.

The method signature can contain more parameters other than the one that defines the trigger. You can have the following:

- Input and output bindings marked as such by decorating them with attributes. In the previous sample, the Queue attribute declares that the string (the actual type bound by the runtime) will be saved (because it is an out parameter) in a storage queue called outputQueue when the method ends.
- An ILogger or TraceWriter (TraceWriter is available only for version 1.x) parameter for logging.
- A CancellationToken parameter for graceful shutdown in an async function.
- Binding expression parameters to get trigger metadata.

The arguments of the attribute support binding expressions that provide the possibility to use values defined in the app settings or retrieve special information from the binding.

For example, consider this sample:

```
public static class BindingExpressionsExample
{
    [FunctionName("LogQueueMessage")]
    public static void Run(
        [QueueTrigger("%queueappsetting%")] string myQueueItem,
        DateTimeOffset insertionTime,
        ILogger log)
    {
      log.LogInformation($"Message content: {myQueueItem}");
      log.LogInformation($"Created at: {insertionTime}");
    }
}
```

The name of the trigger queue is defined in the app settings using the `queueappsetting` key, as shown in the next snippet:

```
{
  "IsEncrypted": false,
  "Values": {
  "AzureWebJobsStorage": "UseDevelopmentStorage=true",
  "FUNCTIONS_WORKER_RUNTIME": "dotnet",
  "queueappsetting" : "inputqueue"
  }
}
```

While the value contained in the `insertionTime` parameter is retrieved from the message creation time in the storage queue.

 You can find all the possible triggers, binding parameters, and binding expressions in the official documentation. For Queue (based on storage account), the official documentation is located at `https://docs.microsoft.com/en-us/azure/azure-functions/functions-bindings-storage-queue`.

Once you write your function, you can build it (you'll learn how later in the chapter) and the build process will generate a folder structure like the following diagram:

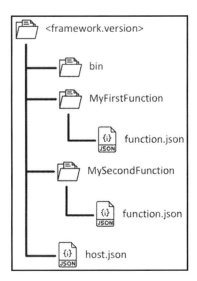

As you can see, the build tool creates, as usual, the `bin` folder where you can find all the mandatory assembly for your code. Then, it also creates two essential files:

- `function.json`: In this file, you can find the metadata of the single function in terms of triggers, bindings, and assembly. For example, if you build a project that contains the previous `LogQueueMessage` function, the `function.json` file will look like this:

```
{
    "generatedBy": "Microsoft.NET.Sdk.Functions-1.0.24",
    "configurationSource": "attributes",
    "bindings": [
        {
            "type": "queueTrigger",
            "queueName": "%queueappsetting%",
            "name": "myQueueItem"
        }
    ],
    "disabled": false,
    "scriptFile": "../bin/MyFunction.dll",
    "entryPoint": "MyFunction.BindingExpressionsExample.Run"
}
```

  The `configurationSource` property tells the runtime that the code uses the attribute approach for trigger and bindings while the `bindings` section contains the complete definition for each binding involved in the function.

  You can find other examples of `function.json` in the Azure Functions GitHub repository (`https://github.com/Azure/azure-functions-host/wiki/function.json`), while the JSON schema is available at `http://json.schemastore.org/function`.

- `host.json`: This file contains the global configuration for the entire function app. For example, you can find the runtime version to use for hosting functions here. If you are using .NET Core 2.x, you can also put your configuration data in `appsettings.json` or `local.settings.json` (only for local test and debugging).

  You can find more information about the `host.json` schema and configurations at `https://docs.microsoft.com/en-us/azure/azure-functions/functions-host-json`, while more information about `appsetting.json` is available at `https://docs.microsoft.com/en-us/azure/azure-functions/functions-app-settings`.

The entire Azure Functions ecosystem is open source, and a set of GitHub repositories contains all the different components related to the Azure Functions world. Here is the list of GitHub repositories currently available:

- Azure Functions: `https://github.com/Azure/Azure-Functions`
- Azure Functions host: `https://github.com/Azure/azure-functions-host`
- Azure Functions portal: `https://github.com/azure/azure-functions-ux`
- Azure Functions templates: `https://github.com/azure/azure-functions-templates`

Azure Functions Core Tools

The Azure Functions runtime (runtime for short) is part of Azure Functions Core Tools, a set of **Command-Line Interface (CLI)** tools that allow you to run, test, and deploy your functions and that you can install on your PC or server.

There are two versions of Azure Function Core Tools:

- **Version 1.x**: This version can run only on Windows and supports version 1.x of the Azure Functions runtime. It supports .NET Framework 4.7.1 only.
- **Version 2.x**: This version can run on Windows, macOS, and Linux and supports the 2.x version of the Azure Functions runtime.

The 2.x version of the tool contains the 2.x version of the Azure Functions runtime. It is based on .NET Core and can run on all platforms that support .NET Core 2.x and 3.x (Windows, macOS, and Linux).

 Azure Functions Core Tools (both v1.x and v2.x) is open source under the MIT License, and you can find it on GitHub at `https://github.com/Azure/azure-functions-core-tools`.

The first step to use the tool is, therefore, to install .NET Core on your machine. You can install the tool in different ways depending on whether you are on Windows, macOS, or Linux.

If you are on Windows, you can use Chocolatey or npm.

Chocolatey and npm are two package managers for Windows: using them, you can install tools and applications using CLI (you don't need to care about finding the right installation package, download it and install):

1. For example, to install the latest version of Azure Functions Core Tools using Chocolatey, you can open Command Prompt and write the following command:

```
C:>choco install azure-functions-core-tools
```

2. If you prefer npm, you can open Command Prompt and write this command:

```
C:>npm install -g azure-functions-core-tools
```

3. If you are on macOS, you have to use Homebrew:

```
brew tap azure/functions
brew install azure-functions-core-tools
```

4. Finally, if you are on Linux (Ubuntu or Debian), you have to use APT, and in particular, you have to register the Microsoft product key as a trusted key:

```
curl https://packages.microsoft.com/keys/microsoft.asc | gpg --
dearmor > microsoft.gpg
sudo mv microsoft.gpg /etc/apt/trusted.gpg.d/microsoft.gpg
```

5. Then, you can add the APT source and install the package:

```
sudo sh -c 'echo "deb [arch=amd64]
https://packages.microsoft.com/repos/microsoft-ubuntu-$(lsb_release
-cs)-prod $(lsb_release -cs) main" >
/etc/apt/sources.list.d/dotnetdev.list'
sudo apt-get update
sudo apt-get install azure-functions-core-tools
```

Of course, you can also use a more productive tool, such as Visual Studio or Visual Studio Code, but it's important to understand that you can perform all the basic operations using Azure Functions Core Tools and that all your functions run inside the Azure Functions runtime.

Once you install the tools, you can start your journey into the Azure Functions development world.

You can show the help for Azure Function Core Tools by merely running the `func` command (without any parameters):

```
C:\MasteringServerless>func
```

The following screenshot shows the output of the preceding command:

As you can see, Azure Function Core Tools has the concept of context; the context is the scope in which you want to work, for example, `function` is the context to manage Azure Functions, while `durable` is the context to work on Azure Durable Functions.

The scope mentioned earlier (the context) is why the name is Azure Functions Core Tools, and you can imagine every single context as a separate tool that works on a particular scope. You can show the help for each context using the following command:

```
C:\MasteringServerless>func <context>
```

For example, if you try to get help for the `function` context, Azure Functions Core Tools generates the following output:

```
Administrator: Command Prompt                                                    —  □  ×

C:\MasteringServerless>func function

                        %%%%%%%
                        %%%%%%%
              @         %%%%%%%%         @
             @@         %%%%%%%         @@
            @@@        %%%%%%%%%%%%     @@@
           @@        %%%%%%%%%%%%%%       @@
            @@             %%%%%         @@
             @@            %%%         @@
              @@          %%         @@
                          %%
                          %

Usage: func function [context] <action> [-/--options]

Actions:
new     Create a new function from a template. Aliases: new, create
    --language [-l] Template programming language, such as C#, F#, JavaScript, etc.
    --template [-t] Template name
    --name [-n]     Function name
    --csx           use old style csx dotnet functions


C:\MasteringServerless>
```

The context isn't mandatory because Azure Function Core Tools has a set of commands that are common for every context; for example, if you want to create a function app to host all your functions, you can use the following command:

```
C:\MasteringServerless\MyFirstFunctionApp>func init --worker-runtime dotnet
```

This command initializes inside the current folder (in the previous snippet, the `MyFirstFunctionApp` folder), your functions project, so before you create your first project, you should create the folder that will contain it.

The `init` command has many arguments but the only one that is mandatory, `--worker-runtime`, which allows you to choose which type of programming language you want to use.

When the command completes its job, you will find a bunch of files in the folder:

.vscode	3/21/2019 12:12 PM	File folder	
.gitignore	3/21/2019 12:12 PM	Text Document	5 KB
host.json	3/21/2019 12:12 PM	JSON File	1 KB
local.settings.json	3/21/2019 12:12 PM	JSON File	1 KB
MyFirstAppFunction.csproj	3/21/2019 12:12 PM	Visual C# Project f...	1 KB

The project directory contains the `host.json` and `local.settings.json` files and the `.gitignore` file configured for Visual Studio, and, of course, the `.csproj` project file.

You can consider this directory as equivalent to the function app in Azure.

If you choose to use Azure Functions version 2.x (the default version for Azure Functions Core Tools), every function in the app function must be developed using the same programming language (C# in the previous sample), so you must declare what type of language you want to use (the `--worker-runtime` option in the `init` command). In version 1.x, you must specify the language each time you create a function, not when you create the function app.

To complete your job, you must create an Azure Function, and you can do this using another command of Azure Functions Core Tools:

```
C:\MasteringServerless\MyFirstFunctionApp>func function new --template
HttpTrigger --name MyHttpFunction
```

When you use the `new` option, you must specify the template you want to use to create the function (in the previous sample, we created an HTTP trigger function) and, of course, the function name. If you don't specify the necessary parameters, the tools will prompt you.

The command creates a `.cs` file containing the code for the Azure Function, but don't update the project file to add the new function to the project—you need to update the project file only if you want to work on the project using Visual Studio (or Visual Studio Code); otherwise, you can run your function using the following Azure Functions Core Tools command:

```
C:\MasteringServerless\MyFirstFunctionApp>func host start
```

In this case, the tool restores the NuGet packages and builds the project as shown in the following screenshot:

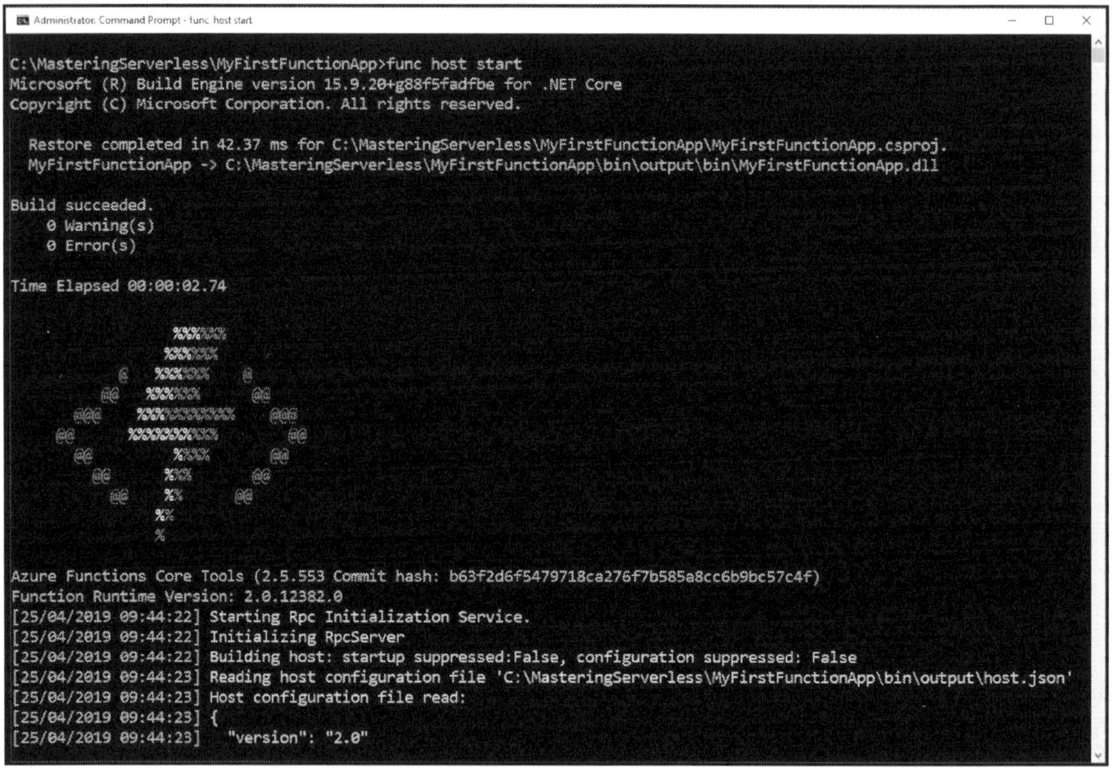
Administrator: Command Prompt - func host start
C:\MasteringServerless\MyFirstFunctionApp>func host start
Microsoft (R) Build Engine version 15.9.20+g88f5fadfbe for .NET Core
Copyright (C) Microsoft Corporation. All rights reserved.
Restore completed in 42.37 ms for C:\MasteringServerless\MyFirstFunctionApp\MyFirstFunctionApp.csproj.
MyFirstFunctionApp -> C:\MasteringServerless\MyFirstFunctionApp\bin\output\bin\MyFirstFunctionApp.dll
Build succeeded.
0 Warning(s)
0 Error(s)
Time Elapsed 00:00:02.74
Azure Functions Core Tools (2.5.553 Commit hash: b63f2d6f5479718ca276f7b585a8cc6b9bc57c4f)
Function Runtime Version: 2.0.12382.0
[25/04/2019 09:44:22] Starting Rpc Initialization Service.
[25/04/2019 09:44:22] Initializing RpcServer
[25/04/2019 09:44:22] Building host: startup suppressed:False, configuration suppressed: False
[25/04/2019 09:44:23] Reading host configuration file 'C:\MasteringServerless\MyFirstFunctionApp\bin\output\host.json'
[25/04/2019 09:44:23] Host configuration file read:
[25/04/2019 09:44:23] {
[25/04/2019 09:44:23] "version": "2.0"

If the build succeeds, then the tool starts the Azure Functions runtime to host the function:

```
Administrator Command Prompt - func host start                                      —    □    ×
[25/04/2019 09:44:23]     "BatchSize": 1000,
[25/04/2019 09:44:23]     "FlushTimeout": "00:00:30",
[25/04/2019 09:44:23]     "IsEnabled": true
[25/04/2019 09:44:23] }
[25/04/2019 09:44:23] SingletonOptions
[25/04/2019 09:44:23] {
[25/04/2019 09:44:23]     "LockPeriod": "00:00:15",
[25/04/2019 09:44:23]     "ListenerLockPeriod": "00:00:15",
[25/04/2019 09:44:23]     "LockAcquisitionTimeout": "10675199.02:48:05.4775807",
[25/04/2019 09:44:23]     "LockAcquisitionPollingInterval": "00:00:05",
[25/04/2019 09:44:23]     "ListenerLockRecoveryPollingInterval": "00:01:00"
[25/04/2019 09:44:23] }
[25/04/2019 09:44:23] Starting JobHost
[25/04/2019 09:44:23] Starting Host (HostId=maxdell-1192019585, InstanceId=c8d1cf39-e585-462e-b1b4-00687b1edbb9, Version
=2.0.12382.0, ProcessId=27600, AppDomainId=1, InDebugMode=False, InDiagnosticMode=False, FunctionsExtensionVersion=)
[25/04/2019 09:44:23] Loading functions metadata
[25/04/2019 09:44:23] 1 functions loaded
[25/04/2019 09:44:23] WorkerRuntime: dotnet. Will shutdown other standby channels
[25/04/2019 09:44:23] Generating 1 job function(s)
[25/04/2019 09:44:23] Found the following functions:
[25/04/2019 09:44:23] MyFirstFunctionApp.MyHttpFunctionfunc.Run
[25/04/2019 09:44:23]
[25/04/2019 09:44:23] Host initialized (167ms)
[25/04/2019 09:44:23] Host started (178ms)
[25/04/2019 09:44:23] Job host started
Hosting environment: Production
Content root path: C:\MasteringServerless\MyFirstFunctionApp\bin\output
Now listening on: http://0.0.0.0:7071
Application started. Press Ctrl+C to shut down.

Http Functions:

        MyHttpFunctionfunc: [GET,POST] http://localhost:7071/api/MyHttpFunctionfunc
```

When the Azure Functions runtime starts, it scaffolds your assemblies to find all the Azure Functions and shows them in the console log, so you can immediately check whether all your implementations are OK. If the Azure Functions runtime finds issues in some functions (for example, you are using a binding, and it isn't configured in the right way), it excludes the functions from the scaffolding, shows you a warning in the log console, and you cannot use them.

As you can see in the previous screenshot, `MyHttpFunction` is listening on the `http://localhost:7071/api/MyHttpFunction` endpoint, and you can try to execute an HTTP GET:

```
C:>curl —get
http://localhost:7071/api/MyHttpFunction?name=MasteringServerless
```

If you do, you will see this Azure Functions response:

```
C:\>curl --get http://localhost:7071/api/MyHttpFunction?name=MasteringServerless
Hello, MasteringServerless
C:\>
```

Moreover, you can see that the Azure Functions runtime instance you started before still shows the function log during its execution.

You can also use the Azure Functions runtime to host precompiled functions: you can copy the entire output folder (the `bin` folder generated by the build process) and start to host your functions running the `host` command with the `--script-root` option:

```
C:> func host start --script-root C:\MasteringServerless\PrecompiledFolder
```

In this way, you can host your functions outside the Azure environment.

One of the important innovations introduced with Azure Functions 2.0 is the possibility of referencing triggers and bindings only when needed. Azure Functions 2.0 introduces the concept of extension, for example, if you want to use an Azure Cosmos DB binding, you must reference the `Microsoft.Azure.WebJobs.Extensions.CosmosDB` package. You can do this with the Azure Functions Core Tool command:

```
C:\MasteringServerless\MyFirstAppFunction>func extensions install --package
Microsoft.Azure.WebJobs.Extensions.CosmosDB --version 3.0.3
```

In this case, the tool updates the project file to add the NuGet package reference and creates the `extension.json` file inside the output folder. The `extension.json` file contains all the information the runtime needs to use the extensions you referred to.

You can find more information about extensions and the extensions engine later in next chapter.

Developing Azure Functions with Visual Studio

Since 2002, Visual Studio has been the most important IDE for developing solutions with .NET Framework and it is an important tool to use to implement and test your Azure Functions.

In this book, we will always refer to Visual Studio 2019 but most of the operations we will perform on that version can be done on Visual Studio 2017 (Visual Studio 2017 is the oldest version of Visual Studio that supports Azure Functions development).

Visual Studio 2019 allows you to create an Azure Functions project:

1. Simply choose the **File** | **New** | **Project** menu:

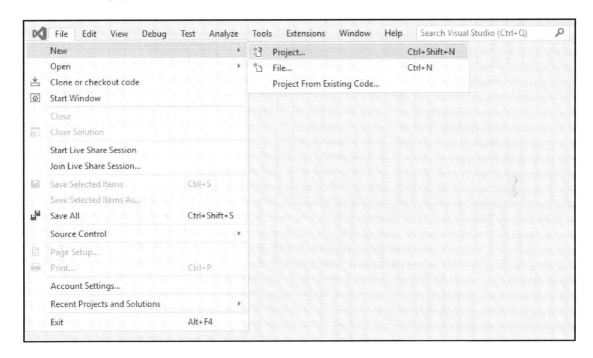

2. This menu option opens the Visual Studio project type window where you can choose the **Azure Functions** project type:

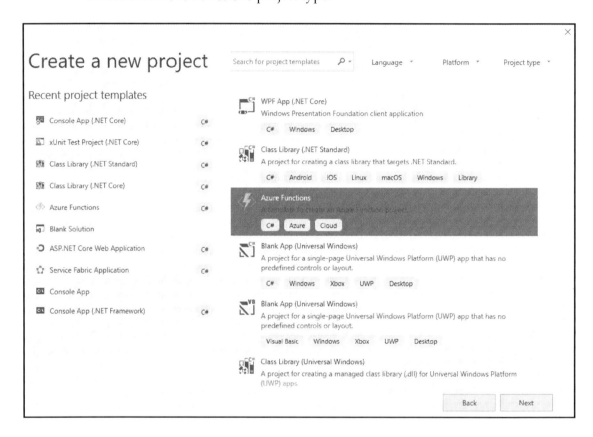

If you don't have the Azure Functions template in the project types list, you probably didn't install the Azure development workload. In this case, you can use the Visual Studio Installer tool to install it.

3. After you select the project template for Azure Functions (the one selected in the previous screenshot), press the **Next** button and choose your project and solution name. You can consider the project as the function app in which you put your functions:

4. Finally, you choose the function runtime, trigger type, and configuration for the trigger:

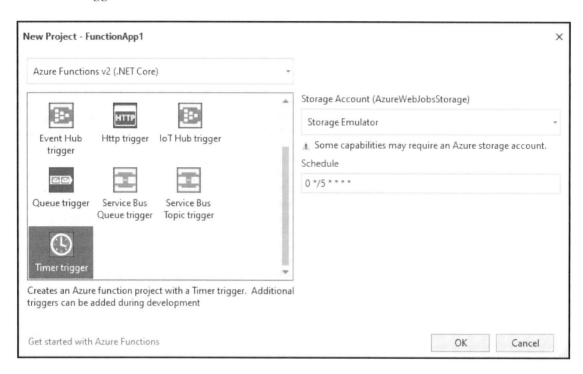

As you can see in the previous screenshot, you can also create Azure Functions for runtime version v1.x. Depending on the trigger you choose, the right-hand part of the window shows the configuration values you must insert for the specific trigger. For example, if you choose a **Time trigger** (as shown in the previous screenshot), the only configuration parameter is the **Schedule** value.

In this step, you also select (using the **Storage Account** combo box) when data will be saved (if a trigger works on data such as a queue or blob). You can choose **Storage Emulator** to use the local storage and test the function locally (without an internet connection).

The value selected in the combo box affects the value of the `AzureWebJobsStorage` key contained in the `local.settings.json` file in the project. In the previous case, choosing the **Storage Emulator** option, you get the following:

```
{
    "IsEncrypted": false,
    "Values": {
        "AzureWebJobsStorage": "UseDevelopmentStorage=true",
```

```
        "FUNCTIONS_WORKER_RUNTIME": "dotnet"
    }
}
```

You can, of course, change this value at any time. Visual Studio uses the `local.settings.json` file only and exclusively for executing code in the local environment. For this reason, you can add sensitive values (for example, access keys to external services) in this file without taking the risk of sharing secrets with other people. The file is, by default, excluded from the source code repository. In fact, Visual Studio creates a `.gitignore` file and sets `local.settings.json` as a file to exclude:

```
## Ignore Visual Studio temporary files, build results, and
## files generated by popular Visual Studio add-ons.
# Azure Functions localsettings file
local.settings.json

# User-specific files
*.suo
*.user
*.userosscache
*.sln.docstates
.
.
.
```

Once the selected trigger configuration is complete, you can complete the process by pressing the **OK** button. Visual Studio creates the solution and the project and, inside the project, the Azure Function.

To run your function, you can just press the *F5* key: Visual Studio, as usual, starts the restore package operation, then builds the solution, and then starts the Azure Functions runtime (in the same way as you saw in the previous paragraph).

You can put breakpoints in the code in the way you do with the other project types in Visual Studio and intercept the function execution.

Visual Studio Code

Visual Studio Code is one of the most diffuse source-code editors in the world and can be used on Windows, macOS, and Linux. It is an open source project managed by Microsoft in collaboration with a wide community of developers and, of course, it supports Azure Functions.

You can download Visual Studio Code from the official website at
`https://code.visualstudio.com/Download`, while the GitHub repository
is at `https://github.com/Microsoft/vscode`.

To develop an Azure Functions project, follow these steps:

1. Install the Azure Functions extension for Visual Studio Code. You can find it by searching in the Extensions tab of Visual Studio Code:

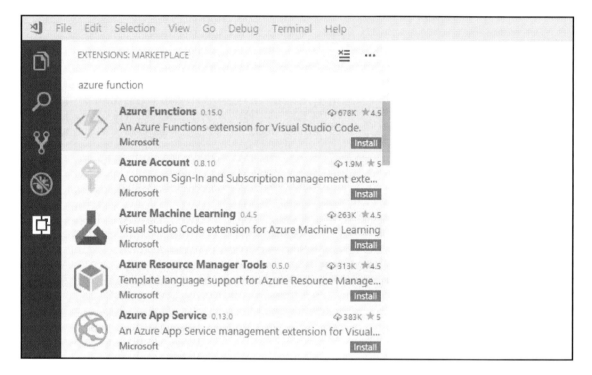

The Azure Functions extension also needs the Azure Account extension to manage your Azure account, and to build and debug Azure Functions, you need the C# for Visual Studio Code extension (powered by OmniSharp).

2. Once you install the extensions, the first thing you will notice is that there is a new tab, identified by the Azure logo, on the left-hand side of the Visual Studio Code window. That is the activity tab you can use to create a new function app:

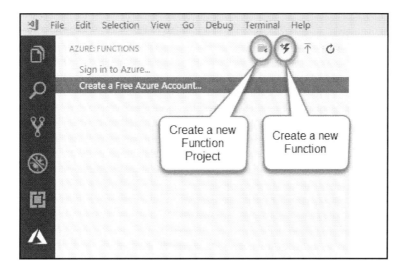

3. When you create a new Azure Functions project by pressing the Create Function... button (at the top of the Azure Functions tab), you must choose the folder where you want to save the project, and then you must select the language you want to use:

4. Once Visual Studio Code completes the project creation, you will see the file created under the folder you chose on the left-hand side of the Visual Studio Code window, in a new workspace:

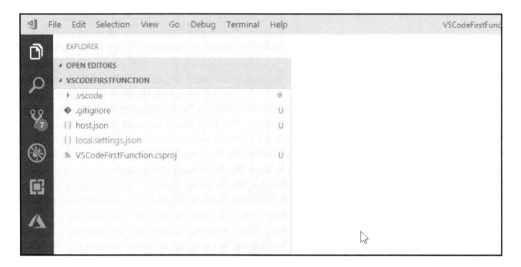

5. The next step allows you to create the Azure Function, and you can do so using the Create new function button at the top of the Azure Functions tab. The Azure Functions extension asks you all the mandatory information for the function (such as the trigger type, the name of the function, its namespace, and the storage configuration) using a wizard. For example, the following screenshot shows the function trigger type selection:

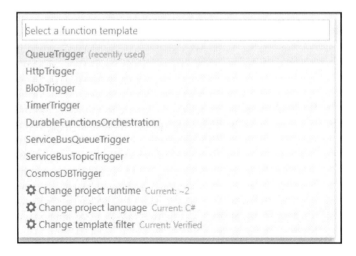

The following one shows a function name request:

6. Finally, if you are developing an `HttpTrigger` function, you must select the **AccessRights** for the function:

At the end of the function configuration wizard, Visual Studio Code creates the class file containing the function:

7. To debug your function, you can use the **Debug** tab and run the configuration named **Attach to C# function created**.

This is the default configuration created by the Azure Functions extension and uses Azure Functions Core Tools in the same way you can do with the command line (or Visual Studio).

The OpenAPI Specification in Azure Functions

If you have worked with SOAP services in your career, surely you have had to deal with the concept of a **Web Services Description Language (WSDL)** manifest. WSDL is the identity card of a SOAP service and fully describes the service itself in terms of the endpoints, ports, and payloads used by the service. Using WSDL, you can understand how a third-party service works and you can create its client automatically.

The OpenAPI Specification is the counterpart of WSDL for REST API services: they are a set of specifications created by the most important players in the computer science world, such as Google, Microsoft, and IBM which join together in open governance structure under the Linux Foundation. The purpose of the OpenAPI specification is to standardize how REST APIs are described using a programming language-agnostic approach based on YAML or JSON files.

 The OpenAPI official website is `https://www.openapis.org` and the specifications are on GitHub (`https://github.com/OAI/OpenAPI-Specification`).

Sometimes, the OpenAPI Specification is also known as **Swagger**, but they are two different sides of the same coin: OpenAPI is the specifications while Swagger is one of the tools you can use to implement the specifications. To make a comparison with the web world: OpenAPI is comparable to W3C's HTML specifications, while Swagger is comparable to one of the browsers that implement such specifications.

At the time of writing this book, the Azure Functions runtime doesn't yet support a native mode to implement OpenAPI specifications in an `HttpTrigger` function but there are, however, ways to implement them using third-party NuGet packages.

First of all, consider the following function:

```
[FunctionName(nameof(GetBooks))]
public static IActionResult GetBooks(
    [HttpTrigger(AuthorizationLevel.Anonymous, "get", Route = "books")]
HttpRequest req,
```

```
        ILogger log)
{
    log.LogInformation($"Call {nameof(GetBooks)}");
    var books = BooksRepository.Books;
    if (req.Query.ContainsKey("title"))
    {
        var titleFilter = req.Query["title"];
        books = books.Where(b => b.Title.Contains(titleFilter));
    }
    return (ActionResult)new OkObjectResult(books);
}
```

The function returns a list of books filtered by title:

```
GET api/books?title=The%20Great%20Gatsby

[
    {
        "title":"The Great Gatsby",
        "price":10.5,
        "author":"F. Scott Fitzgerald"
    }
]
```

The OpenAPI Specification for the function looks like this:

```
{
    "openapi": "3.0.1",
    "info": {
        ....
    },
        "version": "1.0.0"
    },
    "servers": [
        {
            "url": "http://localhost:7071/api"
        }
    ],
    "paths": {
        "/books": {
            "get": {
                "operationId": "books",
                "parameters": [
                    ...
                ],
                "responses": {
                    "200": {
                        ...
```

```
                }
              }
            }
          }
        },
        ...
      }
```

You have an entry in the `path` collections for each API exposed and for each entry. As you can see in the previous sample, you have a complete description of the HTTP verb supported (`GET` in the sample) and all the possible responses supported by the API.

To implement the OpenAPI Specification in the previous Azure Function, you have, at this moment, to use a third-party package. In the following sample, we use the NuGet package called `Aliencube.AzureFunctions.Extensions.OpenApi`. You will find many packages that allow you to implement the OpenAPI Specification in your functions, but we've chosen that because it is simple, it is under MIT license, the code is on GitHub, and it allows you to understand what the steps you need to implement are to expose the JSON (or YAML) file with the OpenAPI description.

 You can find the source code for the `Aliencube.AzureFunctions.Extensions.OpenApi` package in the GitHub repository at `https://github.com/aliencube/AzureFunctions.Extensions`.

The first thing you have to do is to install the package in your Azure Functions project, for example, using the following command in the Package Manager Console (inside Visual Studio):

```
Install-Package Aliencube.AzureFunctions.Extensions.OpenApi
```

Once the package is installed, you need to decorate your function so that the package scaffolding procedure can retrieve the information needed to generate the OpenAPI specification file. The OpenAPI package implements a set of attributes that allow you to define the metadata of the function, its input parameters, and its responses:

```
[FunctionName(nameof(GetBooks))]
[OpenApiOperation("books", Description = "Retrieves a list of books
filtered by the title")]
[OpenApiParameter("title", In = ParameterLocation.Query, Required = false,
Type = typeof(string))]
[OpenApiResponseBody(HttpStatusCode.OK, "application/json",
typeof(IEnumerable<BookModel>), Description ="The books that contains the
filter in the title")]
public static IActionResult GetBooks(
```

```
    [HttpTrigger(AuthorizationLevel.Anonymous, "get", Route = "books")]
HttpRequest req,
    ILogger log)
{
    log.LogInformation($"Call {nameof(GetBooks)}");
    var books = BooksRepository.Books;
    if (req.Query.ContainsKey("title"))
    {
        var titleFilter = req.Query["title"];
        books = books.Where(b => b.Title.Contains(titleFilter));
    }
    return (ActionResult)new OkObjectResult(books);
}
```

As you can see, you can add the following attributes:

- `OpenApiOperation`: This provides some path information, such as the operation ID and the description.
- `OpenApiParameter`: This defines information about an input parameter, such as the name, the direction, the location in the request (for example, a query string), the type, and whether the parameter is mandatory or not. Of course, you must have one attribute for each parameter that your function supports.
- `OpenApiResponseBody`: This defines information about the function response, such as the content type, the type, and the description. You should have one attribute for each status code response your function supports.

In the previous snippet, the `BookRepository` class simulates the data access layer (using it, you can retrieve the full list of books available). You can find its implementation in the GitHub repository for the chapter.

Correctly decorating all functions, however, is not enough because you must implement an endpoint that generates the OpenAPI Specification file. To do this, you can use another function of type `HttpTrigger`:

```
[FunctionName(nameof(RenderOpenApiDocument))]
[OpenApiIgnore]
public static async Task<IActionResult> RenderOpenApiDocument(
    [HttpTrigger(AuthorizationLevel.Anonymous, "get", Route = "openapi")]
HttpRequest req,
    ILogger log)
{
    var ver = OpenApiSpecVersion.OpenApi3_0;
    var ext = OpenApiFormat.Json;
    var settings = new AppSettings();
    var helper = new DocumentHelper();
```

```
        var document = new Document(helper);
        var result = await document.InitialiseDocument()
            .AddMetadata(settings.OpenApiInfo)
            .AddServer(req, settings.HttpSettings.RoutePrefix)
            .Build(Assembly.GetExecutingAssembly())
            .RenderAsync(ver, ext)
            .ConfigureAwait(false);

        var response = new ContentResult()
            {
                Content = result,
                ContentType = "application/json",
                StatusCode = (int)HttpStatusCode.OK
            };

    return response;
    }
```

The function uses the scaffolding features exposed by the Aliencube package to generate (the `Build` method) and render (the `RenderAsync` method) the OpenAPI Specification file and return it as JSON output. In the function, we choose the OpenAPI v3.0 version and JSON format but you can change these options using one of the supporting values of `OpenApiSpecVersion` and `OpenApiFormat` enumeration. You will notice the use of the `AppSetting` class in the previous sample:

```
    class AppSettings : OpenApiAppSettingsBase
    {
        public AppSettings() : base()
        {
        }
    }
```

That class allows you to read the info section for the OpenAPI specification from the app settings:

```
    {
        ...
        "Values": {
            ...
            "OpenApi__Info__Version": "1.0.0",
            "OpenApi__Info__Title": "OpenAPISupport version 1.0.0",
            "OpenApi__Info__Description": "A simple sample to configure OpenAPI
    on Azure Functions.",
            "OpenApi__Info__Contact__Url":
    "https://github.com/masteringserverless/CH01-OpenAPI",
            "OpenApi__Info__License__Name": "MIT",
            "OpenApi__Info__License__Url": "http://opensource.org/licenses/MIT"
```

```
        }
    }
```

Finally, you complete the OpenAPI render function implementation decorated with the `OpenApiIgnore` attribute, which excludes the function from the scaffolding process (so you will not see the render function in the OpenAPI specification file).

If you call the function using, for example, a browser, you receive the following result:

In the next section, we will be using ngrok.

Exposing your Azure Functions on the internet with ngrok

As you have read in the previous paragraphs, you can use the Azure Functions runtime to host your functions, but the host process exposes your function on the localhost, so you cannot reach them from another PC than the one hosting them.

If you want to expose your functions on the internet and, therefore, solve the problem, you can use ngrok. ngrok is software (running on Windows, macOS, and Linux) that allows you to expose a local server to the internet using a secure tunnel, and it also works if your local server is behind a NAT or a firewall.

1. To use ngrok, you need to register yourself on the ngrok website and create an account.

   ngrok has a free plan that allows you to use the software for free with the limitation of only one process at a time with a maximum of four tunnels and a random port, but it is enough to test your functions.

    You can create your own account at https://ngrok.com and download the ngrok client from https://ngrok.com/download. You also find the complete documentation at https://ngrok.com/docs.

2. Once you download the ngrok client, you have to connect your account to the client (you need to do this operation once only) using the following command:

   ```
   ngrok.exe authtoken <your_auth_token>
   ```

You can find your authentication token in the **Auth** section of your account dashboard:

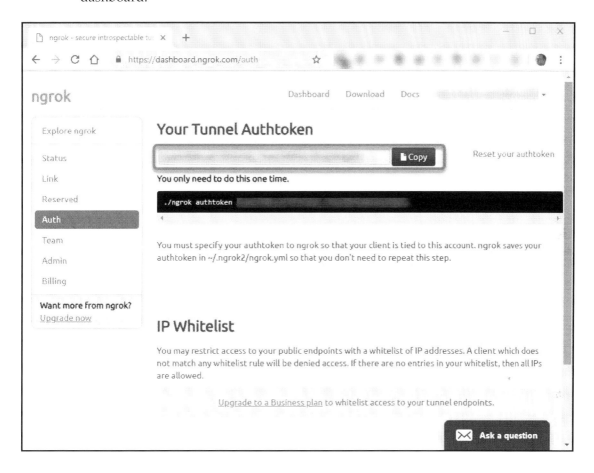

3. To expose your local function using ngrok, simply expose the local port using the `http` command:

```
C:>func host start --port 9999
C:>grok http 9999
```

The following screenshot shows the output of the preceding command:

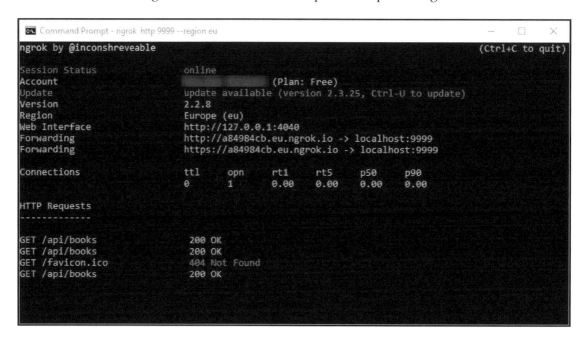

The `http` command starts a tunnel from a random subdomain hosted by the ngrok platform (in the previous screenshot, `a84984cb.eu.ngrok.io`) to your PC. You can call your Azure Functions using the sub-domain instead, `http://localhost`; for example, if your function has the `http://localhost:9999/api/books` URL, you call it using the `http://a84984cb.eu.ngrok.io/api/book` URL.

The ngrok console shows the HTTP requests received through the tunnel, but ngrok also exposes a web GUI you can display using the `http://localhost:4040` URL. The web console shows you all the requests received by the ngrok tunnel, as you can see in the following screenshot:

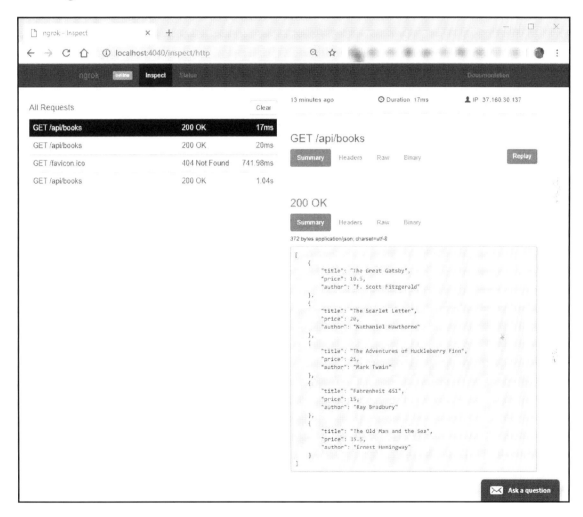

This is a screenshot of the web console which shows you all the requests received by the ngrok tunnel. The text and numbers in this image are intentionally illegible

And it also shows you the metrics about your connection, as you can see in the following screenshot:

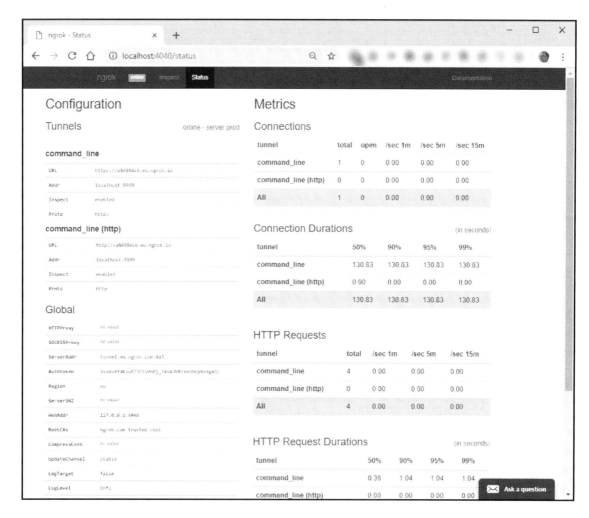

This is a screenshot of the web console which shows you the metrics about your connection. The text and numbers in this image are intentionally illegible

The web GUI allows you to inspect every single request received and gives you information about the tunnel and statistics about the requests (for example, connections and request duration).

Debugging an Azure Function

Implementing a software solution is only the first step; once you've written your code (or if something goes wrong in your test environment), you need to be able to debug it.

Visual Studio and Visual Studio Code give you all the tools to debug an Azure Function both locally and remotely.

In this section, we will use the features of Visual Studio, but these features are also available in Visual Studio Code.

Debugging your function locally

Using the Visual Studio debugger (or the Visual Studio Code debugger), you can debug your function locally as you do for any other program written in .NET: you can insert breakpoints, run the software step by step, or use the debug console.

The issue, when you debug an Azure Function, is that your function, generally, doesn't live alone: it writes data to Blob storage, reads items from a storage queue, or inserts documents into a Cosmos DB database.

The question is: *how can you emulate the binding endpoints?*

Of course, if you have an internet connection, you can use Azure resources (for example, Blob storage) directly but your debug experience will not be the best. On the other hand, if you haven't got an internet connection (for example, you need to debug your function while you are on a flight), you won't have access to the Azure resources you need and you won't be able to debug your code.

Fortunately, you can *emulate* some of the resources involved in the function bindings using Microsoft Azure Storage Emulator or Azure Cosmos Emulator.

Microsoft Azure Storage Emulator provides you with a local environment that emulates the services exposed by Queue, Table, and Blob storage.

 Microsoft Azure Storage Emulator is a component of the Azure SDK (https://azure.microsoft.com/downloads/) but you can install it on your PC using the standalone installer (https://go.microsoft.com/fwlink/?linkid=717179amp;clcid=0x409).

At the time of writing this book, the Microsoft Azure Storage Emulator runs only on Windows, but there is an open source version called **Azurite** (`https://github.com/azure/azurite`) that runs on Linux.

Microsoft Azure Storage Emulator uses a local Microsoft SQL instance (SQL Server 2012 Express LocalDB) and the filesystem to emulate the Azure storage services. Microsoft Azure Storage Emulator is a command-line tool, generally installed in the `C:\Program Files (x86)\Microsoft SDKs\Azure\Storage Emulator` folder, and supports a set of commands that allow you to configure the tool as you want. You can retrieve the command list by running `AzureStorageEmulator.exe`:

```
C:\Program Files (x86)\Microsoft SDKs\Azure\Storage Emulator>AzureStorageEmulator
Windows Azure Storage Emulator 5.9.0.0 command line tool
Error: Expected command as first argument.
Usage:
    AzureStorageEmulator.exe init          : Initialize the emulator database and configuration.
    AzureStorageEmulator.exe start         : Start the emulator.
    AzureStorageEmulator.exe stop          : Stop the emulator.
    AzureStorageEmulator.exe status        : Get current emulator status.
    AzureStorageEmulator.exe clear         : Delete all data in the emulator.
    AzureStorageEmulator.exe help [command] : Show general or command-specific help.

See the following URL for more command line help: http://go.microsoft.com/fwlink/?LinkId=392235

C:\Program Files (x86)\Microsoft SDKs\Azure\Storage Emulator>
```

You can start the emulator using the `init` command and configure it to use your specific version of SQL Server:

```
AzureStorageEmulator.exe init –server MySQLServer –sqlinstance
MySQLInstance
```

With the previous command, for example, you start the emulator using the instance of SQL Database called `MySQLInstance` hosted in the `MySQLServer` server.

To use the emulator in your Azure Function, you simply set the `AzureWebJobsStorage` value in `local.settings.json` to `UseDevelopmentStorage=true`. Setting this value, once you start your local debugging, the Azure Functions runtime starts the emulator (if it isn't running yet).

Microsoft Azure Cosmos Emulator provides a local environment that emulates Azure Cosmos DB services. Using Azure Cosmos Emulator, you can debug an Azure Function with Cosmos DB binding locally, without creating a Cosmos DB instance in your Azure subscription. When you're satisfied with how your application is working in Azure Cosmos Emulator, you can switch to using an Azure Cosmos account in the cloud.

Azure Cosmos Emulator uses local resources to emulate some Cosmos DB features, but not all the features that you can find in Azure Cosmos DB instances are implemented. For example, features such as global replication, single-digit millisecond latency for reads/writes, and tunable consistency levels are not implemented.

 You can download Azure Cosmos Emulator from `https://aka.ms/cosmosdb-emulator`.

Azure Cosmos Emulator runs only on Windows systems. If you need to run the emulator on other operating systems, you can install it in a Docker container (more info at `https://github.com/Azure/azure-cosmos-db-emulator-docker`).

Generally, Azure Cosmos Emulator is installed on `C:\Program Files\Azure Cosmos DB Emulator` and, like Microsoft Azure Storage Emulator, it provides a CLI that allows you to configure, as you want, the emulator. To get all the possible options supported by the emulator, you can run the following command:

```
C:\Program Files\Azure Cosmos DB Emulator>CosmosDB.Emulator.exe /?
```

If you run the emulator with the default settings, it uses the
`%LocalAppdata%\CosmosDBEmulator` folder to store the data and provides you with a
web UI on port `8081` (`https://localhost:8081/_explorer/index.html`):

The console is opened automatically when you start the emulator and provides you with
information about the connection string and the primary key to connect to the instance
from your function and allows you to make queries in the Cosmos DB local instance (using
the **Explorer** tab on the left).

Unfortunately, for the other types of binding (for example, SendGrid or Twilio), there aren't
emulators. So, in those scenarios, you can debug your function locally, but you must use
the online services.

Debug your function remotely

Using Visual Studio (or Visual Studio Code) you can attach your debugger directly to the
deployed code.

To do this, you can use the Cloud Explorer extension (you can find it in Azure Marketplace or using the **Manage Extensions** menu option in Visual Studio). This extension allows you to browse the resources contained in your subscriptions and perform actions on them. In the case of the function app resource, it is possible to launch a remote debug session:

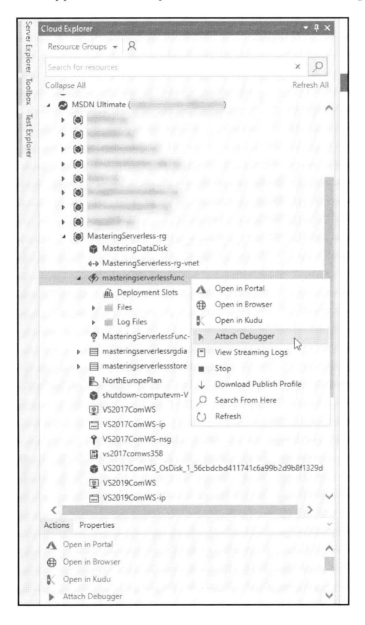

If you have permission to access the resource, Visual Studio attaches the debugger remotely to the function host process, starts it, and you can debug your function in the same way as you perform local debugging: you can set a breakpoint in the code that will be reached every time the function is triggered.

Summary

In this chapter, you learned how to create, build, and debug an Azure Function using Azure Functions Core Tools, Visual Studio, and Visual Studio Code. Also, you discovered how to implement the OpenAPI Specification in our HTTP triggered function and how to expose your local functions on the internet using ngrok.

Azure Functions Core Tools is the main tool you can use to create, host, and manage your Azure Functions. Using this tool, you can write Azure Functions in C#, JavaScript, Java, and Python and build and host them in your local development environment. Along with this tool, you can use a whole series of tools that allow you to enhance your development and debugging experience. Of course, a better development experience is provided by using a modern IDE such as Visual Studio or Visual Studio Code but you can write your functions with your favorite IDE and operating system.

In the next chapter, you will see how you can customize your functions to implement custom triggers and bindings.

Questions

1. Which of these languages is supported by the Azure Functions runtime?
   - C#
   - Golang
   - JavaScript
   - Java
   - Cobol

2. Which of the following tools can you use to create a project containing an Azure Function?
   - Visual Studio
   - Azure Functions Core Tools
   - Storage Emulator
   - Management Studio

3. Can you create Azure Functions written in different programming languages within a function app?
    - Yes, both in V.1.x and in V2.x
    - Yes, only in V1.x
    - Yes, only in V2.x
    - No, never

4. How can you debug your Azure Functions remotely?
    - By installing Visual Studio in the same VM that hosts the Azure Function.
    - Using the Cloud Explorer extension on Visual Studio and the remote debugger.
    - You can't debug an Azure Function remotely.

Further reading

You can find more information about developing and debugging Azure Functions at these URLs:

- *The Azure Functions portal*: https://azure.microsoft.com/en-us/services/functions/
- *Work with Azure Functions Core Tools*: https://docs.microsoft.com/en-us/azure/azure-functions/functions-run-local
- *Code and test Azure Functions locally*: https://docs.microsoft.com/en-us/azure/azure-functions/functions-develop-local
- *Develop Azure Functions using Visual Studio*: https://docs.microsoft.com/en-us/azure/azure-functions/functions-develop-vs
- *Visual Studio tutorial - Create your first Azure Function*: https://tutorials.visualstudio.com/first-azure-function/intro

2
Customizing Your Azure Functions

In real-world scenarios, the triggers and bindings offered by Azure Functions extensions are not always sufficient to meet the requirements that your solutions have.

In this chapter, you will learn how triggers and bindings work and how you can customize them to meet your requirements.

This chapter will cover the following topics:

- Azure Functions extensions
- Creating a custom trigger
- Creating a custom binding

Technical requirements

In this chapter, you will see a lot of code, so it's important that you are familiar with C# and **object-oriented programming** (OOP). Moreover, because you will learn how to customize Azure Functions, it's mandatory to know the Azure Functions framework well and have basic knowledge about triggers and bindings.

You can find the source code for this chapter at `https://github.com/PacktPublishing/Mastering-Azure-Serverless-Computing/tree/master/Chapter02`.

Discovering Azure Functions extensions

As you may have read in the previous chapter, all triggers and bindings (except for `TimerTrigger` and `HttpTrigger`) supported by Azure Functions are available as external packages that must be added in order to be used.

The Azure Functions SDK is based on the Azure WebJobs SDK, so it inherits all the features contained in it and, in particular, it exploits the WebJobs SDK's primitives for the management of extensions.

 You can find more information about the Azure WebJobs SDK in the official GitHub repository located at `https://github.com/Azure/azure-webjobs-sdk-extensions`.

When the Azure Function host job starts, it needs to discover all the extensions Azure Functions want to use: to achieve this, you must create a class (`CustomWebJobsStartup` in the next code snippet) and decorated it with the `WebJobsStartup` attribute to tell the web job what startup class you want to execute in the startup phase:

```
[assembly: WebJobsStartup(typeof(CustomWebJobsStartup))]
public class CustomWebJobsStartup : IWebJobsStartup
{
    public void Configure(IWebJobsBuilder builder)
    {
        // You can add here all the code you want to execute on startup!
    }
}
```

The `CustomWebJobStartup` class must implement `IWebJobsStartup` and you can write your startup code in the `Configure` method.

The `IWebJobsBuilder` parameter exposes only the `IServiceCollection` instance (which can be used to support dependency injection, as you will see in Chapter 6, *Testing and Monitoring*) but there are a number of extension methods that can be used. One of these methods allows you to add a new extension (a trigger or a binding):

```
[assembly: WebJobsStartup(typeof(CustomWebJobsStartup))]
public class CustomWebJobsStartup : IWebJobsStartup
{
    public void Configure(IWebJobsBuilder builder)
    {
        builder.AddExtension<MyCustomExtension>();
    }
}
```

 To use the startup feature provided by the WebJob SDK, you have to change the target framework for the Visual Studio project that contains the `IWebJobsStartup` implementation. To do this, simply change the value present in the `TargetFramework` node of the `.csproj` file and substitute it with the `netstandard2.0` value.

An extension is a class that implements the `IExtensionConfigProvider` interface:

```
public class MyCustomExtension : IExtensionConfigProvider
{
    public void Initialize(ExtensionConfigContext context)
    {
        // Write here the code to initialize your extension
    }
}
```

In the `Initialize` method, you must register your custom trigger or binding.

Another important thing to know about in order to use Azure Functions customization in the right way is the binding process that the runtime uses.

The Azure Functions runtime binding process has two different phases:

- **Startup binding**: The runtime executes this phase only when the host starts. In this phase, the runtime registers the built-in binding (`TimerTrigger` and `HttpTrigger`) and you must add your custom extensions.
- **Runtime binding**: The runtime executes this phase every time a function is triggered by an event.

Let's analyze the individual phases in detail. During the startup binding, the runtime performs the following steps (the startup binding phase):

1. At the start of the host job, the runtime registers its own integrated binding providers. In this step, you can register your custom bindings using the preceding technique.
2. The runtime uses reflection to find all the methods that implement an Azure Function within the referenced assemblies.
3. For each Azure Function found in the previous step, and for each parameter of the function, the runtime will attempt to identify, among the registered binding providers (using the `ITriggerBindingProvider` and `IBindingProvider` interfaces provides by the Azure WebJobs SDK), the provider needed to resolve the binding. If the provider is found, the runtime will use it to bind the parameter.
4. When all the functions have been processed, the runtime creates an internal representation for each of them with all the information necessary for execution during the runtime phase. Functions that do not use bindings correctly (for example, if an unregistered binding is used), are discarded by the runtime and are not available for execution.

5. For each trigger, the runtime creates the corresponding listener and runs it. Now the function is ready to react to events.

Every time an Azure Function is triggered, the runtime performs the following steps (the runtime binding phase):

1. The runtime retrieves the complete definition of the function that it created during the startup phase and, for each binding, executes the `BindAsync` method (`ITriggerBinding.BindAsync`/`IBinding.BindAsync`).
2. The binding has the responsibility of converting the input values to the values actually used by the function.
3. If all binding methods are executed without any exceptions, the function is executed.

Creating a custom trigger

Before starting to implement your custom trigger, is important to understand what the classes involved in the trigger pipeline are and what their responsibility is in that pipeline:

- `TriggerConfigProvider`: This implements the `IExtensionConfigProvider` interface and it has the responsibility of configuring the entire trigger process in terms of:
    - The attribute that defines the trigger
    - The payload associated with the trigger (for example, the HTTP request for `HttpTrigger`)
    - The actual binding provider class to use to create the actual binding object
- `TriggerAttribute`: This is used to decorate a method parameter to identify the function trigger. It inherits from `Attribute` and is decorated by `BindingAttribute`. It has the responsibility of containing the trigger data (for example, the schedule expression for `TimerTrigger`).
- `TriggerBindingProvider`: This implements the `ITriggerBindingProvider` interface and has the responsibility of creating the actual binding object. It is the factory class. In this class, you can read the configuration data from the settings and pass them to the binding class.
- `TriggerBinding`: This implements the `ITriggerBinding` interface and is responsible for creating the listener instance.

- `TriggerListener`: This implements the `IListener` interface and has the responsibility of reacting to events and executing the function. There is a listener for each function you define in your code.

The following diagram shows the interactions between the classes mentioned previously in the different phases of the binding process:

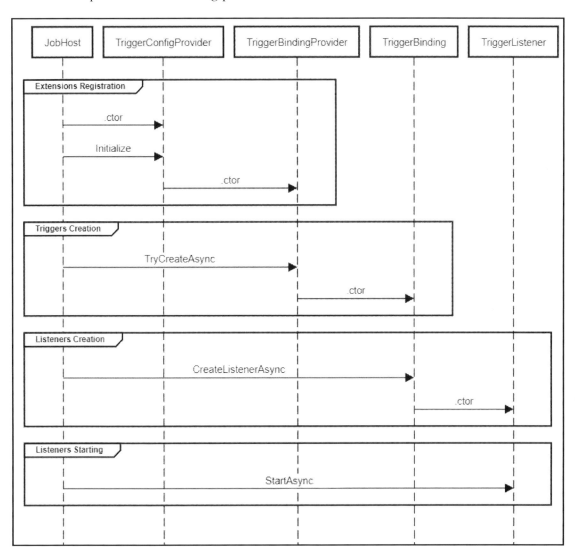

To better clarify the mechanism behind triggers, we'll try to implement a trigger that executes a function when the temperature measured in a city changes:

1. Let's start by implementing the trigger attribute:

```
[Binding]
[AttributeUsage(AttributeTargets.Parameter)]
public class WeatherTriggerAttribute : Attribute
{
    public WeatherTriggerAttribute(string cityName, double
temperatureThreshold)
    {
        CityName = cityName;
        TemperatureThreshold = temperatureThreshold;
    }

    public string ApiKey { get; set; }
    public string CityName { get; internal set; }
    public double TemperatureThreshold { get; internal set; }
}
```

We would like to use OpenWeatherMap services to retrieve the weather information (including the temperature) for a specific city, so we need the city name (for example, *"Rome, IT"* for *Rome in Italy*), the API key to use the OpenWeatherMap API, and the temperature threshold (that is, the difference, in degree Celsius, that fires the trigger).

 OpenWeatherMap provides you with a set of REST APIs to retrieve weather data. It has a free plan that allows you to make 60 calls per minute. You can find more info about it at https://openweathermap.org.

When the function is triggered, the trigger sends us the weather temperature using the following payload:

```
public class WeatherPayload
{
 public string CityName { get; set; }

 public double CurrentTemperature { get; set; }

 public double LastTemperature { get; set; }

 public DateTimeOffset Timestamp { get; internal set; }
}
```

So, an Azure Function that uses our trigger is as follows:

```
[FunctionName(nameof(RomeWeatherCheck))]
public static void RomeWeatherCheck(
    [WeatherTrigger("Rome,IT", 0.1)] WeatherPayload req,
     ILogger log)
{
    var message = $"{req.CityName} [{req.CurrentTemperature}] at
{req.Timestamp}";
    log.LogWarning(message);
}
```

And its execution looks like this:

```
C:\Users\massi\AppData\Local\AzureFunctionsTools\Releases\2.18.5\cli\func.exe                    —    □    ×
[09/04/2019 11:32:53] 1 functions loaded
[09/04/2019 11:32:53] WorkerRuntime: dotnet. Will shutdown other standby channels
[09/04/2019 11:32:53] Generating 1 job function(s)
[09/04/2019 11:32:53] Found the following functions:
[09/04/2019 11:32:53] Functions.WeatherFunctions.RomeWeatherCheck
[09/04/2019 11:32:53]
[09/04/2019 11:32:53] Host initialized (337ms)
[09/04/2019 11:32:53] Host started (351ms)
[09/04/2019 11:32:53] Job host started
Hosting environment: Production
Content root path: E:\Sviluppo\MasteringServerless\CH02-CustomisingAzureFunctions\Functions\bin\Debug\netcoreapp2.1
Now listening on: http://0.0.0.0:7071
Application started. Press Ctrl+C to shut down.
[09/04/2019 11:33:01] Executing 'RomeWeatherCheck' (Reason='', Id=72d21131-b004-4987-9897-a95c9b767aec)
[09/04/2019 11:33:01] Rome,IT [16.6900005340576] at 09/04/2019 11:28:36 +00:00
[09/04/2019 11:33:01] Executed 'RomeWeatherCheck' (Succeeded, Id=72d21131-b004-4987-9897-a95c9b767aec)
[09/04/2019 11:33:02] Host lock lease acquired by instance ID '000000000000000000000006F50611E'.
[09/04/2019 11:53:08] Executing 'RomeWeatherCheck' (Reason='', Id=ed7bf99f-7875-4dbf-be1d-0e13a6a8a988)
[09/04/2019 11:53:08] Rome,IT [16.8500003814697] at 09/04/2019 11:49:52 +00:00
[09/04/2019 11:53:08] Executed 'RomeWeatherCheck' (Succeeded, Id=ed7bf99f-7875-4dbf-be1d-0e13a6a8a988)
[09/04/2019 12:03:12] Executing 'RomeWeatherCheck' (Reason='', Id=e606cb33-0422-438f-a970-a46468376800)
[09/04/2019 12:03:12] Rome,IT [17.0499992370605] at 09/04/2019 12:00:09 +00:00
[09/04/2019 12:03:12] Executed 'RomeWeatherCheck' (Succeeded, Id=e606cb33-0422-438f-a970-a46468376800)
```

Now we'll analyze all the classes we need to complete the whole process.

2. Let's start with `TriggerConfigurationProvider`:

```
[Extension("Weather")]
public class WeatherTriggerConfigProvider :
IExtensionConfigProvider
{
    // .... Field definitions (look at GitHub repo for the full
code)

 public WeatherTriggerConfigProvider(INameResolver nameResolver,
ILoggerFactory loggerFactory, IWeatherService weatherService)
 {
     // .... dependency assignment (look at GitHub repo for the
```

```
full code)
  }

  public void Initialize(ExtensionConfigContext context)
  {
      var triggerAttributeBindingRule =
context.AddBindingRule<WeatherTriggerAttribute>();
      triggerAttributeBindingRule.BindToTrigger<WeatherPayload>(
          new WeatherTriggerBindingProvider(this._nameResolver,
this._loggerFactory, this._weatherService));
  }
}
```

WeatherTriggerConfigProvider is decorated with the Extension attribute to mark it as an extension, and the Initialize method is where we define our binding rule. In this case, add a binding rule using the trigger attribute and set the trigger binding with the BindToTrigger method. This method tells the runtime that we use the WeatherPayload class to take the trigger data and WeatherTriggerBindingProvider as the provider to generate the binding class.

3. Once we define our configuration provider, we have to add it in the binding pipeline, and to do this we must use the startup method seen previously:

```
[assembly: WebJobsStartup(typeof(ExtensionsStartup))]
public class ExtensionsStartup : IWebJobsStartup
{
    public void Configure(IWebJobsBuilder builder)
    {
        builder.AddExtension<WeatherTriggerConfigProvider>();
    }
}
```

In a real application, the startup method contains a lot of code (for example, the registration of the services in the dependency resolver container or a more complex configuration of the extensions), and for this reason, generally, extension methods are implemented for the registration of individual extensions:

```
[assembly: WebJobsStartup(typeof(ExtensionsStartup))]
public class ExtensionsStartup : IWebJobsStartup
{
    public void Configure(IWebJobsBuilder builder)
    {
        builder.UseWeatherTrigger();
        // Other configurations
    }
```

```
}

public static class WebJobBuilderExtensions
{
    public static IWebJobsBuilder UseWeatherTrigger(this
IWebJobsBuilder builder)
    {
        if (builder == null)
            throw new NullReferenceException(nameof(builder));
        builder.AddExtension<WeatherTriggerConfigProvider>();
        // Add here all the configuration code for the extension
        return builder;
    }
}
```

You will notice that the constructor of the `WeatherTriggerConfigProvider`
class has three parameters but there is no trace of these parameters in the
registration (the `AddExtension` method). This is because you can take advantage
of the type resolution natively supported by the WebJobs SDK. In this case, when
the platform has to create an instance of `WeatherTriggerConfigProvider`, it
will try to resolve the types automatically. The `INameResolver` (used to read the
configuration) and `ILoggerFactory` types are registered automatically by the
platform, while for the resolution of `IWeatherService` (our service for access to
the OpenWeatherMap API), it is necessary to use the type registration:

```
builder.Services.AddTransient<IWeatherService, WeatherService>();
```

4. The next class we create is the `WeatherTriggerBindingProvider` class:

```
public class WeatherTriggerBindingProvider :
ITriggerBindingProvider
{
    // .... Field definitions (look at GitHub repo for the full
code)

    public WeatherTriggerBindingProvider(INameResolver
nameResolver,
        ILoggerFactory loggerFactory, IWeatherService
weatherService)
    {
        // .... dependency assignment (look at GitHub repo for the
full code)
    }

    public Task<ITriggerBinding>
TryCreateAsync(TriggerBindingProviderContext context)
    {
```

```
        // TryCreateAsync implementation
    }

    private string
GetTriggerAttributeApiKey(WeatherTriggerAttribute triggerAttribute)
    {
        // retrieves the configuration for the trigger
    }
}
```

In general, the implementation of `TryCreateAsync` will do the following:

- Inspect `ParameterInfo` to see whether it has the specific binding attribute applied to it (in this case, `WeatherTriggerAttribute`)
- Determine whether the `Type` parameter is supported by the binding. If so, the provider constructs and returns an `ITriggerBinding` instance (`WeatherTriggerBinding` in this case):

```
    public Task<ITriggerBinding>
TryCreateAsync(TriggerBindingProviderContext context)
    {
        if (context is null)
            throw new ArgumentNullException(nameof(context));

        var parameter = context.Parameter;
        var triggerAttribute =
parameter.GetCustomAttribute<WeatherTriggerAttribute>(inherit:
false);
        if (triggerAttribute is null)
            return Task.FromResult<ITriggerBinding>(null);

        triggerAttribute.ApiKey =
GetTriggerAttributeApiKey(triggerAttribute);

        return Task.FromResult<ITriggerBinding>(
            new WeatherTriggerBinding(parameter, _nameResolver,
_weatherService, triggerAttribute));
    }
```

In this method, you can also validate the `triggerAttribute` parameter or read values from app settings (using the `nameResolver` instance passed in the constructor):

```
    private string
GetTriggerAttributeApiKey(WeatherTriggerAttribute triggerAttribute)
    {
        if (string.IsNullOrEmpty(triggerAttribute.ApiKey))
        {
            var apiKey = _nameResolver.Resolve("Weather.ApiKey");
            if (string.IsNullOrEmpty(apiKey))
                throw new InvalidOperationException("ApiKey is
mandatory");
            return apiKey;
        }
        return triggerAttribute.ApiKey;
    }
```

The `TryCreateAsync` method returns the instance of `ITriggerBinding` the runtime uses to create the listener. In our scenario, `ITriggerBinding` is implemented by the `WeatherTriggerBinding` class:

```
public class WeatherTriggerBinding : ITriggerBinding
{
    public Type TriggerValueType => typeof(WeatherPayload);
    public IReadOnlyDictionary<string, Type> BindingDataContract {
get; } = new Dictionary<string, Type>();
    // .... other Field definitions (look at GitHub repo for the
full code)

    public WeatherTriggerBinding(ParameterInfo parameter,
INameResolver nameResolver, IWeatherService weatherService,
WeatherTriggerAttribute attribute)
    {
        // .... dependency assignment (look at GitHub repo for the
full code)
    }

    public Task<ITriggerData> BindAsync(object value,
ValueBindingContext context)
    {
        return Task.FromResult<ITriggerData>(new TriggerData(null,
new Dictionary<string, object>()));
    }

    // This is the most important method of the class. It has the
    responsibility to create the listener for the function.
```

```
    public Task<IListener>
CreateListenerAsync(ListenerFactoryContext context)
    {
        return Task.FromResult<IListener>(new
WeatherTriggerListener(context.Executor, this._weatherService,
this._attribute));
    }

    public ParameterDescriptor ToParameterDescriptor()
    {
        // look at GitHub repo for the full code
    }
}
```

The ITriggerBinding interface exposes three methods and two properties.

The BindAsync and BindingDataContract pair allows you to create triggers that support binding expressions in the trigger parameters. You can see an example of binding expressions in the following snippet of code:

```
[FunctionName("ResizeImage")]
public static void Run(
    [BlobTrigger("sample-images/{filename}")] Stream image,
    [Blob("sample-images-sm/{filename}", FileAccess.Write)] Stream
imageSmall,
    string filename,
    ILogger log)
{
    log.LogInformation($"Blob trigger processing: {filename}");
    // ...
}
```

The {filename} expression in the BlogTrigger parameter, is a binding expression. The BindingDataContract property exposes a dictionary (of string and Type) that enumerates all the allowed binding expressions for the trigger. If you look at the BlobTrigger implementation in the GitHub repository, you will find the following:

```
private static IReadOnlyDictionary<string, Type>
CreateBindingDataContract(IBlobPathSource path)
{
    var contract = new Dictionary<string,
Type>(StringComparer.OrdinalIgnoreCase);
    contract.Add("BlobTrigger", typeof(string));
    contract.Add("Uri", typeof(Uri));
    contract.Add("Properties", typeof(BlobProperties));
    contract.Add("Metadata", typeof(IDictionary<string, string>));
```

```
    IReadOnlyDictionary<string, Type> contractFromPath =
path.CreateBindingDataContract();

    if (contractFromPath != null)
    {
        foreach (KeyValuePair<string, Type> item in
contractFromPath)
        {
            // In case of conflict, binding data from the value
type overrides the built-in binding data above.
            contract[item.Key] = item.Value;
        }
    }

    return contract;
}
```

The `BindAsync` method is called by the runtime during the binding phase to convert the trigger parameters into an `ITriggerData` instance using the `BindingDataContract` seen previously.

You can find the implementation of `BlobTrigger` in the GitHub repository at `https://github.com/Azure/azure-webjobs-sdk`.

In our sample, we don't support binding expressions, so we return an empty dictionary for the `BindingDataContract` property and a `TriggerData` instance without any data for the `BindAsync` method.

`CreateListenerAsync` is the most important method of the class: it is responsible for creating the listener for the function. The listener should be initialized with all the parameters mandatory for the function (in the previous sample, the weather service, and the attribute information) and with the `ITriggerFunctionExecutor` instance used to invoke the function inside the listener when it needs to.

The `ToParameterDescriptor` method has the responsibility of returning a `ParameterDescriptor` instance that describes the trigger parameter. The descriptor can be used by some tools to display parameter information on dashboards.

Finally, the `TriggerValueType` property defines the type of value returned by the trigger—in our sample, the `WeatherPayload` we use in the function signature.

5. The last class we have to implement is the listener, the heart of the trigger process. It is responsible for checking whether the trigger event is fired (in our sample, if the selected city temperature increases by a configured threshold) and if it is, it executes the function:

```
public class WeatherTriggerListener : IListener
{
    // .... Field definitions (look at GitHub repo for the full
code)
    private CancellationTokenSource _listenerStoppingTokenSource;
    private Task _listenerTask;

    public WeatherTriggerListener(ITriggeredFunctionExecutor
executor,
          IWeatherService weatherService, WeatherTriggerAttribute
attribute)
    {
        // .... dependency assignment (look at GitHub repo for the
full code)
    }

    public void Cancel()
    {
        // .....
    }

    public Task StartAsync(CancellationToken cancellationToken)
    {
        // .....
    }

    public async Task StopAsync(CancellationToken
cancellationToken)
    {
        // .....
    }
}
```

The `IListener` interface exposes only three methods that allow the runtime to manage the listener.

The `Cancel` and `StopAsync` methods are used by the runtime to close the listener (for example, because the function host needs to be moved to another server). The listener needs to manage the async pattern used for function invocation in the right way, and this is the reason why you find the `CancellationToken` in the parameter of the `IListener` interface methods:

```
public void Cancel()
{
    StopAsync(CancellationToken.None).Wait();
}

public async Task StopAsync(CancellationToken cancellationToken)
{
    if (_listenerTask == null)
        return;
    try
    {
        _listenerStoppingTokenSource.Cancel();
    }
    finally
    {
        await Task.WhenAny(_listenerTask, Task.Delay(Timeout.Infinite,
cancellationToken));
    }
}
```

The `StartAsync` method is used by the runtime, in the startup phase, to start the listener. The listener is like a game loop that periodically checks whether the trigger event is fired:

```
public Task StartAsync(CancellationToken cancellationToken)
{
    try
    {
        _listenerStoppingTokenSource = new CancellationTokenSource();
        var factory = new TaskFactory();
        var token = _listenerStoppingTokenSource.Token;
        _listenerTask = factory.StartNew(async () => await
ListenerAction(token), token);
    }
    catch (Exception)
    {
        throw;
    }
    return _listenerTask.IsCompleted ? _listenerTask : Task.CompletedTask;
```

```
    }

    private async Task ListenerAction(CancellationToken token)
    {
        // this is the code that the listener use to check if the trigger is
    fired
    }
```

The `StartAsync` method simply starts a task that is an infinite loop (closed by the `CancellationToken` cancellation request). Inside the loop, we use the weather service to retrieve the city weather information and if the city temperature increased by the threshold (which is our trigger event), we create the weather payload and execute the function using the `ITriggeredFunctionExecutor` instance passed from the trigger binding:

```
    private async Task ListenerAction(CancellationToken token)
    {
        this._weatherService.ApiKey = this._attribute.ApiKey;
        var cityData = new CityInfo();
        double lastTemperature = 0;
        while (!token.IsCancellationRequested)
        {
            // get weather info and check if the city temperature is over the
    threshold (look at GitHub repo for the full code)
            // If the listener need to fire the function (the temperature is
    over the threshold) use the next statement to fire the function
            await _executor.TryExecuteAsync(new TriggeredFunctionData() {
    TriggerValue = weatherPayload }, token);
            await Task.Delay(TimeSpan.FromMinutes(1), token);
        }
    }
```

Remember that you have a listener for each function, so the scalability of the function depends on how you implement the trigger. The listener executes a function and only when it finishes, it can check if another trigger event has been fired. This is why Azure Functions should not have a long duration. If you know that your functions may have a long duration, you have to write the listener to achieve this goal (for example, you could create a new task that performs the long-duration operation by exploiting multithreading and not blocking the execution of the listener).

Creating a custom binding

You need to create a custom trigger when you want to run your Azure Function as a reaction to your custom events. In the example we saw in the previous section, we would like to run our function when the temperature of a city rises by a threshold: exceeding the threshold represents our custom event.

You must create a custom binding, instead, when you want to interact with an external data source within your Azure Function and you want to demand at runtime the responsibility for the creation and life cycle management of the binding. In that case, your function receives the instance of the binding from the runtime and doesn't care about its creation or release.

In fact, you also can interact with an external source by creating your data access class inside the body of the Azure Function (for example, using the constructor), but in this scenario, you are responsible for creating and managing the life cycle while, if you use the binding approach, you let the runtime do the job for you.

As we did for custom triggers, before starting to implement your custom binding, it's important to understand what the classes involved in the binding pipeline are and what their responsibility is in that pipeline.

The binding pipeline is similar to the custom trigger pipeline, and the involved classes depend on what kind of binding you want to implement.

The classes involved in the pipeline are as follows:

- `BindingAttribute`: This is used to decorate a function parameter to identify the function binding. It inherits from `Attribute` and is decorated by `BindingAttribute` (like the trigger attribute you saw in the previous paragraph). It has the responsibility of containing the binding data (for example, the queue name for `QueueBinding`) specifically for the function in which you use it.

- `BindingConfigProvider`: This implements the `IExtensionConfigProvider` interface and has the responsibility of configuring the rules for binding. Defining a rule means that you do the following:
  - Declare what kind of binding attribute identifies the rule. When the runtime discovers that a binding attribute is used in a function, then it uses the corresponding rule.
  - Add, if you want, a validator for the attribute (for example, you can check that a connection string is formally valid).
  - Add the behavior for the rule. The behavior depends on what kind of object you, actually, want to use to implement the binding feature. You can have three types of binding:
    - `BindToInput`: You just declare that your binding type is an object. You use this kind of behavior when you want to bind your data to a single input (for example, a single row in `CloudTable`).
    - `BindToCollector`: You declare that you support a list in your binding; that means your binding object is a collection that implements the `IAsyncCollector` interface (for example, you want to add multiple items to a queue).
    - `BindToStream`: You want to support a stream as binding.
- `BindingConverter`: This class has the responsibility of creating the actual binding class for the binding (the behavior mentioned before). It must implement the `IConverter` interface.
- **Binding class**: The binding class is the class that actually binds to the data source. Its structure depends on the binding behavior you choose.

The following diagram shows the interactions between the classes mentioned previously in the different phases of the binding process:

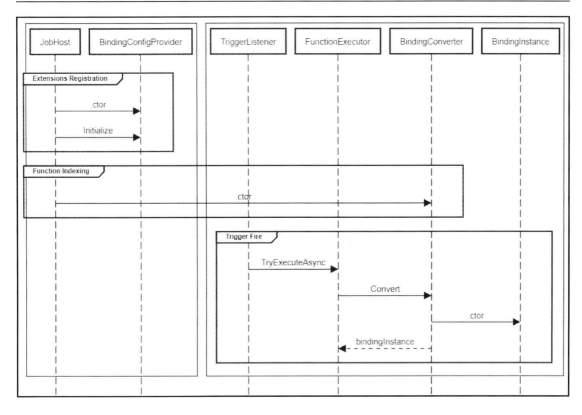

As we did for the custom trigger, we'll try to implement a custom binding that allows your functions to send tweets using a Twitter account:

> We'll use the TweetinviAPI package, a simple and open source library for accessing the Twitter REST API. The NuGet package is available at `https://www.nuget.org/packages/TweetinviAPI/`, and the source code is available on GitHub (`https://github.com/linvi/tweetinvi`).

1. First of all, you define the binding attribute:

```
[Binding]
[AttributeUsage(AttributeTargets.Parameter |
AttributeTargets.ReturnValue)]
public class TwitterBindingAttribute : Attribute
{
    [AppSetting(Default = "Twitter.ConsumerKey")]
    public string ConsumerKey { get; set; }

    [AppSetting(Default = "Twitter.ConsumerSecret")]
    public string ConsumerSecret { get; set; }
```

```
        [AppSetting(Default = "Twitter.AccessToken")]
        public string AccessToken { get; set; }

        [AppSetting(Default = "Twitter.AccessTokenSecret")]
        public string AccessTokenSecret { get; set; }
}
```

2. Using this attribute, you can write the function:

```
[FunctionName(nameof(PeriodicTweet))]
public static void PeriodicTweet(
        [TimerTrigger("0 */5 * * * *")] TimerInfo timer,
        [TwitterBinding()] IAsyncCollector<string> tweetMessages,
        ILogger log)
{
  // .....
}
```

You will notice that the attribute properties are marked with the
AppSetting attribute. This attribute tells the runtime that the property must be
resolved by reading the values from the app settings file and, by default, the
value is contained in the key defined by the Default property. So, in the
previous snippet of code, the runtime will look for app settings like this:

```
{
    "IsEncrypted": false,
    "Values": {
        ..
        "Twitter.ConsumerKey": "smv2pDr......Rbko4",
        "Twitter.ConsumerSecret": "JWH8......73RUnV",
        "Twitter.AccessToken": "111........EZLZv8m8w",
        "Twitter.AccessTokenSecret": "E7H.....eMmKize0"
    }
}
```

The use of the AppSetting attribute allows the developer to create code like the
following:

```
[FunctionName(nameof(PeriodicTweet))]
public static void PeriodicTweet(
        [TimerTrigger("0 */5 * * * *")] TimerInfo timer,
        [TwitterBinding(ConsumerKey="myConsumerKeySetting")]
IAsyncCollector<string> tweetMessages,
        ILogger log)
{
  // .....
}
```

This means that the runtime will look for the value of `ConsumerKey` in the `myConsumerKeySettings` key of the app settings.

You can also use the `AutoResolve` attribute, which allows the developer to use binding expressions inside the attribute declaration. For example, if you have the following code:

```
[Binding]
[AttributeUsage(AttributeTargets.Parameter |
AttributeTargets.ReturnValue)]
public class TwitterBindingAttribute : Attribute
{
    [AutoResolve]
    public string ConsumerKey { get; set; }
    ....
}
```

You can use the following declaration:

```
[FunctionName(nameof(PeriodicTweet))]
public static void PeriodicTweet(
        [TimerTrigger("0 */5 * * * *")] TimerInfo timer,
        [TwitterBinding(ConsumerKey="%PrefixKey%%PostfixKey%")]
IAsyncCollector<string> tweetMessages,
        ILogger log)
{
 // .....
}
```

This means that the runtime will look for the `PrefixKey` and `PostfixKey` in app settings and then set `ConsumerKey` with the concatenation of the two values.

3. Once you have defined the attribute that identifies your binding, you must create, as you did in the previous paragraph for the custom trigger, `ExtensionConfigProvider`:

```
[Extension("Twitter")]
public class TwitterBindingConfigProvider :
IExtensionConfigProvider
{
    // .... Field definitions (look at GitHub repo for the full
code)

    public TwitterBindingConfigProvider(INameResolver nameResolver,
            ILoggerFactory loggerFactory, ITwitterService
twitterService)
    {
```

```
            // .... dependency assignment (look at GitHub repo for the
full code)
    }

    public void Initialize(ExtensionConfigContext context)
    {
        var bindingRule =
context.AddBindingRule<TwitterBindingAttribute>();
        bindingRule.AddValidator(ValidateTwitterConfig);
bindingRule.BindToCollector<OpenType>(typeof(TwitterBindingCollecto
rConverter),
            _nameResolver, _twitterService);
bindingRule.BindToInput<TwitterBinder>(typeof(TwitterBindingConvert
er),
            _nameResolver, _twitterService);
    }

    private void ValidateTwitterConfig(TwitterBindingAttribute
attribute, Type paramType)
    {
        // Attribute validation code
        if (string.IsNullOrEmpty(attribute.AccessToken))
            throw new InvalidOperationException($"Twitter
AccessToken must be set either via the attribute property or via
configuration.");
        // ..... look at GitHub repo for the full code
  }
}
```

In the `Initialize` method, you can create all the binding rules you need (using the `AddBindingRule` method of the `ExtensionConfigContext` class). This method returns a `FluuntBindingRule` instance that you can use to configure the rule itself. In the previous sample, we added a validation using `AddValidator` and configured the rule to use the `TwitterBindingCollectorConverter` class and `TwitterBindingConverter` to create the actual binding instances.

The validation method will be called by the runtime in the indexing phase; that is when the runtime discovers all the functions and sets up the triggers and binding. If the attribute passed by the parameter is not valid, you can throw an exception and the runtime will exclude the function from the available functions.

When the runtime tries to execute a function that uses your binding (because a trigger listener invokes it), the runtime creates the binding object using the converter you define in the `BindTo` method and based on what kind of binding class you request.

For example, let's say the function looks like the following:

```
[FunctionName(nameof(PeriodicTweets))]
public static async Task PeriodicTweets(
        [TimerTrigger("0 */5 * * * *")] TimerInfo timer,
        [TwitterBinding] IAsyncCollector<string> tweetMessages,
        ILogger log)
{
    // .....
}
```

The runtime uses an instance of `TwitterBindingCollectorConverter` to create an instance of the `tweetMessages` parameter:

```
public class TwitterBindingCollectorConverter :
    IConverter<TwitterBindingAttribute, IAsyncCollector<string>>
{
    private readonly INameResolver _nameResolver;
    private readonly ITwitterService _twitterService;

    public TwitterBindingCollectorConverter(INameResolver
nameResolver, ITwitterService twitterService)
    {
        _nameResolver = nameResolver;
        _twitterService = twitterService;
    }

    public IAsyncCollector<string> Convert(TwitterBindingAttribute
attribute)
    {
        return new TwitterBindingAsyncCollector(attribute,
_twitterService, _nameResolver);
    }
}
```

Instead, if the function looked like the following:

```
[FunctionName(nameof(PeriodicTweet))]
public static async Task PeriodicTweet(
        [TimerTrigger("0 */5 * * *")] TimerInfo timer,
        [TwitterBinding()] TwitterBinder twitter,
        ILogger log)
{
    // .....
}
```

The runtime would invoke an instance of `TwitterBindingConverter` to create the `TwitterBinder` instance passed in the `twitter` parameter:

```
public class TwitterBindingConverter :
    IConverter<TwitterBindingAttribute, TwitterBinder>
{
    private readonly INameResolver _nameResolver;
    private readonly ITwitterService _twitterService;

    public TwitterBindingConverter(INameResolver nameResolver,
ITwitterService twitterService)
    {
        _nameResolver = nameResolver;
        _twitterService = twitterService;
    }

    public TwitterBinder Convert(TwitterBindingAttribute attribute)
    {
        return new TwitterBinder(attribute, _twitterService,
_nameResolver);
    }
}
```

Both of the converters are responsible for creating the actual binding classes (they are a sort of factory) and you must implement the `Convert` method to create the instances of the binding objects.

The binding classes (`TwitterBindingAsyncCollector` and `TwitterBinder` in the sample) are responsible for managing the interaction between your function and the data source. In our sample, both classes send tweets (the first one allows the developer to send multiple tweets at one time, while the second one supports the sending of only one tweet at a time):

```
public class TwitterBindingAsyncCollector : IAsyncCollector<string>
{
    // .... Field definitions (look at GitHub repo for the full
```

```
code)

    private readonly List<string> _tweetsToSend = new
List<string>();

    public TwitterBindingAsyncCollector(TwitterBindingAttribute
attribute,
        ITwitterService twitterService, INameResolver nameResolver)
    {
        // .... dependency assignment (look at GitHub repo for the
full code)

        this._twitterService.SetSettings(attribute);
    }

    public Task AddAsync(string item, CancellationToken
cancellationToken = default)
    {
        _tweetsToSend.Add(item);
        return Task.CompletedTask;
    }

    public async Task FlushAsync(CancellationToken
cancellationToken = default)
    {
        foreach (var item in this._tweetsToSend)
        {
            await _twitterService.SendTweetAsync(item);
        }
        this._tweetsToSend.Clear();
    }
}
```

TwitterBindingAsyncCollector implements IAsyncCollector<string>
and it allows the developer to add messages to the tweet in the body of the
function (using the Add method) and sends them when the function finishes its
job (the runtime calls the FlushAsync method). When you implement the
IAsyncCollector interface, you should always implement the methods so that
they are thread-safe. In the preceding example, for simplicity, the methods are not
thread-safe:

```
public class TwitterBinder
{
    // .... Field definitions (look at GitHub repo for the full
code)

    public TwitterBinder(TwitterBindingAttribute attribute,
```

```
            ITwitterService twitterService, INameResolver nameResolver)
    {
        // .... dependency assignment (look at GitHub repo for the
full code)

        this._twitterService.SetSettings(attribute);
    }

    public Task TweetAsync(string message)
    {
        return _twitterService.SendTweetAsync(message);
    }
}
```

The `TwitterBinder` class allows the developer to send a single tweet using the `TweetAsync` method and it doesn't implement any interfaces or base classes, so you can design your binding object as you want.

4. Finally, you have to add the configure provider to the `IWebJobBuilder` instance in the host startup method (as you saw in the previous section):

```
[assembly: WebJobsStartup(typeof(ExtensionsStartup))]

public class ExtensionsStartup : IWebJobsStartup
{
    public void Configure(IWebJobsBuilder builder)
    {
        ...
        builder.AddExtension<TwitterBindingConfigProvider>();
        ...
    }
}
```

Summary

In this chapter, you discovered how the trigger and binding pipelines work and how you can leverage pipelines to customize your functions to adapt them to your business scenarios.

The Azure Functions extensions are a powerful tool you can use to adapt function triggers and bindings to your scenarios. You can leverage them to reuse your business code inside your functions with minimal effort. Actually, as you saw in this chapter, it is very simple to implement your custom triggers and bindings, but you always need to remember the serverless nature of Azure Functions: they are born to have great scalability, and triggers and bindings are important ingredients of that scalability. If your custom trigger or binding requires a great amount of memory or takes time to do its job, Azure Functions based on them will probably not be a great example of a serverless solution.

In the next chapter, we will talk about which programming languages are supported by Azure Functions and how you can build your preferred programming language support at runtime.

Questions

1. How many triggers can an Azure Function have?
    - They must always have only one trigger.
    - They cannot have triggers.
    - More than one trigger.
    - Zero or one trigger.

2. How many bindings can an Azure Function have?
    - They must always have only one binding.
    - They cannot have bindings.
    - As many bindings as you want.
    - At most, one binding.

3. What does `TriggerListener` do?
    - Manages custom events and executes Azure Functions when they occur.
    - Opens a socket connection to the Azure Functions runtime and tracks errors.
    - It is used by the runtime only to open HTTP connections to the internet.

4. How can you add a custom extension to the Azure Functions runtime?
   - You need to modify the Azure Functions runtime source code and rebuild it.
   - You can use the `AddExtension` method of the `IWebJobsBuilder` interface in the configuration phase of the startup phase.
   - You cannot add a custom extension to the Azure Functions runtime.
   - You have to create a `TimerTrigger` function that, periodically, adds the extension to the runtime.

Further reading

You can find more information about triggers, bindings, and customizing Azure Functions at the following URLs:

- *Azure Functions triggers and bindings concepts*: `https://docs.microsoft.com/en-us/azure/azure-functions/functions-triggers-bindings`
- *Azure Functions trigger and binding example*: `https://docs.microsoft.com/en-us/azure/azure-functions/functions-bindings-example`
- *Microsoft Azure Learn Path: Execute an Azure Function with triggers*: `https://docs.microsoft.com/en-us/learn/modules/execute-azure-function-with-triggers/`
- *Microsoft Azure Learn Path: Chain Azure Functions together using input and output bindings*: `https://docs.microsoft.com/en-us/learn/modules/chain-azure-functions-data-using-bindings/`
- *Azure GitHub: Creating custom input and output bindings*: `https://github.com/Azure/azure-webjobs-sdk/wiki/Creating-custom-input-and-output-bindings`

3
Programming Languages Supported in Azure Functions

In the previous chapters, you saw a lot of code snippets based on C#. But Azure Functions are not only C#—they support a set of programming languages and, moreover, allow you to create the infrastructure to support your own favorite programming language. After reading this chapter, you will understand how the language extension pattern, implemented by the Azure Functions Runtime, works and how you can extend it to support new languages.

This chapter will cover the following topics:

- Azure Functions and JavaScript
- Azure Functions and Java
- Azure Functions and Python
- Azure Functions and PowerShell
- Language extensibility

Technical requirements

In this chapter, you will see a lot of code snippets written in Node.js, Java, and Python, so a basic knowledge of these languages will help you to understand the concepts.

During this chapter, you will also see the language extension architecture implemented in Azure Functions that allows the support of multiple programming languages. You will need no particular skills to learn about this topic.

Azure Functions and JavaScript

You can implement your Azure Functions using JavaScript. The Azure Functions Runtime leverages Node.js to host and run your functions written in JavaScript.

At the time of writing this book, the runtime uses even-numbered Node.js versions (8.11.1 and 10.14.1 are recommended). You can set the Node.js version using the `WEBSITE_NODE_DEFAULT_VERSION` app settings.

You can retrieve the Node.js version inside any function by using that app's settings or reading the `process.version` property.

You can create your first function using the Azure Functions Core Tools in the same way you do for a C# function:

1. The first step you must perform is to create the project that hosts your functions:

    ```
    func init --worker-runtime node
    ```

    The following screenshot shows the output of the preceding command:

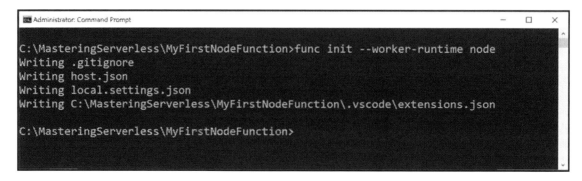

The `--worker-runtime` parameter defines the worker runtime you want to use.

2. In this case, you create the function project using the `node` as the worker runtime, so you can create your function both in JavaScript or TypeScript:

```
func new --name TimerFunction --language javascript --template
TimerTrigger
```

The following screenshot shows the output of the preceding command:

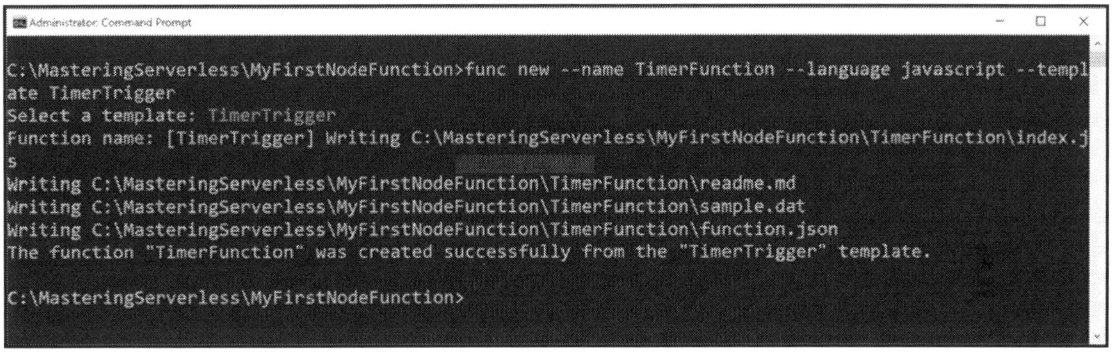

At the time of writing this book (which uses version 2.6.1048 of the Azure Functions Tool), the templates available for the function written in JavaScript are as follows:

- Azure Blob storage trigger
- Azure Cosmos DB trigger
- Azure Event Grid trigger
- Azure Event Hub trigger
- HTTP trigger
- IoT Hub (Event Hub)
- Azure Queue storage trigger
- SendGrid
- Azure Service Bus Queue trigger
- Azure Service Bus Topic trigger
- Timer trigger

The project folder may have the following structure:

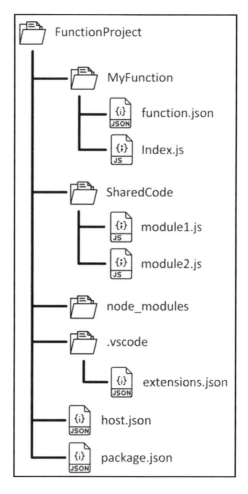

You have a folder for each function in your project, and you can create a SharedCode folder to contain the Node.js code you want to share in more functions.

The host.json file is used to configure the function app (for example, you can use it to define the runtime version or the logging configuration) in the same way that it is used in function apps written in C#.

For each function that you add to the function app (remember what we said in the first chapter: all the functions in the function app need to be written in JavaScript), you will find a folder with at least two files: index.js and function.json.

The `index.js` file contains the code that implements the function, and it is the file that the runtime is looking for when it searches for the functions to execute:

```
module.exports = async function (context, myTimer) {
    var timeStamp = new Date().toISOString();
    if (myTimer.IsPastDue)
    {
        context.log('JavaScript is running late!');
    }
    context.log('JavaScript timer trigger function ran!', timeStamp);
};
```

In this case, the function is very easy, but you will notice the following:

- JavaScript functions must be exported using the `module.exports` declaration.
- The function receives a number of arguments depending on the type of function, but every function receives, at least, the `context` argument. This argument contains the context of the single call and allows you to interact with the runtime (for example, to write a log trace). You can also use the context to interact with the function's binding (instead of using the argument bindings).

If you need to (or want to), you can configure the runtime to search for a different file instead of `index.js`.

The `function.json` file contains the triggers and bindings definition for the function, and it looks like the following:

```
{
    "bindings": [
        {
            "name": "myTimer",
            "type": "timerTrigger",
            "direction": "in",
            "schedule": "0 */5 * * * *"
        }
    ]
}
```

Your function has one input binding of the `timerTrigger` type called `myTimer` with a specific schedule.

Every time you want your function to support other bindings, you must add their definition to this file.

You can define bindings in different ways based on whether their direction is inbound or outbound.

For the inbound bindings (`direction === "in"`), you can do the following:

- Use the arguments of the function (in the same order you declare in the `function.json` file). The `name` property of the JSON must not match the name of the argument in the function signature, but we suggest using the same name to avoid confusion.
- Use the members of the `context` object. Each binding becomes a property of the `context` object with the same name set in the JSON:

```
module.exports = async function (context) {
    var timeStamp = new Date().toISOString();
    if (context.myTimer.IsPastDue)
    {
        context.log('JavaScript is running late!');
    }
    context.log('JavaScript timer trigger function ran!',
timeStamp);
};
```

- Use the objects that are present in the JavaScript argument array. This approach is similar to the use of the signature arguments, but allows you to access the binding dynamically:

```
module.exports = async function (context) {
    var timeStamp = new Date().toISOString();
    if (argument[1].IsPastDue)
    {
        context.log('JavaScript is running late!');
    }
    context.log('JavaScript timer trigger function ran!',
timeStamp);
};
```

For the outbound bindings (`direction === "out"`), you can do the following:

- Return an object (both in the case of a single output and for multiple outputs). In the following example, we are returning an HTTP response and writing an item in a queue:

```
module.exports = async function(context) {
    let retMsg = 'Hello, world!';
    return {
        httpResponse: {
```

```
                body: retMsg
            },
            queueOutput: retMsg
        };
    };
```

- Use the `context` object to assign the return values to its binding properties:

```
module.exports = async function(context) {
    let retMsg = 'Hello, world!';
    context.bindings.httpResponse = {
        body: retMsg
    };
    context.bindings.queueOutput = retMsg;
};
```

The `dataType` property in the JSON file allows you to specify what type of data the binding manages. You can use `binary`, `stream`, or `string`.

Once you have created the function app, you can run it in the same way you run a C# function app:

C:\MasteringServerless\MyFirstNodeFunction>func start

The following screenshot shows the output of the preceding command:

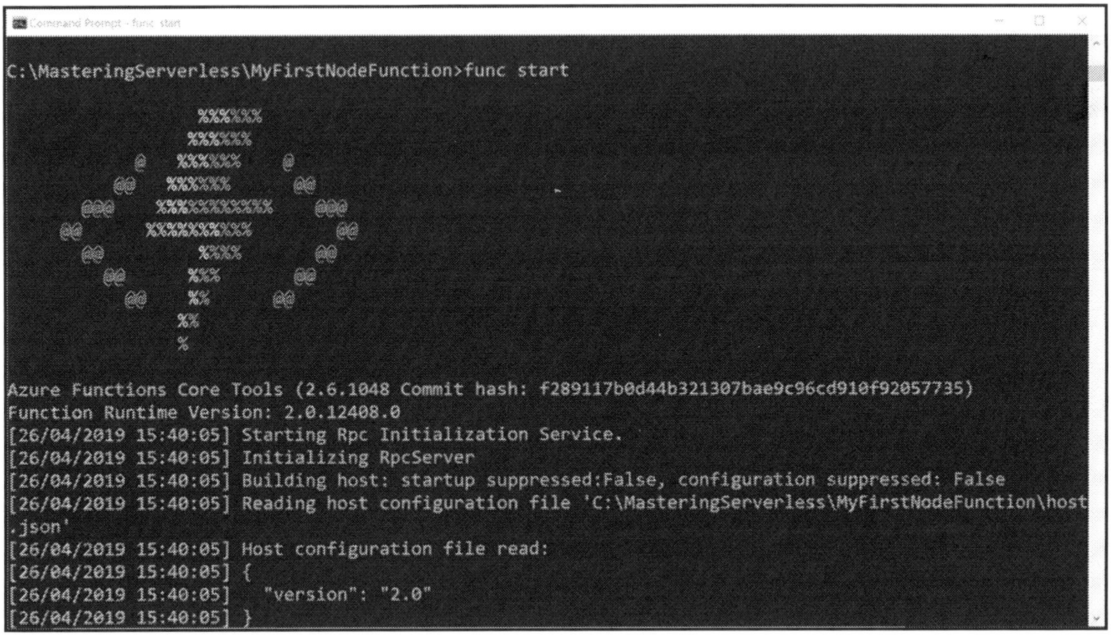

The runtime initializes the host reading the `host.json` file, then starts it and starts the language worker process to support Node.js and JavaScript, as you can see in the following screenshot:

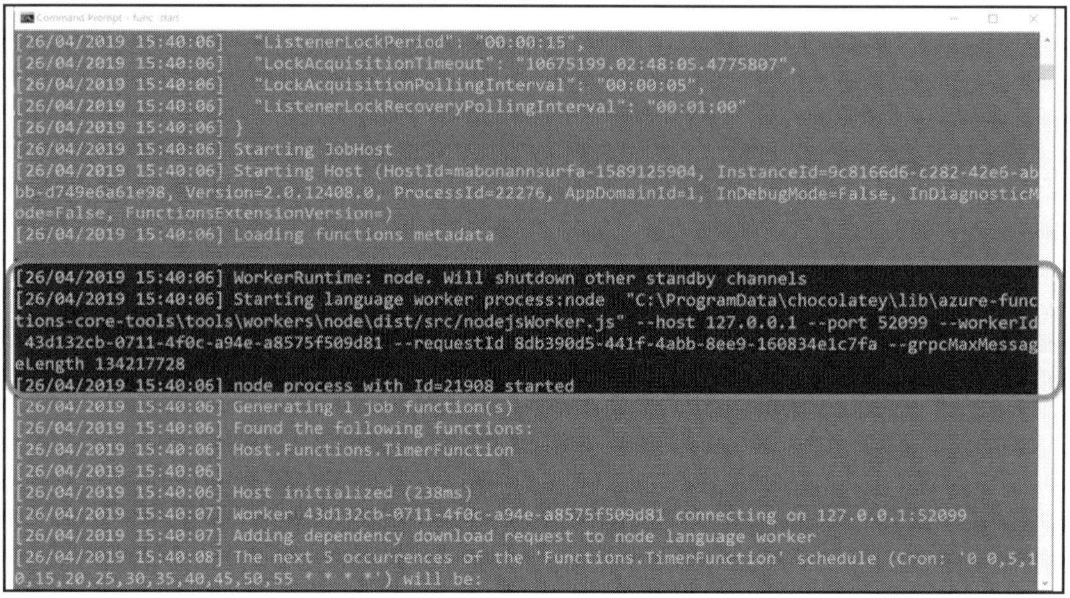

Lastly, the runtime generates one job for every single function discovered, and your functions are alive.

More information about the language worker and language extensibility will be given in later sections.

Azure Functions and Java

Despite the fact that the Azure Functions Runtime supports Java, you cannot create a Java Azure Function using the Azure Function Core Tool in the same way that you created a JavaScript function in the previous section.

To create a Java Azure Function you need the Azure Function Core Tools, but you also must have the following:

- **Java Developer Kit (JDK)** SE LTE version 8 (`https://repos.azul.com/azure-only/zulu/packages/zulu-8/8u181/`)
- Apache Maven version 3.0 or above (`https://maven.apache.org/download.cgi`)

The process to create a Java Azure Function is not simple and linear, but in the end, a Java Azure Function is a public method decorated with the `@FunctionName` annotation (as the `FunctionName` attribute for the C# functions). This method is the entry point for the function and it must be unique in the entire package.

The structure of a project written in Java that contains an Azure Function resembles the following:

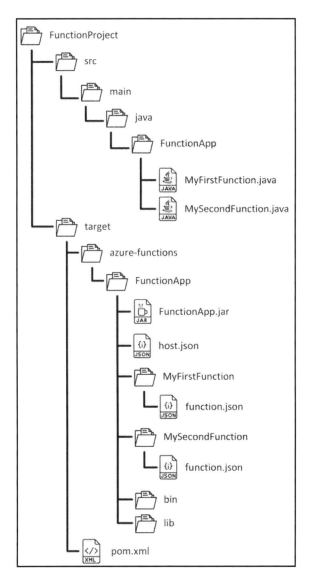

The target folder contains the binaries of the functions, that is, the set of files to deploy.

The host.json file is used, as it is for the C# and Node.js functions, to configure the function app and to define the extensions you want to use inside your functions. Each function has its folder (with the same name as the function), in which you will find the function.json file that contains the definition of the bindings, as shown in the following code:

```json
{
    "scriptFile": "myFirstJavaFunction.jar",
    "entryPoint": "com.example.Function.httpTriggerFunction",
    "bindings": [
        {
            "type": "httpTrigger",
            "name": "req",
            "direction": "in",
            "authLevel": "function",
            "methods": [ "get" ]
        },
        {
            "type": "http",
            "name": "$return",
            "direction": "out"
        }
    ]
}
```

The previous function.json corresponds to the function, as shown in the following code:

```java
public class Function {
    @FunctionName("httpTriggerFunction")
    public String httpTriggerFunction(@HttpTrigger(name = "req", methods =
{"get"}, authLevel = AuthorizationLevel.FUNCTION) String req,
        ExecutionContext context)
    {
        return String.format(req);
    }
}
```

As you can see in the previous function, one of the arguments is an instance of ExecutionContext. It is similar to the context you saw in the Node.js paragraph. It allows you to access log features.

If you want to host your Java functions locally, you have to use Maven, and in particular, you need to run the following commands inside the root folder of your function project:

```
mvn clean package
mvn myFirstJavaFunction:run
```

 You can find more info about Java Azure Function development in the official documentation at https://docs.microsoft.com/en-us/azure/ azure-functions/functions-create-first-java-maven. You can find the developer guide reference at https://docs.microsoft.com/en-us/ java/api/overview/azure/functions/readme?view=azure-java-stable.

Azure Functions and Python

If you want to start writing Azure Functions in Python you need to install Python version 3.6.x (you can download the installation package at https://www.python.org/downloads/; make sure that the minor version is 3.6). If you want to use VS Code to implement your Azure Functions in Python then you also need the *Python extension for VS Code* (you can download it directly inside VS Code or by going to https://marketplace.visualstudio. com/items?itemName=ms-python.python).

Once you have installed Python on your machine, you can create your first Azure Function in the same way you did for C# and Node.js.

First of all, you have to create a virtual environment. You can do this opening Command Prompt and using the following commands:

```
py -3.6 -m venv .env
.env\scripts\activate
```

In this case, you create a virtual environment called .env and activate it. Once you are in the virtual environment, you can initialize your Azure Function project:

```
(.env) C:\MasteringServerless\MyFirstPythonFunction>func init --worker-
runtime python
```

The following screenshot shows the output of the preceding command:

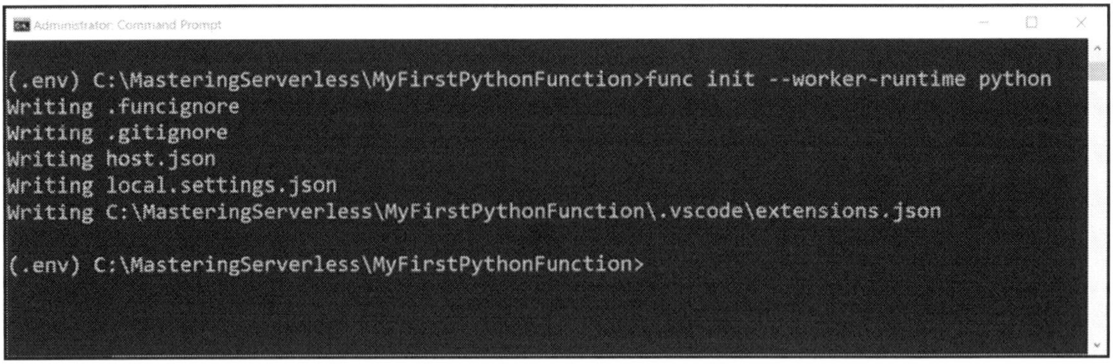

Finally, you can create the Azure Function:

```
(.env) C:\MasteringServerless\MyFirstPythonFunction>func new --name
HttpPythonFunction --template HttpTrigger
```

The following screenshot shows the output of the preceding command:

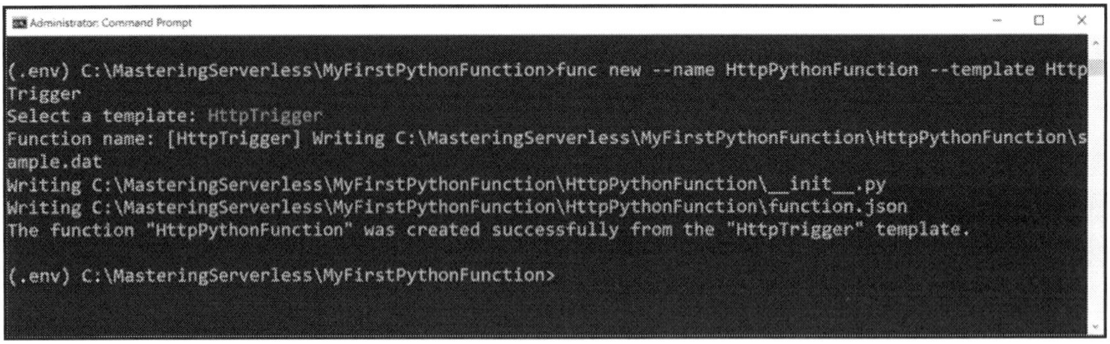

The folder structure for a Python function project is shown in the following diagram:

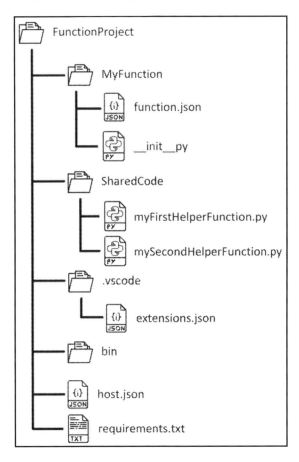

You have a folder for each function in your project and a `SharedCode` folder (if you need it) to contain code that is shared by different functions.

The __init__.py file contains the following function code:

```python
import logging
import azure.functions as func

def main(req: func.HttpRequest) -> func.HttpResponse:
    logging.info('Python HTTP trigger function processed a request.')
    name = req.params.get('name')
    if not name:
        try:
            req_body = req.get_json()
        except ValueError:
            pass
        else:
            name = req_body.get('name')

    if name:
        return func.HttpResponse(f"Hello {name}!")
     else:
        return func.HttpResponse("Please pass a name on the query string or
in the request body", status_code=400)
```

A function in Python should be a stateless method that gets inputs, processes them, and produces output. By default, the Azure Functions Runtime looks for a method called main() in the __init__.py file. If you need or want to, you can change this convention using the scriptFile and entryPoint properties in the function.json file:

```json
{
    "scriptFile": "myScript.py",
    "entryPoint": "myentry",
    ...
}
```

The bindings, as usual, are defined in the function.json file:

```json
{
    ...,
    "bindings": [
        {
            "authLevel": "function",
            "type": "httpTrigger",
            "direction": "in",
            "name": "req",
            "methods": [
                "get",
                "post"
            ]
        },
```

```
        {
            "type": "http",
            "direction": "out",
            "name": "$return"
        }
    ]
}
```

In the Python function, you can write the log using the `logging` handler, which exposes a set of methods, such as `critical()`, `error()`, and `warning()`.

Once you have created your function, you can start and host it:

```
(.env) C:\MasteringServerless\MyFirstPythonFunction>func host start
```

The following screenshot shows the output of the preceding command:

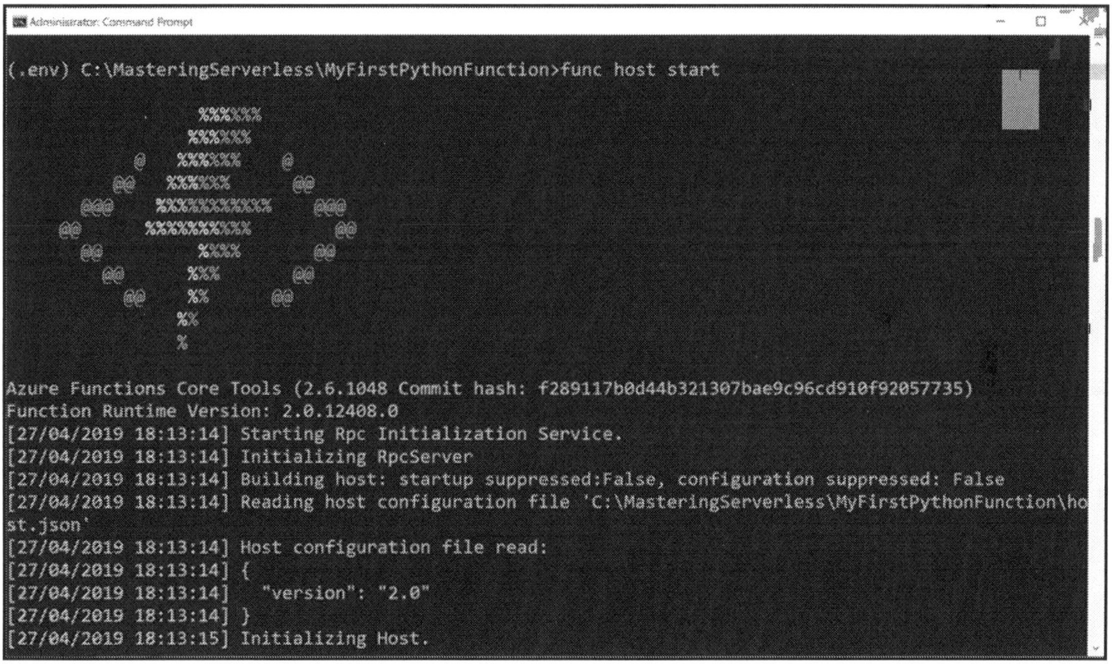

Also, in this case (in the same way you saw for the Node.js), the runtime initializes the host reading the `host.json` file, then starts it and starts the language worker process to support Python, as you can see in the following screenshot:

Finally, the runtime starts one job for each function discovered in the function app folder, and your functions are up and running.

More information about the language worker and language extensibility will be given in later sections.

Azure Functions and PowerShell

Azure Functions support PowerShell, but the support for this language is in preview at the time of writing, so what we will say in this paragraph could change in the future.

The Azure Functions Runtime leverages the features of the PowerShell Core 6 (it is based on .NET Core and can run on Windows, macOS, and Linux) and includes native support for the new Azure AZ module (to interact with the Azure resources).

These features make Azure automation one of the ideal scenarios for using PowerShell within Azure Functions: you can react to an event produced by Azure (for example, a monitor alert) and run some operations on your resources.

When you create an Azure Function using PowerShell, you have all the benefits of the other languages you saw earlier in this chapter, and in particular, you have the following:

- Native bindings to respond to Azure monitoring alerts, resource changes through event grid, HTTP, or timer triggers, and more
- Portal and VS Code integration for authoring and testing scripts
- Integrated security to protect HTTP-triggered functions
- Support for hybrid connections and VNet to help manage hybrid environments
- The ability to run in an isolated local environment

You can create your first Azure Function with PowerShell in the same way you would with the other supported languages:

```
C:\MasteringServerless\myFirstPowershellFunction>func init --worker-runtime
powershell MyFirstPowershellFunction

Writing profile.ps1
Writing requirements.psd1
Writing .gitignore
Writing host.json
Writing local.settings.json
Writing
C:\MasteringServerless\myFirstPowershellFunction\.vscode\extensions.json


C:\MasteringServerless\myFirstPowershellFunction>func new --name
HttpPowershellFunction --template HttpTrigger --language powershell

Select a template: HttpTrigger
Function name: [HttpTrigger] Writing
C:\MasteringServerless\myFirstPowershellFunction\HttpPowershellFunction\run
.ps1
Writing
C:\MasteringServerless\myFirstPowershellFunction\HttpPowershellFunction\sam
ple.dat
Writing
C:\MasteringServerless\myFirstPowershellFunction\HttpPowershellFunction\fun
ction.json
The function "HttpPowershellFunction" was created successfully from the
"HttpTrigger" template.
```

The folder structure for a PowerShell function is shown in the following diagram:

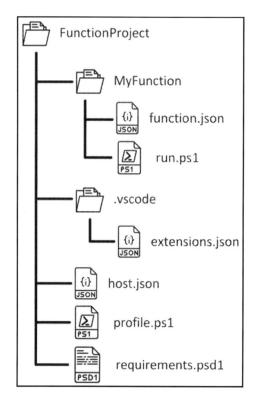

The run.ps1 file inside the folder called as the function contains the PowerShell code for the function itself:

```
using namespace System.Net

# Input bindings are passed in via param block.
param($Request, $TriggerMetadata)

# Write to the Azure Functions log stream.
Write-Host "PowerShell HTTP trigger function processed a request."

# Interact with query parameters or the body of the request.
$name = $Request.Query.Name
if (-not $name) {
 $name = $Request.Body.Name
}

# Analyzes the request and create the response
# ..... look at the github for the complete code
```

```
# Associate values to output bindings by calling 'Push-OutputBinding'.
Push-OutputBinding -Name Response -Value ([HttpResponseContext]@{
  StatusCode = $status
  Body = $body
})
```

In this case, the triggers and bindings are passed as the `param` definition, and you can write the log using the standard `Write-Host` cmdlet.

The triggers and bindings definitions, as usual, are in the `function.json` file with a similar format to the other languages.

The PowerShell language worker can automatically manage the integration of the Azure modules without you needing to reference them in the configuration files (this feature demonstrates that PowerShell in Azure Functions was created with Azure automation in mind). You can enable the integration in the host file by setting the `managedDependency` property to `true`:

```
{
    "version": "2.0",
    "managedDependency": {
        "Enabled": "true"
    }
}
```

The worker also takes care of the critical and security updates on the Azure modules, and you can enable this by setting the `Az` property in the `requirements.psd1` file:

```
@{
  Az = '1.*'
}
```

Finally, the `profile.ps1` file is used by the runtime to automatically authenticate the Azure Function host to the Azure services. `profile.ps1` is run when the function app starts, and you can add the common commands to execute for each PowerShell functions in your project in that file:

```
# Azure Functions profile.ps1
#
# This profile.ps1 will get executed every "cold start" of your Function
App.
# "cold start" occurs when:
#
# * A Function App starts up for the very first time
# * A Function App starts up after being de-allocated due to inactivity
#
```

```
# You can define helper functions, run commands, or specify environment
variables
# NOTE: any variables defined that are not environment variables will get
reset after the first execution

# Authenticate with Azure PowerShell using MSI.
# Remove this if you are not planning on using MSI or Azure PowerShell.
if ($env:MSI_SECRET -and (Get-Module -ListAvailable Az.Accounts)) {
 Connect-AzAccount -Identity
}

# Uncomment the next line to enable legacy AzureRm alias in Azure
PowerShell.
# Enable-AzureRmAlias

# You can also define functions or aliases that can be referenced in any of
your PowerShell functions.
```

Once you create your function project, you can run the functions using the following command:

```
C:\MasteringServerless\myFirstPowershellFunction>func start host
```

Next, we will be looking at language extensibility.

Language extensibility

To enable a multilanguage approach in Azure Functions, the runtime is split into two building blocks:

- The host that has the responsibility to manage the function events
- The language worker process in which the functions, written in the different programming languages, run.

The following diagram shows the architecture of the aforementioned building blocks:

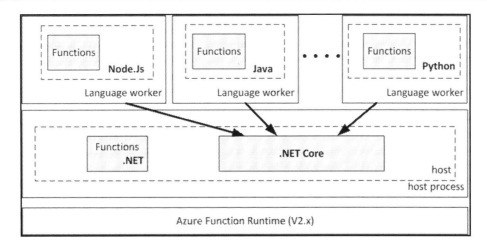

The two layers communicate with each other using the **gRPC** (**Remote Procedure Call (RPC)**), a modern, open source, high-performance RPC framework that can run in any environment and can efficiently connect services in and across data centers. It supports load balancing, tracing, health checking, and authentication.

 You can find more information about the gRPC protocol on the official website at https://grpc.io.

This framework was initially developed by Google, and at this moment it is one of the most commonly used frameworks to implement high-performance communications.

In a gRPC scenario, your client application can directly call a method on a server application as if it were a local object, even if the server application is located on another machine (if you come from a .NET background, you can imagine it as a modern remoting technology) and, of course, you can do it if the client and the server are implemented in different languages (for example, C++ for the server and Ruby for the client):

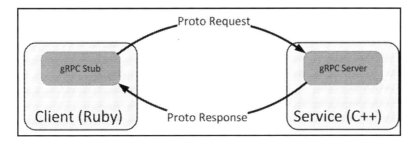

The Azure Functions Runtime and the specific language worker talk to each other using gRPC technology with the following gRPC contract:

```
service FunctionRpc {
    rpc EventStream (stream StreamingMessage) returns (stream
StreamingMessage) {}
}
```

As you can see, every call between the runtime and worker language uses `StreamingMessage` to bring information about the single call. The `StreamingMessage` definition looks like the following:

```
message StreamingMessage {
    string request_id = 1;
    oneof content {
        // Worker signals to host that it has been started
        StartStream start_stream = 20;
        ....

        // Host sends invocation information (function id, binding data,
parameters) to worker
        InvocationRequest invocation_request = 4;

        // Worker sends response to host
        InvocationResponse invocation_response = 5;

        // Structured log from the worker based off the ILogger interface
        RpcLog rpc_log = 2;
    }
}
```

For example, the `InvocationRequest` looks like the following:

```
// Host requests worker to invoke a Function
message InvocationRequest {
    // Unique id for each invocation
    string invocation_id = 1;

    // Unique id for each Function
    string function_id = 2;

    // Input bindings (include trigger)
    repeated ParameterBinding input_data = 3;

    // binding metadata from trigger
    map<string, TypedData> trigger_metadata = 4;
}
```

You can find the full contract definition at `https://github.com/Azure/azure-functions-language-worker-protobuf/blob/dev/src/proto/FunctionRpc.proto`.

Therefore, implementing a language worker for a particular programming language means implementing the gRPC client and all the event handlers defined in the gRPC contract.

Once you have implemented your own language worker, the runtime life cycle for its activation is the following:

1. The host starts up and it starts the gRPC server (inside the runtime).
2. For each function you define in your function app, the runtime creates a language worker. The runtime creates one worker process for each different language (client gRPC), so if the process is already created, the runtime doesn't create it.
3. Once the worker is started, it connects to the server.
4. The host and the worker give each other the version information of the capabilities using `WorkerInitRequest` and `WorkerInitResponse` messages.
5. The host sends the function metadata to the worker using a `FunctionLoadRequest` message and the worker communicates the response to the server using a `FunctionLoadResponse` message.
6. Finally, the host asks the client to execute the function with the `InvocationRequest` message, and the client, after the code execution, responds to the host with `InvocationResponse` message.

As you can imagine, implementing a language worker is not a simple task, but contract definitions and all of the existing language workers are open source, and you can look at them to understand how they work and how you can create them.

You can find all of the gRPC definitions for language workers and some of the language worker implementations at `https://github.com/Azure/azure-functions-host/wiki/Language-Extensibility`.

Summary

In this chapter, you learned that Azure Functions are not only written in C#, but that there are also several programming languages you can use to implement your serverless code, and there is a way to add your own programming language.

Azure Functions can leverage the power of other programming languages to give you the best environment to implement your business scenarios. The language extensibility allows Microsoft and its community to support new programming languages and evolve the Azure Function ecosystem. Azure Functions, thanks to the language extensibility, is a real open-source ecosystem.

In the next chapter, you will see how to deploy your functions on the cloud and how to configure them.

Questions

1. What are the components that compose the Azure Functions Runtime?
   - Host
   - SignalR hub
   - Language worker
   - Azure monitor resource coordinator
   - HTTPS listener

2. Which of the following programming languages are supported by the Azure Functions Runtime?
   - C#
   - Cobol
   - PowerShell
   - Ruby
   - Python

3. What kind of technology does the runtime use to communicate with the language worker process?
   - gRPC
   - COM+
   - Socket
   - Windows Communication Foundation

Further reading

You can find more information about the programming languages supported by Azure Functions by going to the following links:

- *Supported languages in Azure Functions*: https://docs.microsoft.com/en-us/azure/azure-functions/supported-languages
- *Language extensibility GitHub repository*: https://github.com/Azure/azure-functions-host/wiki/Language-Extensibility
- *Azure Functions Java developer guide*: https://docs.microsoft.com/en-us/azure/azure-functions/functions-reference-java
- *Azure Functions Python developer guide*: https://docs.microsoft.com/en-us/azure/azure-functions/functions-reference-python
- *Azure Functions JavaScript developer guide*: https://docs.microsoft.com/en-us/azure/azure-functions/functions-reference-node
- *Azure Functions PowerShell developer guide*: https://docs.microsoft.com/en-us/azure/azure-functions/functions-reference-powershell

Section 2: Azure Functions 2.0 Deployment and Automation

This section shows how to deploy and configure an Azure Function, how to automate those procedures, how to test and troubleshoot the solution, and how to deploy Azure Functions in a container (both in the cloud and on-premises).

It comprises the following chapters:

- Chapter 4, *Deploying and Configuring Your Azure Functions*
- Chapter 5, *Leverage the Power of DevOps with Azure Functions*
- Chapter 6, *Testing and Monitoring*
- Chapter 7, *Serverless and Containers*

Deploying and Configuring Your Azure Functions

4

In the previous chapters, you learned how to create and implement the code behind an Azure Function, but this step is only the first one on the way to building your own solution based on Azure Functions. Once you have your code (and, of course, once you have debugged it), you need to deploy it on Azure and configure it.

This chapter will cover the following topics:

- Creating your Azure function app to contain your Azure Functions
- Deploying your Azure functions on Azure using different techniques
- Understanding what deployment slots are
- Kudu: the Azure Function deployment service
- Configuring your Azure Functions
- Reading the app settings in your Azure Function

Technical requirements

In this chapter, you will learn how to deploy and configure your Azure Functions on Azure environments. Before you learn this, though, you must learn about what Azure is, how it works, and how to use resources and their templates.

You will use the **Azure Resource Manager templates** (**ARM templates**) and PowerShell to prepare the environment and deploy the functions in this environment.

Another important task that you will perform when you put your Azure Functions in production is configuring them. In the second part of this chapter, you will learn how to configure your functions, the best places to put the configuration information, and how you can read it inside your code.

You can find the source code for this book at `https://github.com/PacktPublishing/ Mastering-Azure-Serverless-Computing/tree/master/Chapter04`.

Creating the Azure function app

The first step you have to take when you deploy your Azure Function is creating the host environment that keeps your function alive. This environment is a function app.

You can imagine the function app as the serverless view of an App Service: it hosts your code and gives you a bunch of features that you can use to deploy, monitor, and configure your Azure Function.

When you decide to create a function app, you need the following resources:

- The function app itself.
- A storage account that stores your code. This is mandatory because your code needs a place to be saved.
- An Application Insight component. This isn't mandatory; you will need it only if you want to monitor your code. We will talk more deeply about monitoring in one of the following chapters.
- A hosting plan. This is mandatory when you choose to host your function in a Premium plan or in an App Service plan, but you don't need it if you are creating a function app that runs in the Consumption plan. We will talk more deeply about hosting a plan in one of the following chapters.

Furthermore, in order to maintain all the resources and ensure that they are logically connected, it is appropriate to create a resource group that contains them.

The best way you have to create a function app in Azure is by using an ARM template. An ARM template is a JSON file that contains the definition of your infrastructure in Azure. Using the ARM templates, you can deploy your infrastructure repeatedly and create a test environment on the fly.

For more information about ARM templates, their structure, and their syntax, read the article at `https://docs.microsoft.com/en-us/azure/ azure-resource-manager/resource-group-authoring-templates`.

When using an ARM template, you can think of your infrastructure definition like a programming language's snippet of code. You can version it, store it in a source-control management system (for example, Git), validate it before executing it, and evolve it during the project life cycle.

Generally, when you use an ARM template, you create a template file and a parameter file, and then you can push them on Azure using a PowerShell command.

The first resource you need in your ARM template is the storage account that hosts your function code. So, in the `resources` section of the JSON template, you can put the following:

```
{
    "type": "Microsoft.Storage/storageAccounts",
    "name": "[variables('storageAccountName')]",
    "apiVersion": "2016-12-01",
    "location": "[parameters('location')]",
    "kind": "Storage",
     "sku": {
         "name": "[parameters('storageAccountType')]"
     }
}
```

As you can see in the previous snippet, variables and parameters appear in the storage definition. Variables are placeholders that you can use inside your ARM template to store information for use within resource definition properties (they are similar to the variables in a programming language). Parameters are pieces of information that the ARM template receives from the outside.

The ARM template has special sections to define the `parameters` and `variables`:

```
{
    "$schema":
"https://schema.management.azure.com/schemas/2015-01-01/deploymentTemplate.
json#",
    "contentVersion": "1.0.0.0",
    "parameters": {
        "storageAccountType": {
            "type": "string",
            "defaultValue": "Standard_LRS",
            "allowedValues": [ "Standard_LRS", "Standard_GRS",
"Standard_RAGRS" ],
            "metadata": {
                "description": "Storage Account type"
            }
        },
```

```
        ...
    },
    "variables": {
        ....
        "storageAccountName": "[concat(parameters('appName'), 'storage')]",
        ...
    },
    "resources": [
        ...
    ],
}
```

Every parameter has a type, can have a default value, and can support a set of values.

A variable can be calculated using parameters or other variables (for example, the concat() function in the storageAccountName variable).

The second resource that you need to deploy an Azure Function is the function app, and if you want, you can choose to use a Consumption plan, an App Service plan, or a Premium plan.

We will talk more deeply about the types of plan later in this book, but whether you decide to use the Consumption plan, App Service plan, or Premium plan, you need to configure it, and you can do this with the following snippets.

When you want to run your Azure Functions in a Consumption plan, you simply have to choose it. The Consumption plan, in fact, doesn't need to be defined in terms of server size or operating system type, as shown in the following code:

```
{
    "type": "Microsoft.Web/serverfarms",
    "apiVersion": "2018-02-01",
    "name": "[variables('hostingPlanName')]",
    "location": "[parameters('location')]",
    "sku": {
        "name": "Y1",
        "tier": "Dynamic"
    },
    "properties": {
        "name": "[variables('hostingPlanName')]",
        "computeMode": "Dynamic"
    }
},
```

When you want to use an App Service plan to host your functions, you have to define some server farm properties, as follows:

```
{
    "type": "Microsoft.Web/serverfarms",
    "apiVersion": "2015-04-01",
    "name": "[variables('hostingPlanName')]",
    "location": "[parameters('location')]",
    "properties": {
        "name": "[variables('hostingPlanName')]",
        "sku": "[parameters('sku')]",
        "workerSize": "[parameters('workerSize')]",
        "hostingEnvironment": "",
        "numberOfWorkers": 1
    }
}
```

The properties can have the following values:

- The `workerSize` property defines the size of the hosting plan, and it can be 0, 1, or 2 (small, medium, or large).
- The `sku` property defines the pricing tier of the plan, and you can choose between `Free`, `Shared`, `Basic`, and `Standard`.

As you saw in the previous chapters, you can host your functions in a Linux environment. If you want to do this, you have to set `"kind"="Linux"` in the farm definition.

Finally, if you choose the Premium plan to host your function, the `sku` properties may be one of the following values: `EP1`, `EP2`, or `EP3`:

```
{
    "type": "Microsoft.Web/serverfarms",
    "apiVersion": "2015-04-01",
    "name": "[variables('hostingPlanName')]",
    "location": "[parameters('location')]",
    "properties": {
        "name": "[variables('hostingPlanName')]",
        "sku": "EP1"
    }
}
```

Once you define the host for your function, you need to define the function app with a template that looks like the following:

```
{
    "apiVersion": "2015-08-01",
```

```
        "type": "Microsoft.Web/sites",
        "name": "[variables('functionAppName')]",
        "location": "[parameters('location')]",
        "kind": "functionapp",
        "dependsOn": [
            "[resourceId('Microsoft.Web/serverfarms',
    variables('hostingPlanName'))]",
            "[resourceId('Microsoft.Storage/storageAccounts',
    variables('storageAccountName'))]"
        ],
        "properties": {
            "serverFarmId": "[resourceId('Microsoft.Web/serverfarms',
    variables('hostingPlanName'))]",
            "siteConfig": {
                ...
            }
        }
    }
```

As you can see, the function app is a `Microsoft.Web/sites` resource of
the `"functionapp"` type (function app is a special type of website hosting) and it depends
on (as shown by the `dependsOn` property) the storage account and the server farm. Thanks
to the `dependsOn` property, you can be sure that the function app resource will not be
deployed if the other two resources are not present.

In the function app template, you can also set the configuration using `appSettings` (in
particular, the `siteConfig` section). For example, the next snippet shows how to set the
function's runtime version:

```
"properties": {
        "serverFarmId": "[resourceId('Microsoft.Web/serverfarms',
    variables('hostingPlanName'))]",
        "siteConfig": {
  "appSettings": [
  {
  "name": "FUNCTIONS_EXTENSION_VERSION",
  "value": "~2"
  },
  ....
  ]
  }
    }
```

When you complete your ARM template, you can deploy it using the following PowerShell
script:

```
$resourceGroupName = Read-Host -Prompt "Enter the Resource Group name"
$location = Read-Host -Prompt "Enter the location (i.e. centralus)"
$appName = Read-Host -Prompt "Enter the app name "

Connect-AzAccount

if ((Get-AzResourceGroup -Name $resourceGroupName -Location $location -
ErrorAction SilentlyContinue) -eq $null) {
    New-AzResourceGroup -Name $resourceGroupName -Location $location -Force
-ErrorAction Stop
}

New-AzResourceGroupDeployment -ResourceGroupName $resourceGroupName `
        -TemplateFile C:\MasteringServerless\ConsumptionPlanDeploy.json `
        -Force `
        -appName $appName `
        -ErrorVariable ErrorMessages

if ($ErrorMessages) {
    Write-Output '', 'Template deployment returned the following errors:',
@(@($ErrorMessages) | ForEach-Object { $_.Exception.Message.TrimEnd("`r`n")
})
}
```

The previous script creates the resource group (if it doesn't exist), then calls the New-
AzResourceGroupDeployment cmdlet to create a new deployment in the resource group
and starts it.

The following screenshot shows the PowerShell output:

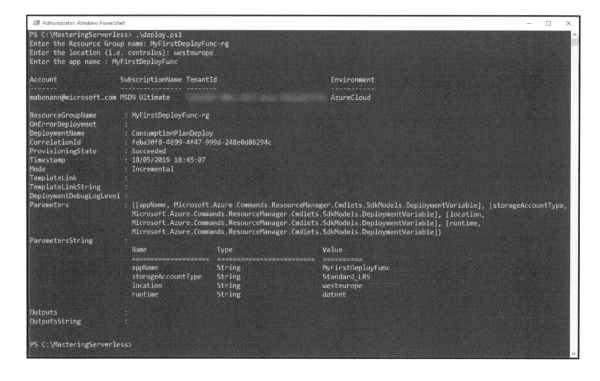

If you use Visual Studio or Visual Studio Code, there is a special type of project available that allows you to manage and create ARM templates. In Visual Studio, this project is called the **Azure Resource Group** project and you can create it in the same way you create a standard code project:

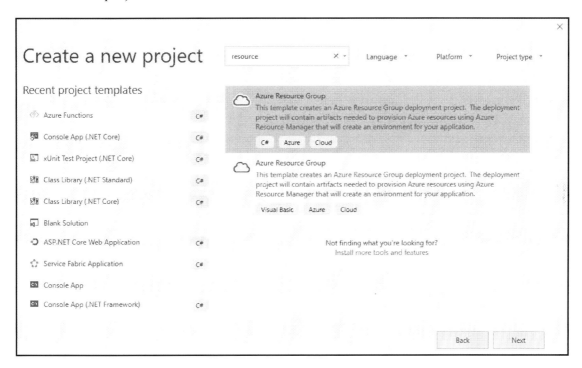

When you choose this kind of project, you can start to write your ARM template from scratch by selecting one of the templates offered by Visual Studio or choosing one of the open-source templates created by the community:

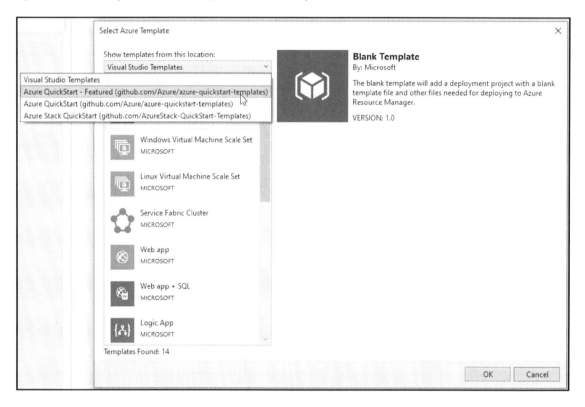

In the next section, we will be looking at deploying the app into the cloud.

Deploying the Azure function app

Once you create the infrastructure to host your function and you implement your function, you need to deploy it into the cloud.

The main tool you can use to do this is Azure Functions Core Tools, which you used in the previous chapters to create and locally debug your functions.

One of the commands that the tool exposes is the `azure` command, which allows you to manage your Azure stuff, and in particular the `functionapp` option (which allows you to manage Azure Functions).

You can use the following command to get help:

```
C:\MasteringServerless\MyFirstFunctionApp> func azure functionapp
```

This will show you the supported options for the `functionapp` command:

As you can see in the previous screenshot, you have four commands that you can use to interact with your function in Azure. The command we are looking for is the `publish` command.

The `publish` command syntax is simple. Using this command, you can *push* your Azure Function directly into the function app.

First of all, you have to connect to your subscription using the following command:

```
C:\MasteringServerless\MyFirstFunctionApp> Connect-AzAccount
```

The preceding command asks you for your Azure credentials and will set your default subscription as the target for the next command.

Pay attention when you try to execute the command because you need to import the `Az.Accounts` module before you run it. If you don't import the module, you could receive the following error:

```
Connect-AzAccount : The 'Connect-AzAccount' command was found in the module
'Az.Accounts', but the module could not be
loaded. For more information, run 'Import-Module Az.Accounts'.
At line:1 char:1
+ Connect-AzAccount
+ ~~~~~~~~~~~~~~~~~
 + CategoryInfo : ObjectNotFound: (Connect-AzAccount:String) [],
CommandNotFoundException
 + FullyQualifiedErrorId : CouldNotAutoloadMatchingModule
```

To solve this issue, you can simply run the following cmdlet:

```
C:\MasteringServerless\MyFirstFunctionApp> Set-ExecutionPolicy -Scope
Process -ExecutionPolicy Bypass
C:\MasteringServerless\MyFirstFunctionApp> Import-Module Az.Accounts
```

If you have more than one subscription and you want to change the subscription target, you can use the `Get-AzSubscription` to retrieve the list of your subscriptions (you need their IDs) and select the desired one with the `Select-AzSubscription` cmdlet.

 You can find more information about everything that the cmdlet contains in the `Az.Accounts` module at https://docs.microsoft.com/en-us/ powershell/module/az.accounts/?view=azps-2.1.0#accounts.

Once you connect to your desired Azure subscription, you can finally deploy your Azure Function using the following command:

```
C:\MasteringServerless\MyFirstFunctionApp> func azure functionapp publish
<functionappname>
```

Here, `<functionappname>` is the name of the function app that you want to host your function:

The `publish` command builds your function if you didn't build it before. Looking at the preceding screenshot, you can see that after the build step, the command creates an *archive* for the directory you are publishing.

This happened because the publishing process, by default, uses a ZIP file to package and deploy your code.

Packaging compiled files for distribution in a single ZIP file provides a number of advantages over distributing individual files:

- Less data is transferred
- All of the files contained in the ZIP file are updated simultaneously

Behind the scenes, the ZIP deployment uses the same engine used by the single-file deployment. This engine is called **Kudu**, and we will talk about it later in this chapter. When you push a ZIP file into a function app, the deployment engine (Kudu) decompresses it and substitutes all the previous files (if they exist) in the target directory.

If you want to use the ZIP deployment approach without using Azure Functions Core Tools, you can create the ZIP file by yourself and use the Kudu API to deploy it as you would for a standard website.

If you want to understand how the ZIP file is structured, you can download the current ZIP file using the Azure portal.

In the function app page, you can find the **Download app content** option, as shown in the following screenshot. You can use it to download the current ZIP file:

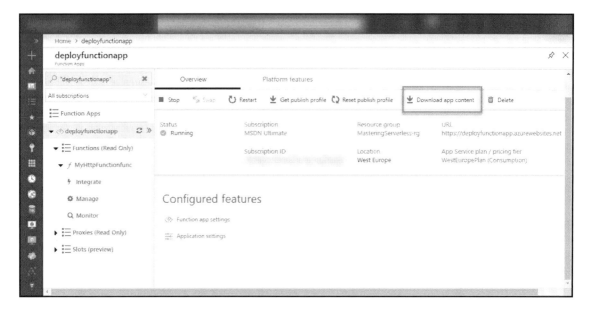

When you click on **Download app content**, you can choose to download the ZIP file or the Visual Studio project. The structure of the ZIP file is shown in the following diagram:

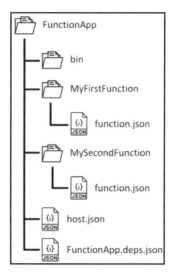

Next, we will be looking at deployment slots.

Using the deployment slots

Azure Functions run inside App Services, and they inherit many of the features available for App Services. One of these is deployment slots.

Deployment slots enable you to deploy different versions of your function app with different URLs.

You can imagine a deployment slot as like another function app contained in the main function app. You create a slot with a name and you can use it to deploy your functions in the same way that you would with a normal function app. In the following screenshot, you can see a slot called beta:

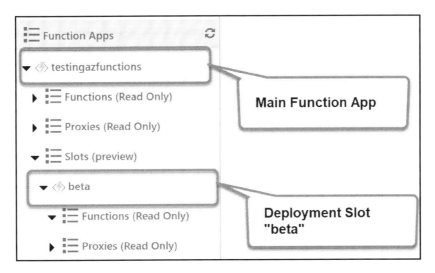

If the function app is called testingazfunctions, its URL will be
http://testingazfunctions.azurewebsites.net. If you create a slot called beta, its URL will be http://testingazfunctions-beta.azurewebsites.net.

The process of deploying a function app inside a slot is completely identical to what was seen previously. After you deploy the function app inside a slot, you can swap it with another slot (even with the main slot), as shown in the following code:

The swap operation also involves the configuration, as you can see in the preceding screenshot.

Kudu – the Azure Function deployment service

Kudu is the open source engine used by Azure to deploy Azure websites. It can also run outside Azure and is used to deploy the Azure Functions.

Kudu is also used by Azure when you deploy something from a Git repository.

Every App Service you create in Azure has a service site identified by the initials `scm`, which runs an instance of Kudu and a set of website extensions.

If your website is `http://mysite.azurewebsite.net`, the service site URL will be `http://mysite.scm.azurewebsite.net`.

The `scm` service site has the following properties:

- If you configure the website with your custom host name, the service site URL remains the same (`http://mysite.scm.azurewebsites.net`).
- The site uses single sign-on, which means that if you are logged into the Azure portal, you are automatically logged into the `scm` site.
- If you want to use another set of credentials to log into the `scm` site, you have to go to the URL `http://mysite.scm.azurewebsite.net/basicauth` and the site will prompt you for the new credentials.

If you are in the function app blade of the Azure portal, you can enter the Kudu portal using the **Platform features** tab, as shown in the following screenshot:

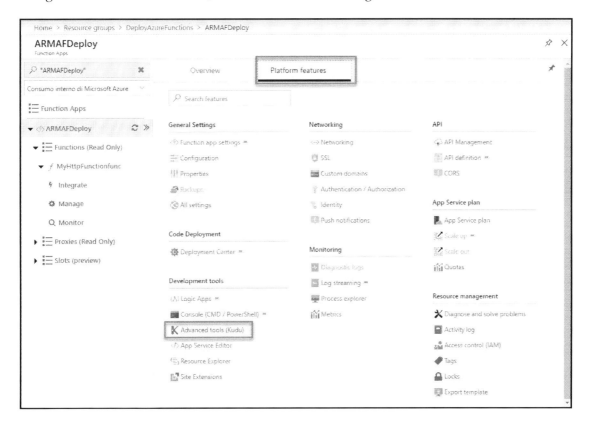

The UI of the Kudu site is simple, and it is shown in the following screenshot:

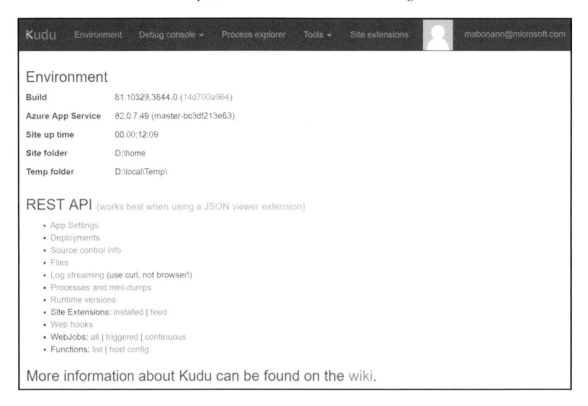

On the homepage, you can find a summary of the environment and the URL for the main REST API, which you can use to retrieve information about the platform.

For example, if you want to retrieve a list of all the deployments you made on the App Service, you can use the second link (the link has the format `https://<mysite>.scm.azurewebsites.net/api/deployments`) and make an HTTP GET request. The result looks like the JSON shown in the following screenshot:

```
1    // 20190523175746
2    // https://████████y.scm.azurewebsites.net/api/deployments
3
4  ▾ [
5  ▾   {
6        "id": "7ea64543480e4af88320aa701fa12d59",
7        "status": 4,
8        "status_text": "",
9        "author_email": "N/A",
10       "author": "N/A",
11       "deployer": "Push-Deployer",
12       "message": "Created via a push deployment",
13       "progress": "",
14       "received_time": "2019-05-22T07:03:45.4323229Z",
15       "start_time": "2019-05-22T07:03:46.0729204Z",
16       "end_time": "2019-05-22T07:03:50.341709Z",
17       "last_success_end_time": "2019-05-22T07:03:50.341709Z",
18       "complete": true,
19       "active": true,
20       "is_temp": false,
21       "is_readonly": true,
22       "url": "https://armafdeploy.scm.azurewebsites.net/api/deployments/7ea64543480e4af88320aa701fa12d59",
23       "log_url": "https://armafdeploy.scm.azurewebsites.net/api/deployments/7ea64543480e4af88320aa701fa12d59/log",
24       "site_name": "ARMAFDeploy",
25       "provisioningState": null
26     }
27   ]
```

The navigation menu allows you to access the following sections:

- **Environment**: This section shows all the environment configurations in terms of system information (for example, the operating system, number of processors, and so on), app settings, server variables, connection strings, environment variables, path, and HTTP header.
- **Debug console**: You can use this to open a PowerShell or Command Prompt console to execute a cmdlet remotely.
- **Process explorer**: This will give you the list of the processes running in the App Service that host the function app. For each process, you can display the memory occupation and the number of threads, and if you aren't in a free plan, you can start collecting information from the process (profiling the process).
- **Site extensions**: You can use this to display the list of the extensions installed in the App Service and add extensions from the gallery. The site extensions provide a way to add features to the App Service (for example, Application Insight monitoring).

- **Tools**: This section allows you to access a set of tools that you can use to diagnose problems or issues on your App Service. Between these tools, you can find the following:
    - The *Diagnostic Dump* download, which allows you to download the process dumps to analyze the memory consumption of the App Service.
    - The *ZIP Push Deploy*, which allows you to see the ZIP deploy operations you performed on the site.
    - The *Web hooks*, which allows you to see and configure the webhooks for the post-deployment event. Using this tool, you can set an HTTP endpoint (which supports an HTTP POST request) that will be called when a deployment is completed.

One of the features that we are most interested in is the possibility of deployment using REST calls. This feature is not available directly from the Kudu web UI, but it is available at the URL `https://{sitename}.scm.azurewebsites.net/api/zipdeploy`.

To deploy a ZIP file in your function app using Kudu, you have to send a POST call to the previous URL—for example, you can do this using the `curl` command:

```
curl -X POST -u <user:password>
https://{sitename}.scm.azurewebsites.net/api/zipdeploy -T <zipfile>
```

You can find the GitHub repository for the Kudu engine at `https://github.com/projectkudu/kudu`, and the Kudu documentation is at `https://github.com/projectkudu/kudu/wiki`.

Configuring your Azure Functions

The app settings for a function app are similar to the app settings you would configure for a website: in the app settings, you insert the global options that are valid for all of the functions contained in the function app.

When you develop an Azure Function, you can have local settings—that is, the settings you want to use only when you run your functions locally (for example, using the local storage emulator or a test key for a particular service)—and Azure settings—that is, the settings you want to run when you deploy your functions in a function app.

Moreover, you have settings that are related to the runtime (for example, the configured extensions, and the logger settings).

For the local settings, you can use a file called `local.settings.json`. This file is, generally, created by Azure Function Core Tools (or by Visual Studio or Visual Studio Code), and it is located in the same folder that contains the project. If you don't find this file in the folder, you can simply create it. It is a JSON file that looks like this:

```
{
    "IsEncrypted": false,
    "Values": {
        "AzureWebJobsStorage": "UseDevelopmentStorage=true",
        "FUNCTIONS_WORKER_RUNTIME": "dotnet",
        "MySettingValue1": "Value1",
        "MySettingValue2": "Value2"
    }
}
```

If you create the file by yourself, make sure that this kind of file is contained in the `.gitignore` file. To check this, open the `.gitignore` file and check whether there is a line that looks like this:

```
.
.
# Azure Functions localsettings file
local.settings.json
.
.
```

Thanks to this line, the local settings file is not included in the Git source code control, and therefore you can also enter `secrets` (for example, the API key to external services or a connection string to access to your database) inside it, because the file will remain exclusively on the disk of your PC; therefore, there is no possibility that your secrets will be shared with others.

The `local.settings` file allows you to configure the local environment, but when you push your functions to Azure, you need to configure them.

Previously in this section, you saw that you can configure the app settings using ARM template but if you want to configure your function app (and, of course, your functions running in that app), you can use two different ways:

- Azure portal
- PowerShell

If you want to use the Azure portal, you have to go into the function app blade and select the **Configuration** link in the **Platform features** tab:

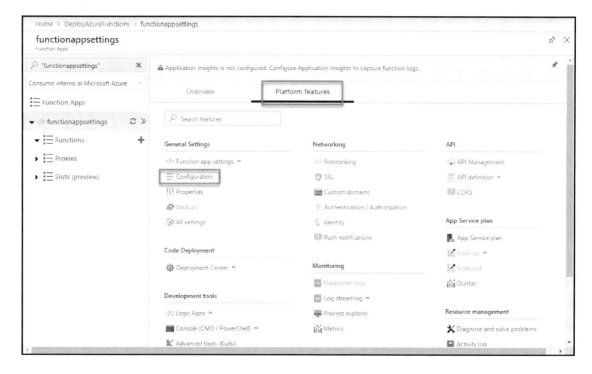

The configuration page for the Azure Functions is exactly the same as you would have for an App Service. The differences are that for the Azure Functions, you cannot define the default documents and the path mappings, as you can do in an App Service.

In the following screenshot you can see the app settings page for a function app:

In the **General settings** tab, you can set the platform configuration, such as the number of bits (32-bit or 64-bit), the type of pipeline version (classic or integrated), whether you want to enable the remote debugger, and so on.

The **Application settings** tab, instead, contains your settings, and in particular the application settings and the connection strings.

If you want to add a new application setting, simply click on **+ New application setting,** and insert the setting name (the key that you will use to retrieve the value) and the value:

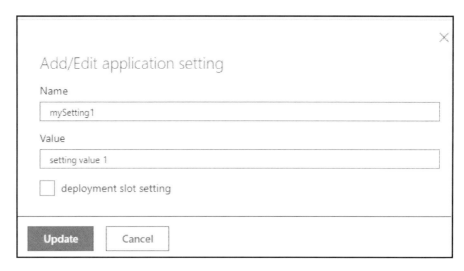

The **Update** button allows you to save the new setting while the **deployment slot setting** option allows you to define the setting only for a slot deployment.

By default, in the setting blade, the setting values are hidden, but you can see them by clicking on the eye icon to the left of the value itself.

If you want to have more security in your settings, you can retrieve the actual value for a setting directly from an Azure key vault. You will learn how to do this later in this section.

The other way you can set the application settings is by using PowerShell, and in particular the Get-AzWebApp and Set-AzWebApp cmdlets

These cmdlets are contained in the AZ.Websites module (so remember to import the module before you use the commands using the Import-Module cmdlet) and allows you to get and push settings from and into the App Service.

Take care when you use the Set-AzWebApp because the cmdlet overwrites the entire set of the setting values, so if you want to add a new setting, you must get the settings using the Get-AzWebApp cmdlet, add a new one to the existing list, and then set the settings using the Set-AzWebApp cmdlet.

The following script shows how you can do this:

```
param (
  [string]$resourceGroupName,
  [string]$appFunctionName
)

Write-Host "Retrieving settings from webapp"
$webApp = Get-AzWebApp -ResourceGroupName $resourceGroupName -Name
$appFunctionName

$newAppSettings = @{}
ForEach ($item in $webApp.SiteConfig.AppSettings) {
    $newAppSettings[$item.Name] = $item.Value
}

$newAppSettings["newAppSetting01"] = "newSettingValue01"
Write-Host "Set new settings into web app"
$webApp = Set-AzWebApp -AppSettings $newAppSettings -ResourceGroupName
$resourceGroupName -Name $appFunctionName
```

When you run the script, it retrieves all the app settings configured in the App Service, copies them into a new hashtable, modifies the newAppSetting01 value, and then applies the new hashtable into the App Service. If the newAppSetting01 exists, the script modifies it; otherwise, if the value doesn't exist, the script inserts it.

You can use a KeyVault to store secrets and tell the App Service to retrieve the configuration values directly from the key vault.

Using a KeyVault, you have the advantage that you can hide the actual values you use in a secure place. No one can enter if they don't have the credentials to access the key vault. This is the only way to ensure that sensitive data contained in the settings (for example, password, connection strings, API keys) is secure.

To retrieve a value from a key vault, you simply have to use the following syntax for the value you store in the app settings:

@Microsoft.KeyVault({referenceString})

The value of referenceString may be one of the following:

- SecretUri=secretUri
- VaultName=vaultName;SecretName=secretName;SecretVersion=secretVersion

You can retrieve the information to format the `referenceString` directly in the key vault blade by going through the following steps:

1. Open your key vault blade and select `Secrets` on the left side:

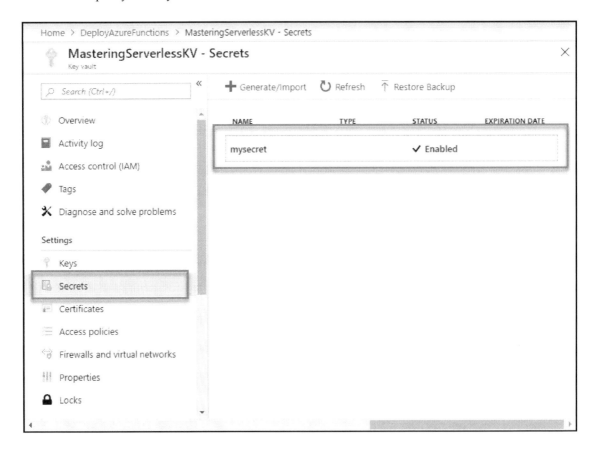

2. Select the secret you want to use (if you don't have the secret, you can create a new one using the **Generate/Import** button at the top of the blade):

3. Retrieve the information you need to format the `referenceString` mentioned before:

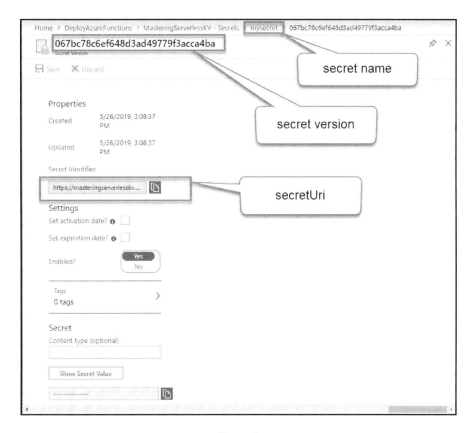

For example, using the information shown in the previous screenshot, the setting value to read the secret in the key vault is as follows:

```
@Microsoft.KeyVault(SecretUri=https://masteringserverlesskv.vault.a
zure.net/secrets/mysecret/067bc78c6ef648d3ad49779f3acca4ba)
```

4. Create an identity for the function app to allow the communication between the function app and the key vault. You can do this using the **Identity** feature that you can find in the **Platform features** tab:

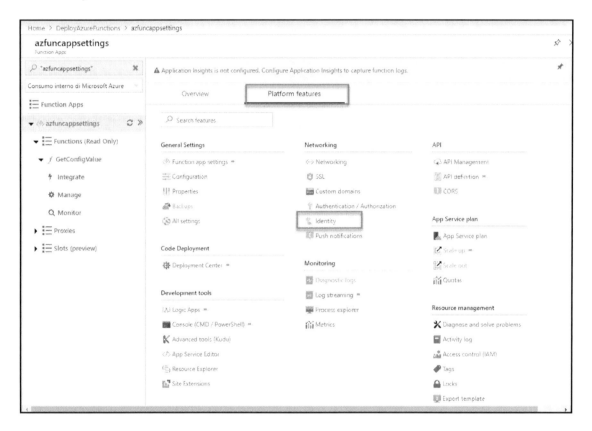

Then, enable the system-assigned identity provided by Azure for the function app:

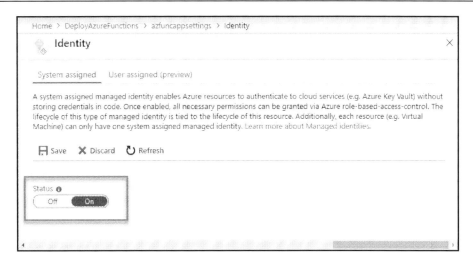

5. Add the system identity created previously in the access policies for the key vault. To do this, go to the **Access policies** tab in the **Key Vault** blade and click on the **+ Add new** button to add a new system identity:

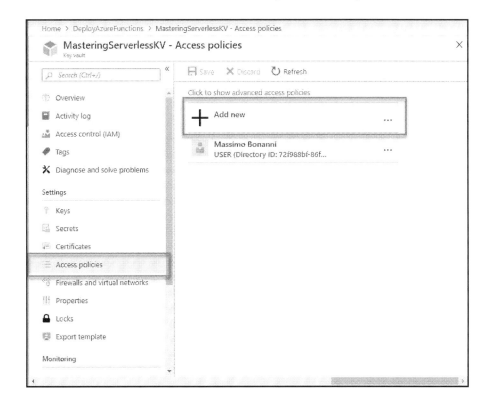

6. Finally, choose the permissions you want to give to the identity (you can do this using a template, as shown in the previous picture, or by selecting the permissions for key, secret, and certificate using the three combinations that are shown under the principal) and the identity itself (it has the same name as the function app):

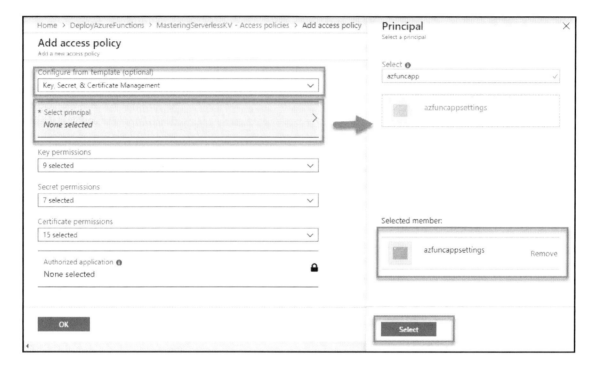

If you don't give the right permission to the function app, then when you read the setting value, you can retrieve the string you insert in the settings and not the value referenced by it in the key vault.

Reading the app settings in your Azure Function

Once you configure your function app, you need to read the values stored in it.

Reading the values contained in the settings is automatic for triggers and bindings in the sense that the infrastructure provides the `INameResolver` interface used by them to access these values. For more information, refer to `Chapter 2`, *Customizing Your Azure Functions*.

However, sometimes you need to access the setting values from the code of your Azure Functions. To do this, you can use the configuration support provided by .NET Core.

The following extension method extends the `ExecutionContext` class to provide the values configured in the settings:

```
public static IEnumerable<KeyValuePair<string, string>>
GetConfigurations(this ExecutionContext context)
{
    if (context == null)
        throw new NullReferenceException(nameof(context));
    var config = new ConfigurationBuilder()
        .SetBasePath(context.FunctionAppDirectory)
        .AddJsonFile("local.settings.json", optional: true,
reloadOnChange: true)
        .AddEnvironmentVariables()
        .Build();
    return config.AsEnumerable();
}
```

The `ConfigurationBuilder` class is contained in the `Microsoft.Extensions.Configuration` namespace, and you can use one of the extension methods provided by Microsoft to add different configuration providers. In the previous snippet, we use `AddJsonFile` to also support the `local.settings.json` file, but you can use `AddXmlFile` (for example) to store the configuration in an XML file instead of a JSON file.

The following extension method allows you to retrieve the single value when given the value name:

```
public static string GetConfig(this ExecutionContext context, string
keyName)
{
    if (string.IsNullOrWhiteSpace(keyName))
        throw new ArgumentException(nameof(keyName));
    var config = GetConfigurations(context);
    var pair = config.FirstOrDefault(k => k.Key == keyName);
    if (pair.Equals(default(KeyValuePair<string, string>)))
        return null;
    return pair.Value;
}
```

The following function is an example of how you can use the previous extension methods inside an Azure Function. The function has an HTTP trigger and returns the value of the setting for the specific name passed in the query string:

```
[FunctionName("GetConfigValue")]
public static IActionResult Run(
    [HttpTrigger(AuthorizationLevel.Function, "get", Route = null)]
HttpRequest req,
    ILogger log, ExecutionContext context)
{
    string key = req.Query["key"];
    log.LogInformation($"Retrieve config for {key}");
    if (key == null)
        return new BadRequestObjectResult("Please pass a key on the query
string");
    var configValue = context.GetConfig(key);
    return new OkObjectResult(new { key, value = configValue });
}
```

You can use one of the signatures of an Azure Function method that supports the `ExecutionContext` as one of the parameters.

Summary

In this chapter, you learned how to create an Azure function app, deploy Azure Functions inside it, and configure them.

Using the ARM template, you can create a function app on the fly and update it with minimum effort, and you can use Azure Functions Core Tools to deploy the Azure Functions. In some scenarios (for example, test environments), you can rapidly create an environment by simply running the ARM template and deploying the function app using the Core Tools, and you can do it programmatically.

In the next chapter, you will see how you can use DevOps methodologies with your Azure Functions.

Questions

1. What is an ARM template?
    - A PowerShell script
    - A JSON file
    - An XML file
    - A C# snippet

2. Which of these resources are essential for a function app?
    - An Azure storage
    - A function app
    - An Azure SQL database
    - An Application Insight account
    - A firewall

3. What is the property that you can use in an ARM template to state that a resource can be created only after creating other resources?
    - `kind`
    - `location`
    - `sku`
    - `dependsOn`

4. How can you make sure that the `local.settings.json` file is not saved in the source code repository?
    - You cannot do it.
    - Enable the option **Don't save local file** in the Visual Studio project.
    - Add the right line in the `.gitignore` file.
    - Change the file extension in JSON.

5. Can you store values in the key vault and reference them in the app settings?
    - Yes, but the function app needs to have the right permission.
    - Yes, but not in the Consumption plan.
    - No, you cannot access the value contained in the key vault.

Further reading

You can find more information about creating, deploying, and configuring Azure Functions by going to the following links:

- *Automate resource deployment for your function app in Azure Functions*: `https://docs.microsoft.com/en-us/azure/azure-functions/functions-infrastructure-as-code`
- *App settings reference for Azure Functions*: `https://docs.microsoft.com/en-us/azure/azure-functions/functions-app-settings`
- *host.json reference for Azure Functions 2.x*: `https://docs.microsoft.com/en-us/azure/azure-functions/functions-host-json`
- *Project KUDU official GitHub repository*: `https://github.com/projectkudu/kudu`
- *Zip deployment for Azure Functions*: `https://docs.microsoft.com/en-us/azure/azure-functions/deployment-zip-push`
- *Use Key Vault references for App Service and Azure Functions*: `https://docs.microsoft.com/en-us/azure/app-service/app-service-key-vault-references`

5
Leverage the Power of DevOps with Azure Functions

Today, it is very important to be agile and have a quick time to market. Application solutions, especially those in the cloud, change quickly, and it isn't possible to keep pace if a release strategy is adopted based on the manual intervention of a human operator. This is one of the reasons why it may make sense to implement **continuous integration** (**CI**) and **continuous deployment** (**CD**) pipelines to bring your latest version into production as quickly as possible.

In this chapter, you will learn how to bring the power of DevOps methodology into your Azure Functions solution using Azure DevOps, its CI/CD pipelines, and its integration with Git and GitHub.

This chapter will cover the following topics:

- Understanding Azure DevOps and Azure Pipelines
- Creating a build pipeline for a simple Azure Function and configuring it for CI
- Creating a release pipeline that allows you to deploy your Azure Function in a cloud environment using CD

Technical requirements

In this chapter, we will talk about Azure DevOps, so it will be helpful if you know about DevOps techniques and the benefits of using them.

You can find the source code for this chapter at `https://github.com/PacktPublishing/Mastering-Azure-Serverless-Computing/tree/master/Chapter05`.

Understanding Azure DevOps

Azure DevOps is a suite of tools, hosted in Azure, that allows you to implement your DevOps methodologies and manage your code, building, and deployment tasks.

You can access the Azure DevOps features using a browser or an IDE, such as Visual Studio, and Azure DevOps also exposes a set of RESTful APIs that you can leverage to create your custom tools.

 You can start your journey into Azure DevOps at `https://azure.microsoft.com/en-us/services/devops/`. You can create an account using a Microsoft account or a GitHub account.

Azure DevOps offers a plan with the first five users free and a monthly fee for additional users. You can find more info about pricing at `https://azure.microsoft.com/en-us/pricing/details/devops/azure-devops-services/`.

Azure DevOps is composed of five pillars. Each of the pillars allows you to manage a part of your software project and is integrated with the other pillars. The pillars are described as follows:

- **Azure Boards**: This provides you with a set of tools to manage your teamwork. Task, bug, and user stories can be created and tracked by the team using the web interface or the IDE interface (for example, Visual Studio). It allows you to create dashboards and queries to understand the progress of your project. It natively supports Scrum, agile, and CMMI project templates, but you can customize the template you use in a simple way.

- **Azure Repos**: This provides you with a set of version-control tools that you can use to manage your code. Azure DevOps provides you with two different types of version control:
  - **Git**: This is one of the most widely used version control systems, and is free and open source. You can find more information about it at `https://git-scm.com/`. It is a distributed version control system, which means you can have a copy of your code repository locally and, of course, you can synchronize it with the server counterpart (and with all of your team).
  - **Team Foundation Version Control (TFVC)**: This is a centralized version control system based on a Microsoft product called Team Foundation Server. In this case, every developer has only one version of each file on their PC and the historical sequence is maintained on the server.

- **Azure Pipelines**: This is a cloud service that allows you to host your build and release pipelines. You can imagine a pipeline as a task chain in which you build your project or deploy it on an environment. You can use any programming language (it is language-agnostic) and you can address every type of environment (on-premises, Azure, AWS, and so on). You can write your pipeline using a sort of designer tool or you can use YAML.

- **Azure Artifacts**: This allows you to share your Maven, npm, and NuGet packages with your team. You can integrate it with the CI/CD pipelines to automate the sharing process.

- **Azure Test Plans**: This provides you with a set of tools that you can use to test your apps. With this pillar, you can create manual/exploratory tests or implement continuous testing.

You can configure every team project in Azure DevOps to use only a subset of the five pillars exposed by the platform. Later in this section, for example, we will use only the pipelines pillar and use GitHub as the code repository.

Azure DevOps also offers you collaboration tools, such as customizable team dashboards with configurable widgets to share information, wikis for sharing documentation, configurable notifications, and more.

In addition, the Azure DevOps platform provides support for adding extensions and integrating with other popular services—such as Slack, Trello, and UserVoice—and developing your own custom extensions.

Azure DevOps is your main tool to manage your software project. You can configure it to use only what you need and you can integrate it with your favorite tools.

Azure Pipelines and Azure Functions

In this section, you will learn how to implement CI/CD pipelines to build your function app and deploy it on Azure. Let's set them up by going through the following steps:

1. First of all, you must have an organization in Azure DevOps; then you can create a team project to host your pipelines. In this example, we will assume that your code is on GitHub.

2. To create your team project, use the **Create project** button in Azure DevOps:

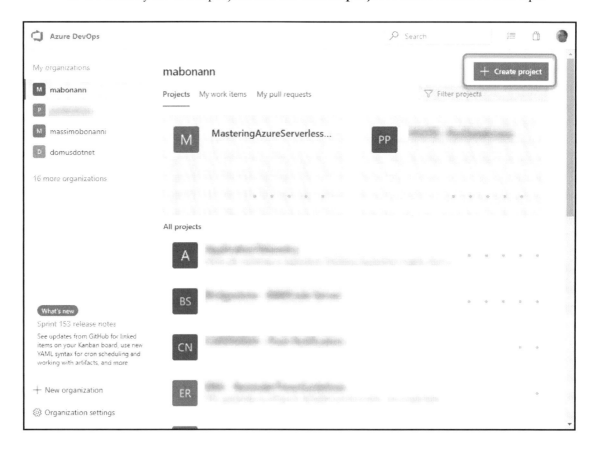

3. Then configure it:

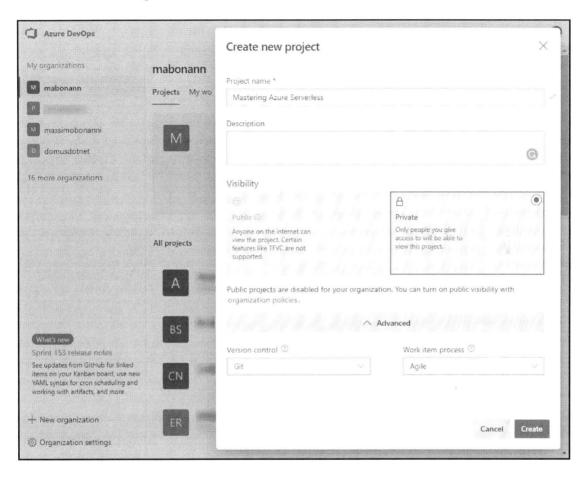

4. You can set a description to describe your project. In this case, the advanced configurations are useless as you will not be using Azure Boards and Azure Repos (instead, you will connect your Azure DevOps team project to the GitHub repository).

5. Finally, to integrate Azure Pipelines with GitHub, you must enable Azure Pipelines on your GitHub repository. You can find the Azure Pipelines extension in the marketplace:

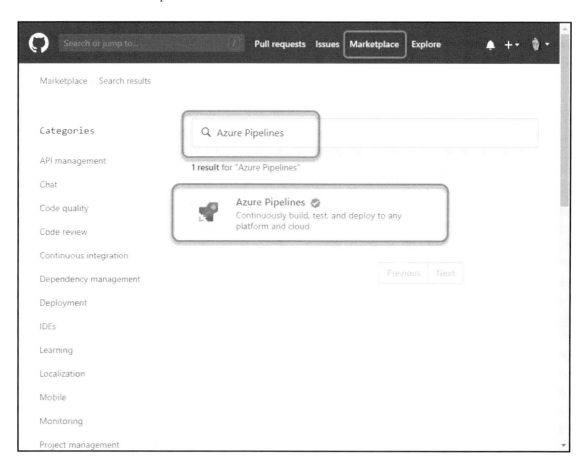

6. Select it and choose the plan you prefer:

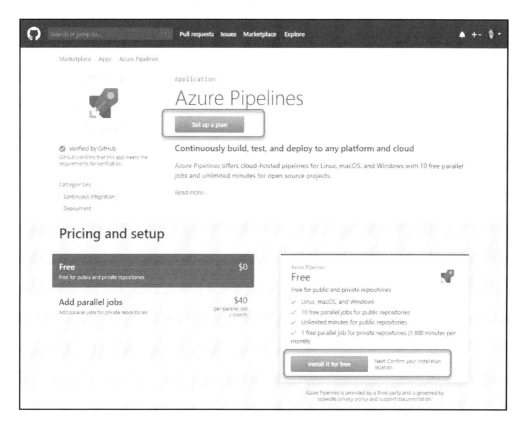

7. Once you enable Azure Pipelines in your repository, you can create your pipelines in Azure DevOps and link your GitHub repository.

In the following screenshot, you can see the solution we used to implement CI/CD. You will find it in the GitHub repository at the link in the *Technical requirements* section:

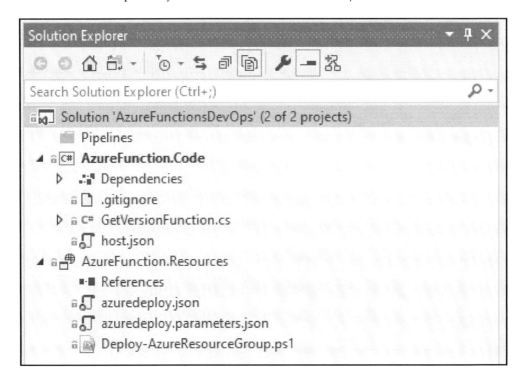

The solution is composed of two projects:

- `AzureFunction.Resources`: This contains the ARM template definition for the resources you need to create to host your functions (function app, storage, app plan, and so on), as you saw in the previous chapter.
- `AzureFunction.Code`: This contains the Azure Functions code that implements the sample function.

In a few words, the goal of this chapter is to create an automatic process (for the build and release pipelines) that allows you to change something in your solution, push it to the Git repository, and, after a certain period of time, automatically have the new code and resources on an environment in Azure.

The function code that we will use as an example is very simple:

```
public static class GetVersionFunction
{
    private static string Version = "1.0.0.0";

     [FunctionName("GetVersion")]
     public static IActionResult Run(
         [HttpTrigger(AuthorizationLevel.Function, "get", Route = null)]
HttpRequest req,
         ILogger log)
     {
         log.LogInformation("C# HTTP trigger function processed a
request.");
         return (ActionResult)new OkObjectResult($"Your awesome function
version {Version}");
     }
}
```

The function is an HTTP-triggered function that responds to an HTTP GET verb and returns the message `Your awesome function version 1.0.0.0`. When you complete the implementation of the pipelines, you can change something (for example, the version number to 1.1.0.0), push the changes to the Git repository, and finally, the function is deployed on Azure and responds with `Your awesome function version 1.1.0.0` without any human interaction during the build and release process.

Creating your first build pipeline

A build pipeline is a set of tasks that you want to execute when you want to create an artifact that will be pushed to a software environment. The purpose of a build pipeline is to create an *immutable* artifact that can be used in different environments (for example, first in a test environment, then preproduction, and then production). When you think about the build pipeline, you must remember that it only builds something—it does not deploy—and that the artifact you generate must be immutable in order to guarantee that you will always deploy a consistent version of your code.

To create your build pipeline, go through the following steps:

1. Select the **Builds** option on the left-hand side of the pipelines in Azure DevOps.
2. Use the **New** drop-down at the top of the page and select the **New build pipeline** option:

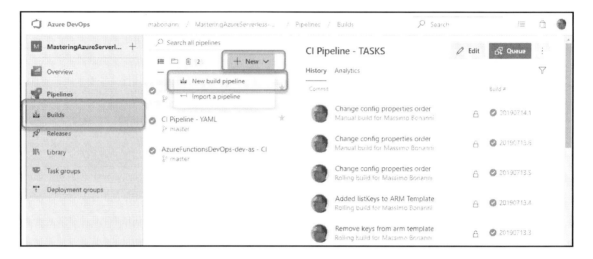

Azure DevOps supports two types of pipelines:

- **Task-based pipelines**: Here, you define your pipeline by choosing tasks from a predefined set or from the marketplace and using a web-browser designer
- **YAML pipeline**: Here, you define your pipeline using YAML

3. When you choose to create a new build pipeline, bear in mind that Azure DevOps uses the YAML approach. If you want to define your pipeline using a graphical approach, you must choose **Use the classic editor**, as shown in the following screenshot:

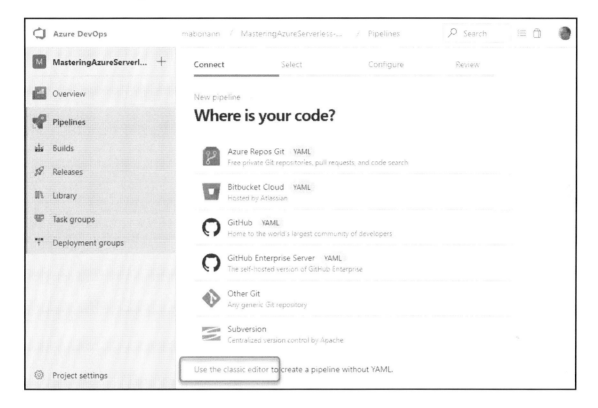

4. The first step you must take when you create a pipeline is to choose where your code is located:

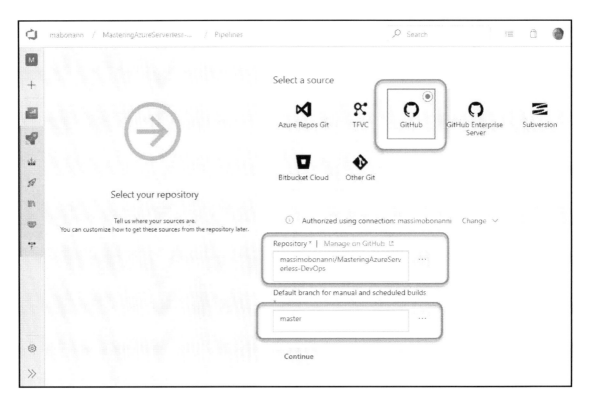

5. In our example, your code is on GitHub, and so you need to choose what the repository is, as well as the branch you want to use for your build pipeline. The first time you perform this operation, Azure DevOps will ask you to authorize its connection to GitHub. As you will see, you can use a wide set of source control systems.

6. Once you have selected the source control for your code, you can select what kind of pipeline you want to implement by choosing the template:

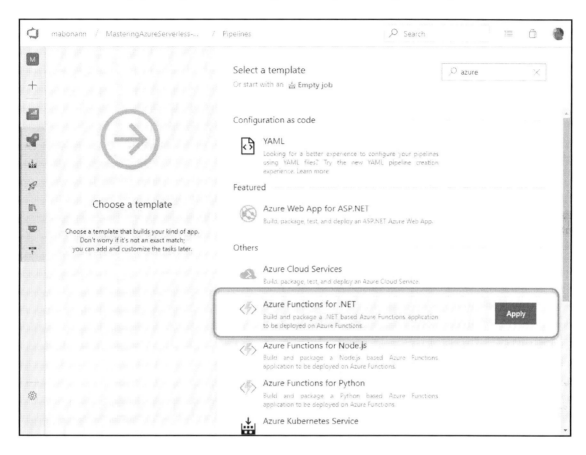

7. You can start from an empty job if you want to create the pipeline from scratch (for example, if you don't find a template for your scenario), or you can choose the YAML approach, but for Azure Functions, there is a template you can select to add the basic tasks you need to build an Azure Function.

8. Once you click on the **Apply** button, Azure Pipelines will create a new pipeline with a set of predefined tasks to accomplish the Azure Function building:

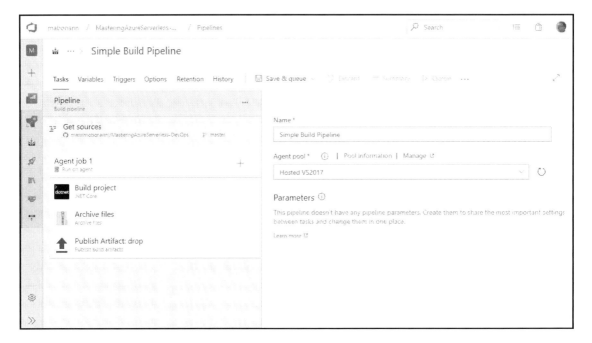

As you can see in the preceding screenshot, the pipeline has different tabs that you can use to define and configure it.

The main one is the **Tasks** tab. Before we look at it in more detail, let's look at the other tabs.

The Variables tab

The **Variables** tab allows you to define or change the pipeline variables:

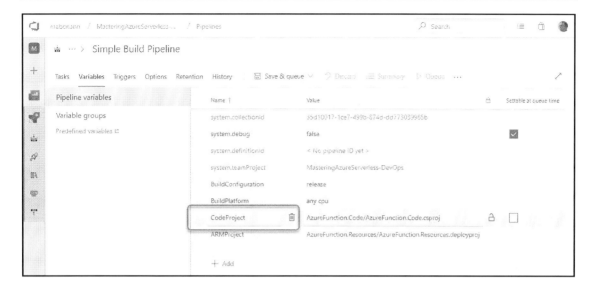

The pipeline variables are a sort of placeholder you can use inside your tasks or YAML to centralize values all over the pipeline.

In the preceding screenshot, you can see the `CodeProject` variable (which contains the value `AzureFunction.Code/AzureFunction.Code.csproj`). Every time you use the placeholder `CodeProject` in a task, the pipeline engine will substitute it with the right value during the build process.

Every variable can be a plain value (a text everybody can see as the `CodeProject`) or a secret (where only the owner of the pipeline can see it). You can change the mode using the lock icon on the left.

You can also choose whether a variable can be set when someone executes the build pipeline using the **Settable at queue time** option on the left.

Finally, you have a set of predefined variables that are defined and filled by the pipeline engine, which you can use inside your tasks. The variables are as follows:

- `Build.BuildId`: The ID of the build
- `Build.BinariesDirectory`: The local path used by the build agent to store the output binaries of the build
- `Build.SourceBranch`: The source branch for the build

You can find more information about predefined variables at `https://docs.microsoft.com/en-us/azure/devops/pipelines/build/variables?view=azure-devops`.

The Triggers tab

In the **Triggers** tab, you can set when your pipeline will start:

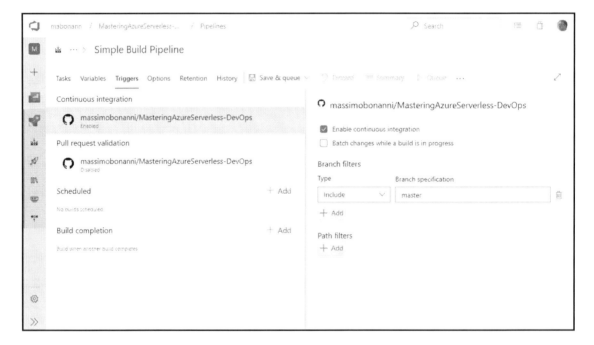

You can configure the following triggers:

- **Continuous integration**: This is the trigger that allows you to use the CI pipeline. Every time someone pushes new commits to your repository, the pipeline starts. To enable it, you simply check the flag shown in the preceding screenshot. You can configure what branch you want to include or exclude (if you include a branch, the pipeline will also start if someone pushes new commits to that branch) and what disk paths will be included or excluded (for example, you may want to exclude a source folder that contains only documentation files so that a build is not performed if someone changes the documentation).

- **Pull request validation**: You can also use the pipeline to verify that the code inserted after a pull request, at least, compiles (and reject it in the event of a failure of the build).
- **Scheduled**: You can use this option to implement a *nightly build*—for example, you can configure your pipeline to start every night at midnight.
- **Build completion**: You can set up your pipeline to start if another build pipeline completes its job without errors. With this option, you can implement a chain of build pipelines.

Of course, you can set any one or more of the previous options simultaneously.

The Options tab

The **Options** tab allows you to set some options for the pipeline and the job behind the pipeline:

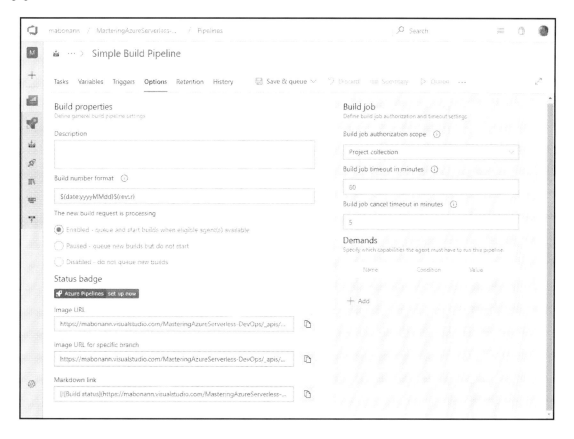

The **Build properties** section allows you to set information about the pipeline itself:

- **Description**: This is a detailed description you can use to explain what the pipeline does.
- **Build number format**: This is the number that the build engine sets over the build execution when the pipeline starts. You can use a fixed value, but the best approach is to generate the build number dynamically with an incremental value or by using the time at the moment the pipeline starts, as shown in the preceding screenshot. In the preceding screenshot, in fact, the build number is `$(date:yyyyMMdd)$(rev:.r)`, which means that the build engine uses the current date at the start of the pipeline and generates a number composed by the concatenation of the year, the month, and the day followed by a daily revision number (for example, if the pipeline starts on July 7, 2019, the build number is `20190707.1`).
- **Status badge**: In this section, you can find the **Image URL** and **Markdown link** to show the status badge of the build on your website.

The **Build job** section allows you to set up the timeout for the job executed by the agent (you will learn more about the agent and how it works later, in the *The Tasks tab* section):

- **Build job authorization scope**: This allows you to define the authorization scope for the build job. You must choose **Project collection** when you access multiple team projects; select **Current project** when you want to isolate the job to a particular team project.
- **Build job timeout in minutes**: Here, you can set the maximum amount of time a job can run before it is canceled by the server. For example, if you set it to 60 minutes, then if a job, for some reason, remains active for more then 60 minutes (for example, if it is blocked by some errors), the server will automatically cancel it and the build will fail. You can set an infinite timeout by simply putting zero in the textbox, but remember that you have a free fixed number of minutes for a build for a month, and if you set the timeout to be infinite, then you could consume them unnecessarily. For more information about the values you can set in this field, go to `https://docs.microsoft.com/en-us/azure/devops/pipelines/process/phases?view=azure-devopstabs=yamlviewFallbackFrom=vsts#timeouts`.
- **Build job cancel timeout in minutes**: This allows you to set a limit for the job cancel time.

The History tab

Every time you change something in your pipeline and save it, Azure DevOps creates a new version of the pipeline:

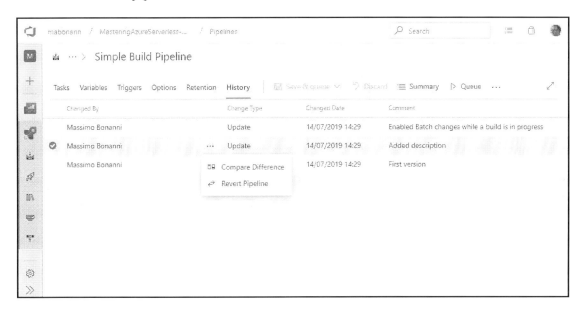

In this tab, you can find one record for each version of your pipeline with the change type (for example, update or add), the change date, the user that made the change, and, if it exists, the comment the user left when they saved the pipeline. The topmost record is the current version.

It is a source-control system integrated into Azure DevOps for the pipeline. If you are using YAML, your pipeline will be described by a file in your source control (for example, GitHub), and this tab is used by Azure DevOps to historicize changes to the build process (for example, variables or triggers defined in the web interface).

You can use the ... menu to execute an operation over a particular version:

- **Compare Difference**: This allows you to check the difference between two versions.
- **Revert Pipeline**: This allows you to promote an old version as a new current version.

The Tasks tab

The **Tasks** tab is the place where you can find the definition of the pipeline. As you've learned already, in the previous section, the goal of a build pipeline is to create an immutable artifact that you use every time you deploy the exact version of your application.

Remember that, when you talk about the DevOps pipeline, there is a net separation between the build process (the build pipeline) and the deploy process in one or more environments (deployment pipeline).

A build pipeline has a name and a set of agents. An agent is a task orchestrator that takes care of a job, and a job is a set of tasks run in a sequence as a unit to create the artifact. A build pipeline can have one or more agents. An agent may be of two different types:

- **Agent job**: An agent job is a process that runs on a virtual machine. It has access to the hard drive of the VM (the VM can also be in your servers). You use this type of agent when you have to build source code or a ZIP file (for example). An agent job can run a wide set of tasks.
- **Agentless job**: An agentless job is a kind of virtual process that runs on Azure DevOps servers. It doesn't need a physical agent process on a VM and supports only a few types of tasks (for example, when retrieving a work item from Azure DevOps boards, getting an HTTP request to an on-premises server, and so on). You use this kind of job when you need to aggregate data for the build (for example, when creating a release note for the artifact) or you have to implement a manual intervention in the build.

Once you define a build pipeline and run it, it executes on an agent. Instead of managing each agent individually, Azure DevOps organizes them in agent pools. You can define your own agent pool (for example, located on your on-premises servers) or use one of the pools provided by the platform. Before you start to create your agent pool (called a self-hosted pool) or use one of the pools provided by Azure DevOps, it's important to remember that a pool is scoped to the entire organization, not the single team project.

At the beginning of this section, you create your pipeline using the Azure Functions template:

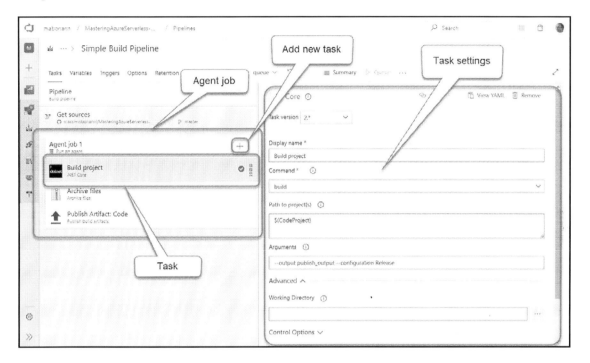

If you press the **+** button to add a new task to the pipeline, you can choose from a wide set of tasks provided by Azure DevOps, as shown in the following screenshot:

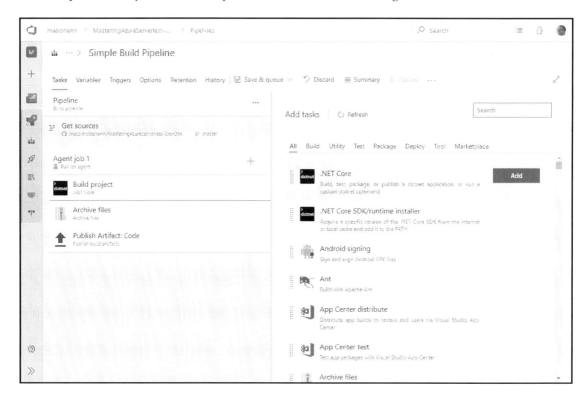

As you can see in the preceding screenshot, you have tasks related to Microsoft technologies (for example, a .NET Core task) but you can also find non-Microsoft technologies (for example, Android or Ant tasks). You can search your task or you can use the **Marketplace** tab to install new third-party tasks.

Every task has a name, a version, and a set of settings that you can configure to customize it and the behavior of the pipeline when the task is executed.

Looking at the .NET Core task shown in the preceding screenshot, we can see that it implements the `dotnet` command for .NET Core (you can find more information at `https://docs.microsoft.com/en-us/dotnet/core/tools/dotnet`), so you can find the command argument (for example, build, restore, publish, and so on). If you try to change the command selected from the drop-down, you will see that all the other settings will change to adapt the input to the actual parameters the command needs.

For example, for the build command selected in the screenshot, you should find the path to the project or solution to build and the argument for the compiler. As you can see, inside the **Path to project(s)** textbox, you can use one of the variables defined in the **Variables** tab.

Whatever task you decide to use, there are common settings that control the behavior of the pipeline following the task result:

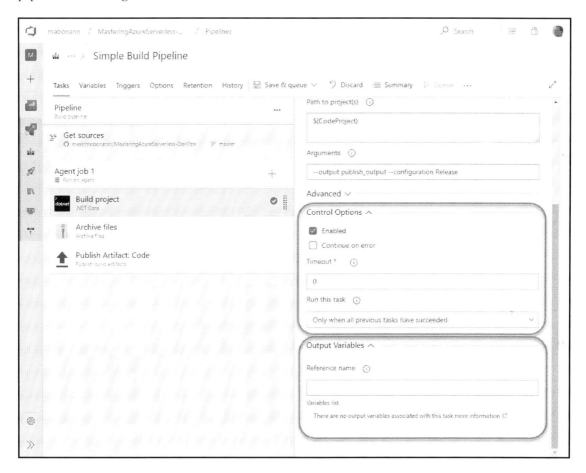

The **Control Options** section allows you to define the behavior of the pipeline if the task fails. You can decide to stop the execution of the pipeline if the task fails (for example, the pipeline must stop if your code doesn't build) or let it continue through the error. You can also control when to run the task (for example, after the completion of the previous task, or if the previous task fails) and the task timeout.

The **Output Variables** section allows you to pass data from one task to the following one: when you define a set of variables here, you publish those variables to the server and they become available for the whole pipeline. So you can use them inside the next tasks as a variable that you define in the **Variables** tab.

If you look at the pipeline created by the wizard, you can see the tasks, which are listed as follows:

- `Build project`: This task uses the `dotnet` command to build the project, which contains the function code (the `AzureFunction.Code` project in your solution):

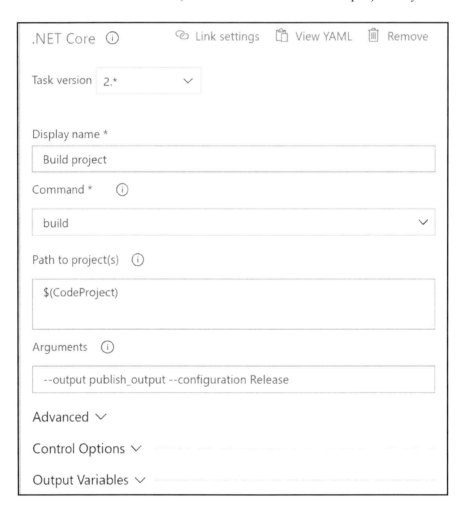

The dotnet command arguments contain the --output publish_output option, which tells the task to save the compilation result in the publish_output folder.

- Archive files: This task creates a ZIP file containing all the build files:

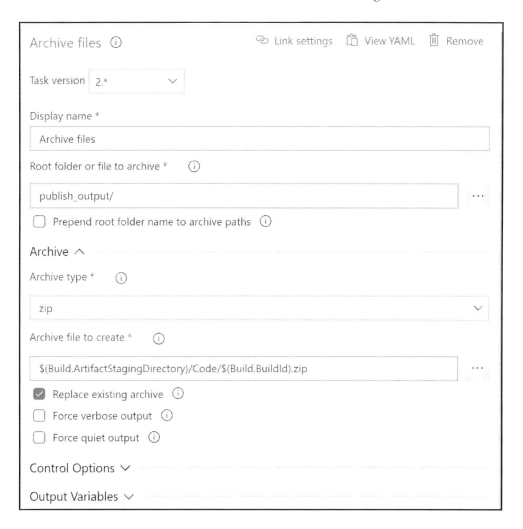

The Archive files command creates a ZIP file (named using the build identifier stored in the Build.BuildId variable) with all the files contained in the publish_output folder and saves it in the Code subfolder of the folder defined in the Build.ArtifactStagingDirectory variable.

- `Publish Artifact: Code`: This task brings the ZIP created by the previous task and pushes it into a repository hosted in Azure DevOps that contains the build artifacts of your whole build pipeline. This is precisely the idea of an immutable artifact; every time you must deploy the version you create with this pipeline, you should bring it from the artifact repository. This is the only way you can be sure that the binary of your code will be the same:

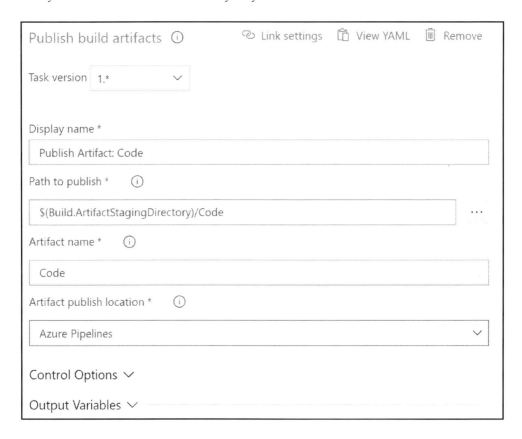

The task brings all the files contained in the `$(Build.ArtifactStagingDirectory)/Code` folder (the folder used by the previous task to save the zipped file) to a location called `Code` in the artifact repository in Azure DevOps. Every build has its own space in the artifact repository, so two different build executions will occupy different space in the repository: the `Code` location for the first is different from the `Code` from the second. Anyway, the artifact repository management is completely transparent to you; it is the responsibility of Azure DevOps, so you can just use it.

To complete the pipeline, you should do two things: add a task in the current agent to restore the NuGet package before starting the build `dotnet` task and create another agent to build the `AzureFunction.Resources` project in your solution.

To do the first operation, go through the following steps:

1. Select the `dotnet` task, click the **+** button, select another `dotnet` task, and click on **Add**. The designer inserts the new task after the first, but don't worry: you can drag-and-drop it in the first position.
2. Once you insert the new task, you can configure it as shown in the following screenshot:

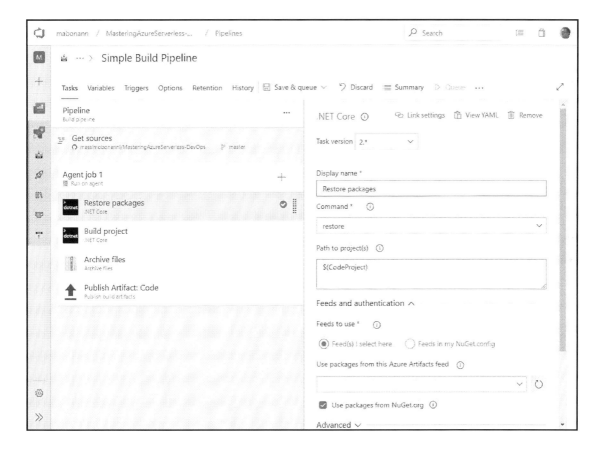

3. When you complete the task configuration, you can save the build definition using the **Save & queue** drop-down button located at the right of the **Pipelines** tab:

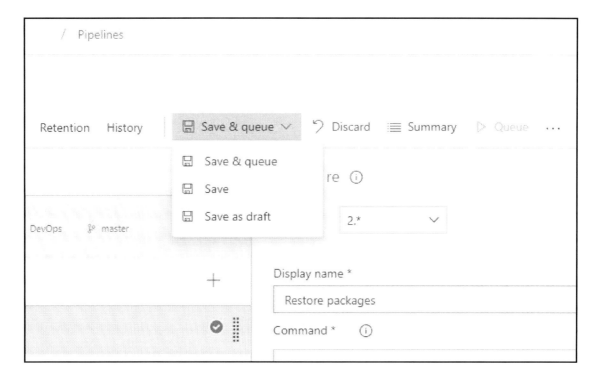

This menu allows you to do the following:

- **Save**: Saves the definition and makes the new one the current version
- **Save as draft**: Saves the definition, but it remains a draft and doesn't become the current version
- **Save & queue**: Saves the definition as the **Save** option and, after that, runs a new build using the new version

In any case, when you save a build definition, Azure DevOps will ask you to insert a comment that can be useful to describe the operation in question. This comment will appear inside the **History** tab:

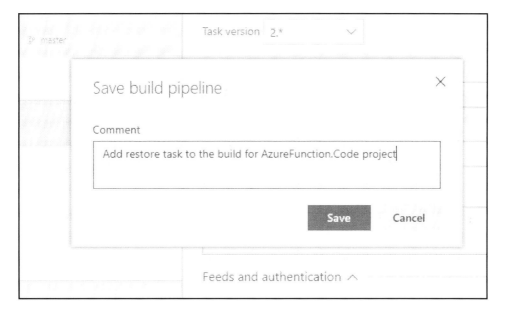

Your solution will also contain a project for the ARM template that defines the infrastructure used to host your function, so the second thing to do in your build pipeline is to create an agent to build that project. Let's set this up by going through the following steps:

1. To create a new agent, you can use the **...** menu to the right of the **Pipeline** header:

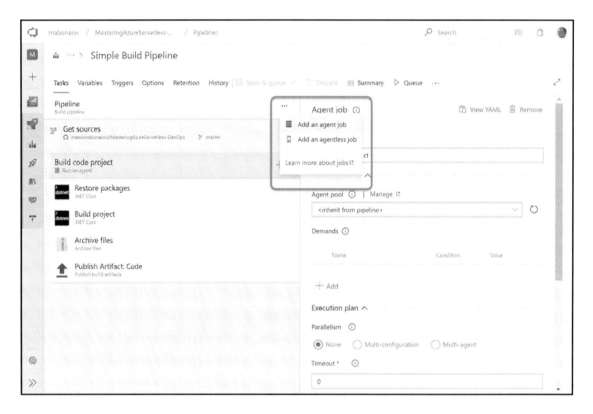

2. Once you select the **Add an agent job**, the designer adds a new agent to the bottom of the pipeline.

The job to build the ARM template is composed of the following tasks:

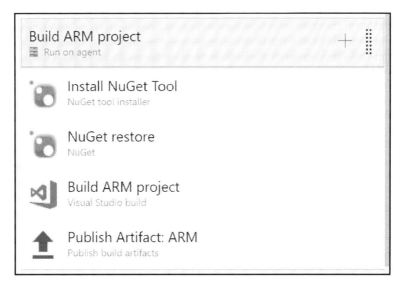

- **Install NuGet Tool (NuGet tool installer)**: This task installs the NuGet tool on the agent machine. You need to install it because you need it to restore the NuGet packages used in the project, and the agent machine may not have it (the machine could be created from scratch). The task doesn't need any configuration:

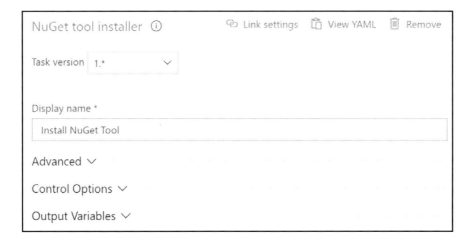

- **NuGet restore (NuGet)**: This task wraps the `restore` command for the NuGet tool (you can find more info about the NuGet `restore` command at `https://docs.microsoft.com/en-us/nuget/consume-packages/package-restore`). In this task, you must configure the command parameter (`restore`) and the project to restore in the **Path to solution, packages.config, or project.json** textbox:

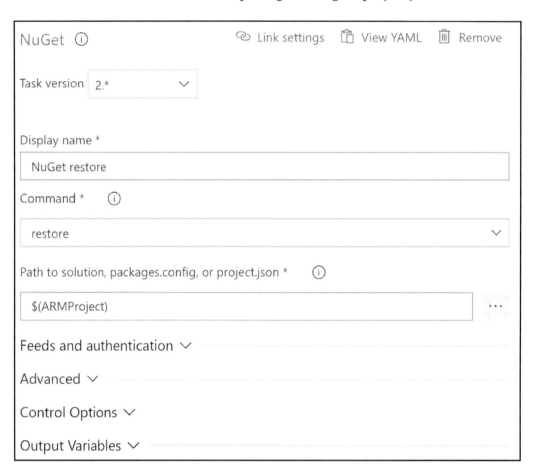

- **Build ARM Project (Visual Studio build)**: This task builds the ARM project (`AzureFunction.Resources`). It uses MSBuild to build the project. The configuration is shown in the following screenshot:

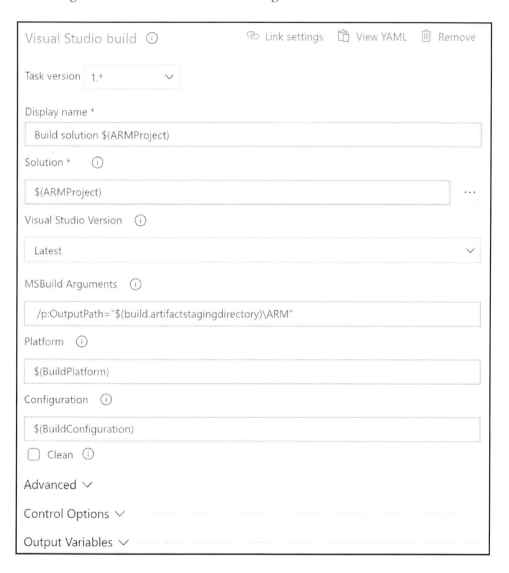

- **Publish Artifact ARM (Publish build artifact)**: This task copies all the files created by the build task in the artifact repository (in the location called ARM):

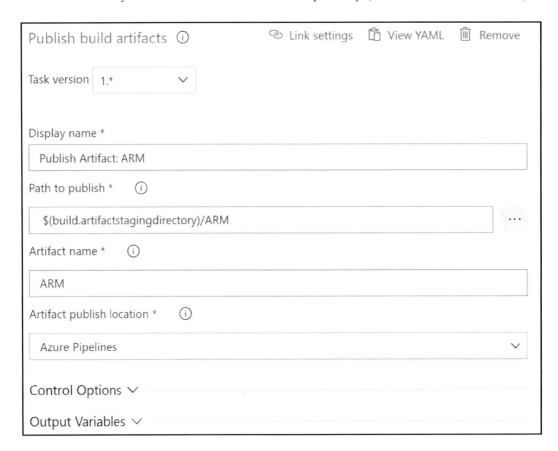

Now your pipeline is complete, and you can run it in two different ways:

- Every time someone pushes a new commit into the Git repository because you set **Continuous integration** in the **Triggers** tab. In this case, the build starts silently and it uses the default value for the variables.
- Manually, if you use the `Queue` command. In this case, you can override the default value of the variables you define in the definition.

If you are using a hosted agent, then when a build definition starts, Azure DevOps will look for an available agent and then, finally, assign the build to the agent and run it.

You can find all the build definitions executed in the **History** tab:

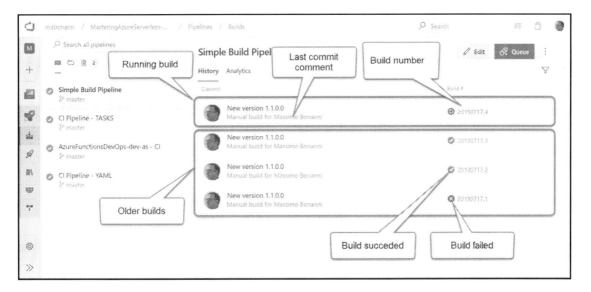

If you click on the build, you can see its log (if it is running, you can see the log in real time):

You can download every single artifact you create with the build using the **Artifacts** drop-down.

Using YAML definition

You defined your first build pipeline using the task approach and the web designer, but you can also do it using YAML files.

When you use YAML, your pipeline is completely defined inside the YAML file, which is managed like a standard code file (it is stored in your Git repository and versioned like every other code file in your projects).

 YAML is a human-readable data serialization format used in configuration files that use whitespace indentation to define their structure. For more information, go to `https://yaml.org/`.

A YAML file that describes a pipeline has the following structure:

```
Pipeline
 └── Variables
 └── Trigger
 └── Jobs
     └── Job
         Steps
          └── Task
          └── Task
     └── Job
         Steps
          └── Task
          └── Task
```

The job collections contain all the agent definitions, while the steps collections contain the tasks.

For example, the pipeline you defined in the previous section will be as follows:

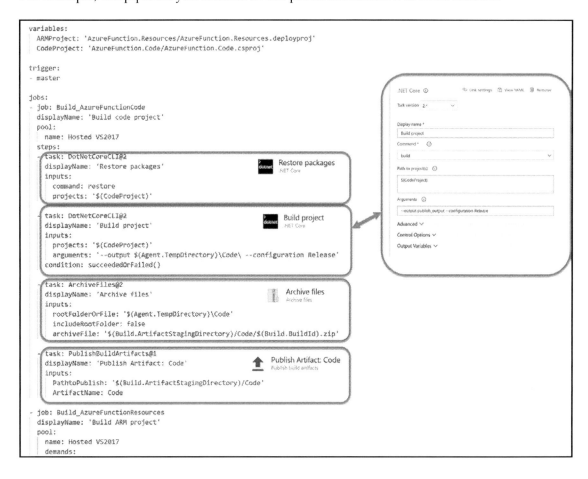

```
variables:
  ARMProject: 'AzureFunction.Resources/AzureFunction.Resources.deployproj'
  CodeProject: 'AzureFunction.Code/AzureFunction.Code.csproj'

trigger:
- master

jobs:
- job: Build_AzureFunctionCode
  displayName: 'Build code project'
  pool:
    name: Hosted VS2017
  steps:
  - task: DotNetCoreCLI@2
    displayName: 'Restore packages'
    inputs:
      command: restore
      projects: '$(CodeProject)'

  - task: DotNetCoreCLI@2
    displayName: 'Build project'
    inputs:
      projects: '$(CodeProject)'
      arguments: '--output $(Agent.TempDirectory)\Code\ --configuration Release'
    condition: succeededOrFailed()

  - task: ArchiveFiles@2
    displayName: 'Archive files'
    inputs:
      rootFolderOrFile: '$(Agent.TempDirectory)\Code'
      includeRootFolder: false
      archiveFile: '$(Build.ArtifactStagingDirectory)/Code/$(Build.BuildId).zip'

  - task: PublishBuildArtifacts@1
    displayName: 'Publish Artifact: Code'
    inputs:
      PathtoPublish: '$(Build.ArtifactStagingDirectory)/Code'
      ArtifactName: Code

- job: Build_AzureFunctionResources
  displayName: 'Build ARM project'
  pool:
    name: Hosted VS2017
    demands:
```

You can create your YAML file from scratch or start from the task pipeline. Every agent definition or task definition in the designer has a **View YAML** option you can use to generate the YAML snippet:

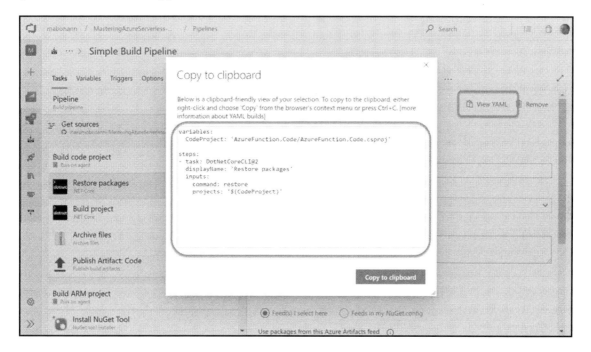

If you want to create your pipeline using YAML, you can create the pipeline as you did in the previous section, but you must choose YAML as a template instead of choosing Azure Functions:

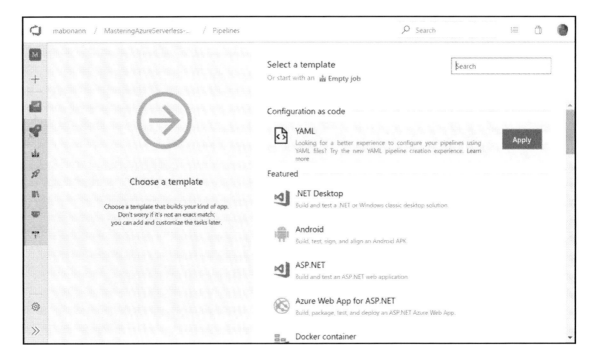

Select the YAML definition file from your repository:

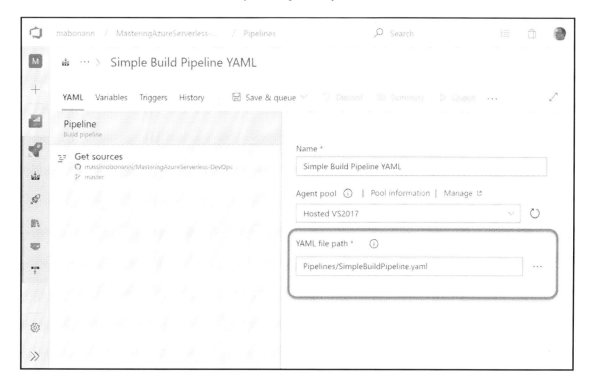

 You can find more information about the schema reference for YAML in Azure DevOps at `https://docs.microsoft.com/en-us/azure/devops/pipelines/yaml-schema?view=azure-devopstabs=schema`.

Creating the release pipeline

In the previous section, you created your first build pipeline to create your artifact. Now is the time to create your first release pipeline in order to deploy an artifact to an environment (for example, Azure).

A release pipeline starts from one or more artifacts and defines one or more stages to deploy them:

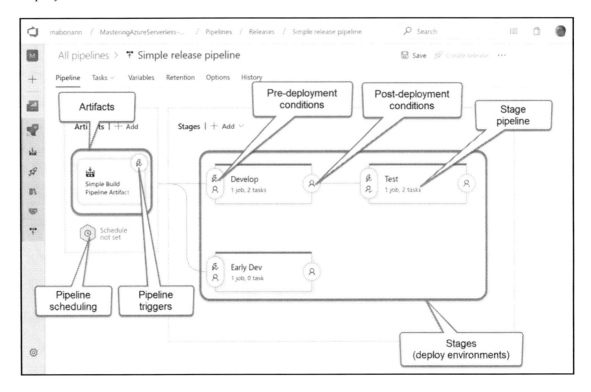

The **Artifacts** box contains all the artifacts that the release pipeline uses. For each artifact, you can configure the trigger (the continuous deployment trigger and pull request trigger) that activates the release. You can also configure schedules for the release (for example, to implement a nightly release).

When a trigger is fired, Azure DevOps creates a new release that is simply a potential release for one of the stages in the pipeline. Then, this new release can run the deployment on one or more stages, depending on the pre-deployment conditions you set for every environment.

A release can have one or more stages (you can imagine each stage as an environment). For each stage, you can configure the pre-deployment conditions:

- **Triggers**: The triggers define when a release must be started (after every release, after another stage, or manually)

- **Artifact filtering**: You can filter the artifacts and start a stage only if a particular artifact changes
- **Schedule**: The release can start at a specific time (nightly release)
- **Pre-deployment approval**: The release is deployed only if a user approves it
- **Gates**: You can define a delay time to evaluate the release before the pipeline automatically deploys it

You can also set post deployment conditions. These conditions are applied after a stage is deployed and before the release is available for the next stage in the stage chain.

In the previous screenshot, for example, the `Test` stage can be released only if the `Develop` stage is deployed successfully, while `Early Dev` can be deployed immediately when the release from the artifact is ready.

In a release pipeline, similar to the build pipeline, you can define the variables to be used within the various tasks that compose the pipeline. These variables can be global (valid for every stage) or specific to one or more stages:

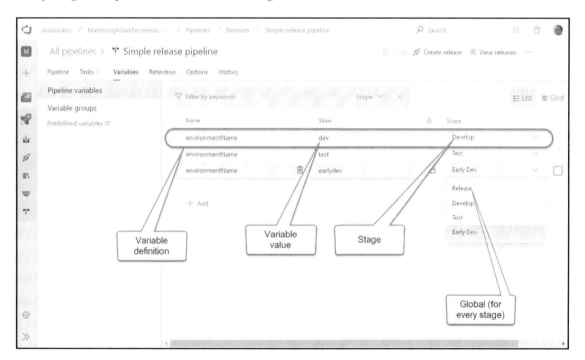

In the example, we used the `environmentName` variable to define each environment name. The pipeline uses this variable to compose the name of every resource it deploys. For example, the resource group name that contains all the resources in the Develop environment will be called `MasteringServerless-dev`.

Finally, every stage has its own pipeline (similar to the build pipeline) with its agent jobs and tasks:

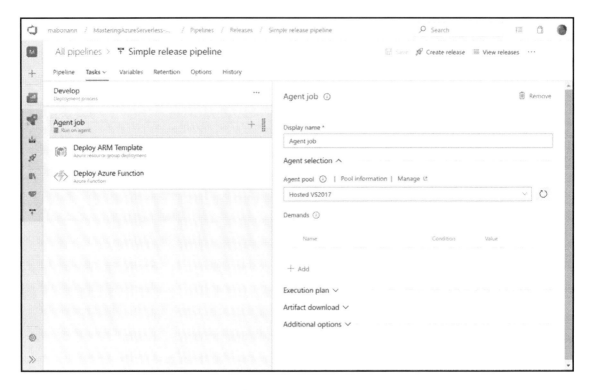

In the sample pipeline, you have the following:

- **Deploy ARM Template (Azure resource group deployment)**: This task uses the ARM template artifact built by the build pipeline to create (if it does not already exist) the resource group that contains your function app. It also creates all the resources defined in the template:

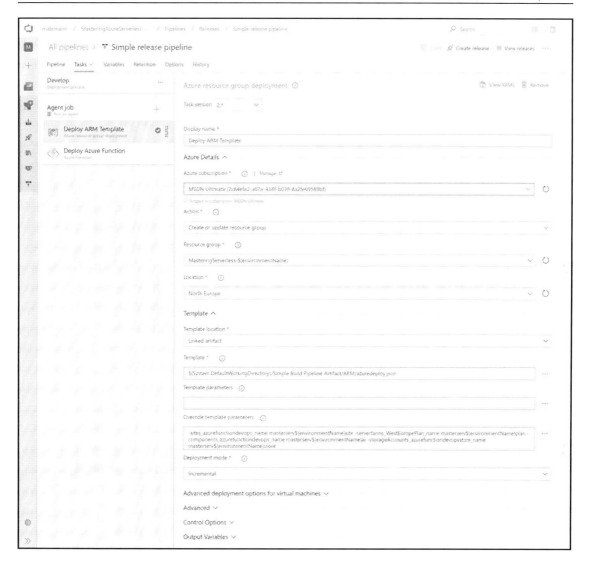

You might note that the resource group name is generated by composing the MasteringServerless- string and the environmentName variable. This means that the resource group name for the Develop stage will be MasteringServerless-dev while the resource group name for the Test stage will be MasteringServerless-test.

The task uses the `azuredeploy.json` file in the artifact and overrides the template parameters that create the resource name with the variables. For example, the name of the function app is `masterserv$(environmentName)site`, which means the actual name of the `Develop` stage will be `masterservdevsite`.

- **Deploy Azure Function (Azure Function)**: This task brings the ZIP created by the build pipeline and contained in the `Code` artifact folder and deploys it as an Azure Function on the function app called `masterserv$(environmentName)site`:

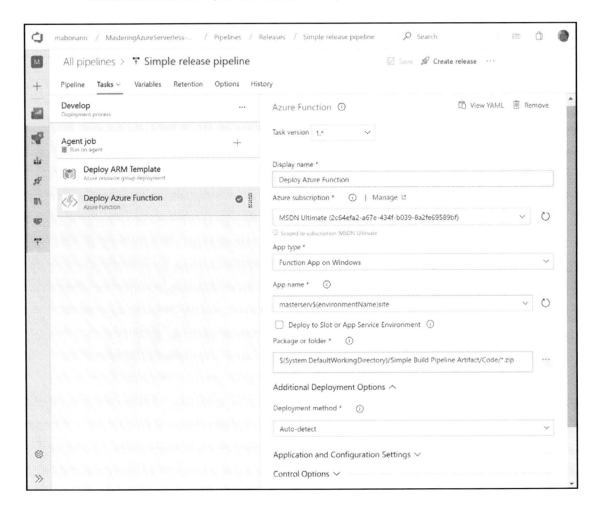

This simple stage pipeline can be cloned for the `Test` stage. Of course, you can add some other tasks, as you did in the build pipeline, and every single stage can have a different set of tasks. You should always remember that the release pipeline is intended to release resources and not build them.

CI/CD at a glance

Once you define the build and release pipelines and set them for CI (the build pipeline) and CD (the release pipeline), your developers can change the source code, push it to the GitHub repository, and then the following will occur automatically:

- The build pipeline will build a new artifact version and store it in the artifact repository
- The release pipeline will get the new artifact and try to release it on the configured stage:

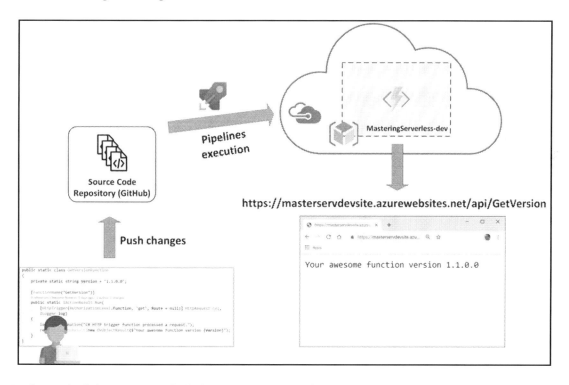

At the end of the process, if all the pipelines complete their jobs successfully, your users can use the new version of your function.

Summary

In this chapter, you learned how to leverage the power of Azure DevOps and its pipelines to automate your build and deploy tasks. Automating these kinds of operations ensures that human interaction (and therefore human error) will be minimized. These operations are generally repetitive and we humans tend to make mistakes when repeatedly performing the same operation over and over again. Furthermore, thanks to the automation, the new versions of the solution can go immediately into production, significantly reducing the time to market. Finally, you learned how to improve the code quality by adding test tasks or code analysis tasks in the pipelines.

In the next chapter, you will learn how to test and monitor your Azure Functions.

Questions

1. Which of the following are Azure DevOps pillars?
   - Azure Boards
   - Azure Monitor
   - Azure Pipelines
   - Azure Repos
   - Azure CLI

2. Which of the following are types of pipelines?
   - Task-based pipeline
   - JSON pipeline
   - YAML pipeline
   - C# pipeline

3. Which of the following are valid triggers for a build pipeline?
   - Continuous integration
   - Pull Request Validation
   - Scheduled
   - SMS
   - Email

4. How many artifacts can you use in a release pipeline?
   - None
   - Only one
   - At least one

Further reading

You can find more information about Azure DevOps pipelines at the following links:

- *What is Azure DevOps?*: https://docs.microsoft.com/en-us/azure/devops/user-guide/what-is-azure-devops
- *Get started with Azure Pipelines*: https://docs.microsoft.com/en-us/azure/devops/pipelines/get-started/overview
- *Continuous deployment for Azure Functions*: https://docs.microsoft.com/en-us/azure/azure-functions/functions-continuous-deployment
- *Azure DevOps Projects*: https://docs.microsoft.com/en-us/azure/devops-project/

6
Testing and Monitoring

In the previous chapters, you learned how to implement, debug, deploy, and configure your functions. These steps are important, but in software engineering, there are two other very important phases that you cannot underestimate or ignore: testing and monitoring.

This chapter will cover the following topics:

- Implementing unit testing over your Azure Functions
- Supporting the inversion of control and the dependency injection patterns in Azure Functions
- Monitoring your functions using Application Insights

Technical requirements

In this chapter, you will see a lot of code, so it is important that you are familiar with C# and object-oriented programming. Moreover, you will learn how to create unit testing for your Azure Functions; it is important that you have a good understanding of what the unit testing approach is.

You can find the source code for this chapter at `https://github.com/PacktPublishing/Mastering-Azure-Serverless-Computing/tree/master/Chapter06`.

Testing your Azure Functions

Debugging your functions is not enough to guarantee that your code reacts appropriately to all the possible scenarios in which it is involved. Furthermore, you cannot automatically repeat the debug procedures every time part of your code changes.

Unit testing helps you. You can run your code automatically and consistently in a manner, covering all possible scenarios that your code might encounter.

Before we look at how to implement unit tests for your functions, it is important to clarify some definitions about unit testing.

Unit testing is a particular type of test where individual units/components of your code are tested. The purpose of the unit test is to validate that the behavior of a component is exactly the behavior of your design.

Unit testing is the first type of test that you execute in the software development pipeline, and, generally, it is created and managed by the developer.

Implementing unit tests gives you the following benefits:

- It increases your confidence in changing or maintaining code. You can refactor or change your code with no worries because if the tests you have prepared give a positive result after refactoring or changing the code, it means that the behavior of the software has not changed.
- Your code is more reusable because if you want to make unit tests, you have to write code that is more modular, so it will probably be more reusable.
- Fixing a bug during unit testing (during the first phase of your test, when your code is not in production yet) is cheaper than fixing a bug when your code is in production.

But unit tests also have the following disadvantages:

- Using the unit test approach, you will be able to capture errors caused by the code present in the code unit being tested, but it is not easy to find errors that are caused by the interaction of different components (you must use integration tests for this purpose)
- In complex software, it is practically impossible to write a test for every possible scenario envisaged by your code unit

Of course, implementing unit tests is not simple, and you have to design your code to support them.

In the real world, your code will include references to external objects (for example, your methods could call external services or write to a database). In order to be unit testable, your code should be able to replace external references with components whose behavior is known. This is because, otherwise, your test will not only run on your code, but also on the code of external references, and this would mean that the code being tested is no longer unitary. So instead of these external resources, the code being tested uses friendly components. These *friendly* components are called **mocks** or **stubs**, and the way to use them is by using a mock library that helps you to create the mock components in a declarative way.

In the example snippet of this section, we will use the Moq library to implement these mocks, but, of course, you can use your favorite mock library.

 Moq is an open source mocking library, and its repository is at `https://github.com/moq/moq4`.

If you look at one Azure Function signature, you can find the following dependencies:

- **Trigger**: As you saw in the previous sections, the function trigger is implemented by an attribute and a payload (generally a simple class that contains the trigger data).
- **Bindings**: The bindings are also implemented with an attribute and, generally, a class or an interface that models the interaction with the binding source.
- **Logger**: The logger is passed to the function using the `ILogger` interface.

To simplify, let's suppose we have the following function, which calculates a mortgage loan:

```
[FunctionName(FunctionNames.MortgageCalculatorFunction)]
public static async Task<IActionResult> Run(
    [HttpTrigger(AuthorizationLevel.Function, "get", Route = null)]
HttpRequest req,
    [Table("executionsTable", Connection = "StorageAccount")]
ICollector<ExecutionRow> outputTable,
    ILogger log)
{
    // Code to retrieve info from the request and calculate the loan
}
```

The preceding code contains the following elements:

- The `req` parameter is an instance of `HttpRequest` and contains the information of the `HttpTrigger` (defined by the `HttpTriggerAttribute` attribute).
- The `outputTable` parameter is an instance of `ICollector<T>`, and it is the handle you can use in the function to interact with the storage table.
- The parameter log is an instance of the `ILogger` interface, and you can use it to write your log.

When the function runs in the runtime environment, all the parameter instances are managed by the runtime itself, but when you test the function, you can mock them because they are simple classes or instances of an interface.

An example of a unit test for the `MortgageCalculatorFunction` function you saw previously is as follows:

```
[Fact]
public async Task Run_RightParametersInQueryString_CalculateTheRate()
{
    var request = new Mock<HttpRequest>();
    request.Setup(e => e.Query["loan"]).Returns("100000");
    request.Setup(e => e.Query["interest"]).Returns("0.06");
    request.Setup(e => e.Query["nPayments"]).Returns("180");

    var table = new Mock<ICollector<ExecutionRow>>();
    table.Setup(t => t.Add(It.IsAny<ExecutionRow>()))
        .Verifiable();

    var logger = new Mock<ILogger>();

    var actual = await MortgageFunctions.Run(request.Object, table.Object,
logger.Object);

    // Assert
}
```

The test is written using the `xUnit.net` test framework, but you can use your favorite testing engine.

 xUnit.net is an open-source unit testing tool for .NET Framework. The official website is `https://xunit.net/` and the GitHub repository is `https://github.com/xunit/xunit`.

The HTTP request, the collector, and the logger are mocked using the Moq library and are passed to the function. Of course, you have to set up all the mock methods that the function will call in the scenario you are testing (that is, in the previous sample, the method to access the query string of the request or the `Add` method of the `ICollector<T>`).

Mocking the parameters of the function is relatively simple, but what happens if you need to use your own service within your function? For example, let's suppose that the mortgage calculation algorithm is implemented within an instance of an interface (for example, `IMortgageCalculator`) and you need to use it inside the `Run` method. In this case, you cannot add the `IMortgageCalculator` in the function signature; otherwise, you will have an error (because it is neither a trigger nor a binding). To solve this, you have to use the dependency injection pattern in your Azure Function.

Dependency injection in Azure Functions

How can you inject your service inside an Azure Function body? In other words, how you can leverage the power of dependency injection in your Azure Functions?

Fortunately, the Azure Functions SDK 1.0.28 (and later versions) has the same dependency injection support that you can use in ASP.NET Core.

To use this dependency injection in your Azure Function, you have to go through the following steps:

1. Convert your Azure Function class from a `static` class to a normal class:

```
public class MortgageFunctions
{
    [FunctionName(FunctionNames.MortgageCalculatorFunction)]
    public async Task<IActionResult> Run(
        [HttpTrigger(AuthorizationLevel.Function, "get", Route =
null)] HttpRequest req,
        [Table("executionsTable", Connection = "StorageAccount")]
ICollector<ExecutionRow> outputTable,
        ILogger log)
    {
        // Function body (look at github repo to check the code)
    }
}
```

2. Define a constructor that supports dependency injection for your services (for example, the instance of the `IMortgageCalculator` interface, shown earlier):

```
public class MortgageFunctions
{
    private readonly IMortgageCalculator mortgageCalculator;

    public MortgageFunctions(IMortgageCalculator
mortgageCalculator)
    {
        this.mortgageCalculator = mortgageCalculator;
    }

    [FunctionName(FunctionNames.MortgageCalculatorFunction)]
    public async Task<IActionResult> Run(
        [HttpTrigger(AuthorizationLevel.Function, "get", Route =
null)] HttpRequest req,
        [Table("executionsTable", Connection = "StorageAccount")]
ICollector<ExecutionRow> outputTable,
        ILogger log)
    {
        // Function body (look at github repo to check the code)

        var calculatorResult = await
this.mortgageCalculator.CalculateMontlyRateAsync(...);

    }
}
```

3. You must create the `Startup` class (like you did for custom extensions in the previous sections) and register your service in the `Services` collection of the `IWebJobsBuilder` instance provided by the runtime:

```
[assembly: WebJobsStartup(typeof(Startup))]
namespace MoneyCalculatorFunctions
{
    public class Startup : IWebJobsStartup
    {
        public void Configure(IWebJobsBuilder builder)
        {
            builder.Services.AddTransient<IMortgageCalculator,
MortgageCalculator>();
        }
    }
}
```

To support the `Startup` class, you must add a reference to the NuGet `Microsoft.Azure.WebJobs` and `Microsoft.Extensions.DependencyInjection` packages.

In the `Startup` class, therefore, you can record both the services to be injected through dependency injection and any custom extensions (the triggers and bindings you saw in the customizing section earlier).

If you don't need to register custom extensions, you can reference only the `Microsoft.Azure.Functions.Extensions` package (it references `Microsoft.Azure.WebJobs` and `Microsoft.Extensions.DependencyInjection`) and write the `Startup` class in the following way:

```
[assembly: FunctionsStartup(typeof(Startup))]
namespace MoneyCalculatorFunctions
{
    public class Startup : FunctionsStartup
    {
        public override void Configure(IFunctionsHostBuilder builder)
        {
            builder.Services.AddTransient<IMortgageCalculator,
MortgageCalculator>();
        }
    }
}
```

Once you have performed the unit tests on your Azure Functions, you can bring your code into the production environment, but you still need to keep an eye on its operation and monitor it. In the next section, you will learn what tools you have available to do this.

Monitoring Azure Functions

Once you deploy your Azure Functions on Azure, you need to monitor them to check when something goes wrong.

The signature of an Azure Function `Run` method provides the instance of `ILogger` that you can use to log information about your code.

Using `ILogger`, you can collect information from your code execution to monitor and triage errors and exceptions.

The Azure Functions platform offers built-in integration with Azure Application Insights. Using Application Insights, you can easily collect and log performance and error data, and Application Insights gives you powerful analytic tools to aggregate log traces to have a better diagnostic experience.

Enabling Application Insights for your function is very easy: just put the Application Insights instrumentation key in the function app settings with the key `APPINSIGHTS_INSTRUMENTATIONKEY`, as shown in the following screenshot:

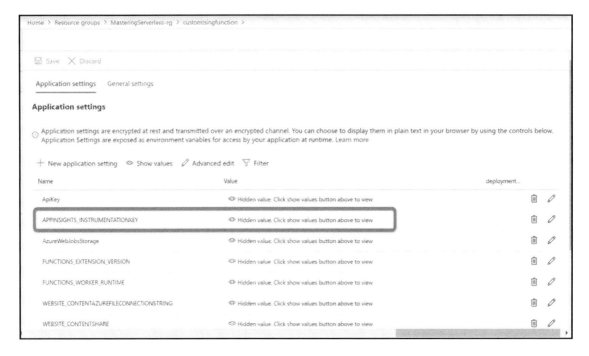

You can find the Application Insights instrumentation key in the **Application Insights** blade, in the **Overview** section:

When you connect Application Insights with your function, all of your log traces that were written using the `ILogger` interface will be stored in Application Insights, but the Application Insights logger provider will also capture other information about your function.

For example, say that you have the following Azure Function:

```
public static class MonitoringFunctions
{
    [FunctionName("TimerTriggerFunction")]
    public static void Run(
        [TimerTrigger("0 */3 * * * *")]TimerInfo myTimer,
        ILogger log)
    {
        log.LogInformation($"C# Timer trigger function executed at:
{DateTime.Now}");
    }
}
```

If you publish it in a function app on Azure, you can go on the Application Insights instance and look at the traces written by the platform:

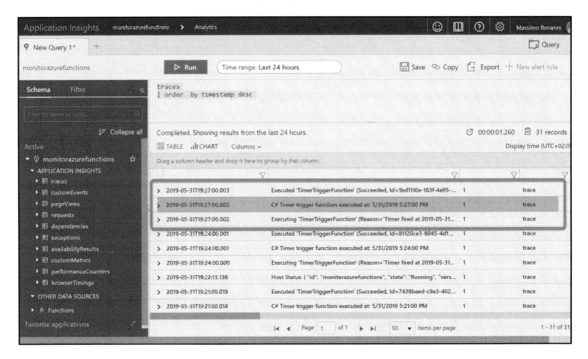

You can see three different traces for each execution, but only one is the trace that you wrote with the `log.TraceInformation()` method.

The other two traces are written by the platform, and each of them contains some important information about the execution context:

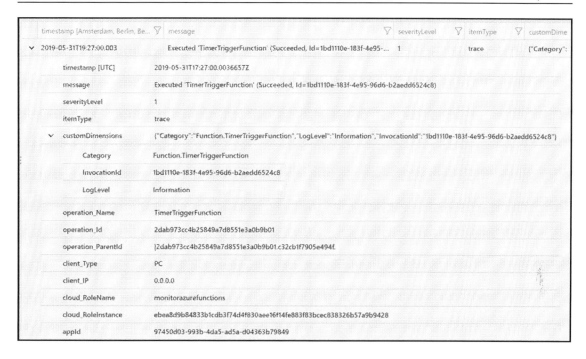

This information depends on the type of the function—for example, if you are monitoring an HTTP trigger function, you can find information about the HTTP request.

The platform writes, by default, some metric information (without you have to add lines of code of your functions but simply enable the monitoring) that you can retrieve using the following query in the analytic interface for Application Insights:

```
customMetrics
| order by timestamp desc
```

This can be seen in the following screenshot:

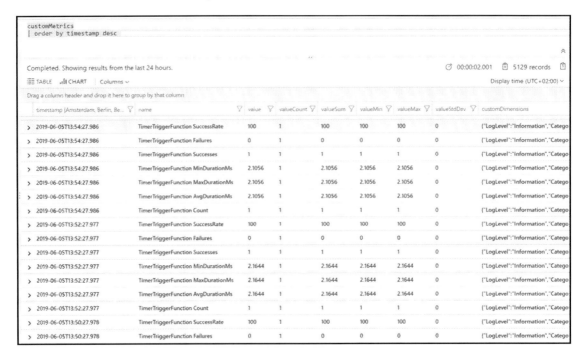

As you can see in the preceding screenshot, the runtime has logged the duration of your functions or the number of functions that succeeded or failed.

Finally, the platform records information about performance counters of the servers that host your function:

```
performanceCounters
| order by timestamp desc
```

This can be seen in the following screenshot:

 The language you use to write queries in the analytics UI for Application Insights is called **Kusto**, and you can find more information about it at https://docs.microsoft.com/en-us/azure/azure-monitor/log-query/query-language.

Of course, you can log whatever you need inside your functions simply by using the ILogger instance the platform gives you, and you can use different degrees of severity for your traces:

```
[FunctionName("TimerTriggerFunction")]
public static void Run([TimerTrigger("0 */5 * * * *")]TimerInfo
myTimer,ILogger log)
{
    var executionTimestamp = DateTime.Now;
    log.LogInformation($"C# Timer trigger function executed at:
{executionTimestamp}");
    log.LogTrace($"Is past due: {myTimer.IsPastDue}");
    log.LogTrace($"Schedule: {myTimer.Schedule}");
    log.LogTrace($"Schedule Status Last: {myTimer.ScheduleStatus.Last}");
    log.LogTrace($"Schedule Status Next: {myTimer.ScheduleStatus.Next}");
    log.LogTrace($"Schedule Status LastUpdated:
{myTimer.ScheduleStatus.LastUpdated}");

    if (IsErrorOccurs())
```

```
        log.LogWarning($"Something happened on your function!!!");

    log.LogMetric("MyCustomMetric", CalculateMyCustomMetric());
}
```

In the preceding snippet, you can see different types of log tracks—for example, you can use the `LogMetric` method to write your own custom metric:

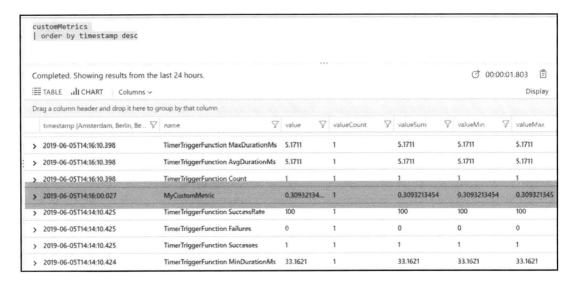

You can also use the `LogWarning` method to signal that something strange happened in your execution:

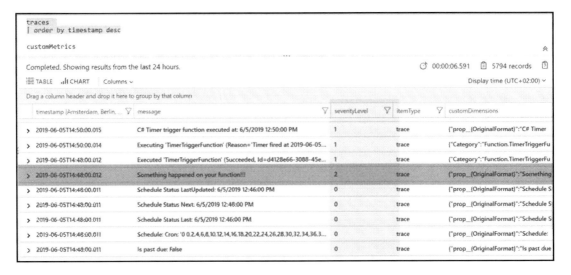

If you look at the traces shown in the preceding screenshot, you can see a column called `SeverityLevel`. The correspondence between `LogLevel` and `SeverityLevel` is shown in the following table:

LogLevel	SeverityLevel
Trace	0
Debug	1
Information	2
Warning	3
Error	4
Critical	5
None	6

You can decide which type of tracks should be written from the log of your function app by editing the `host.json` file. In particular, you have to edit the logging section as shown in the following snippet:

```json
{
    "version": "2.0",
    "logging": {
        "fileLoggingMode": "always",
        "logLevel": {
            "default": "Information",
            "Function": "Warning"
        }
    }
}
```

The Azure Functions Runtime supports the .NET Core logging filter hierarchy, which allows you to filter the types of traces you want in the log category by category.

 You can find more information about .NET Core logging filter hierarchy at `https://docs.microsoft.com/it-it/aspnet/core/fundamentals/logging/?view=aspnetcore-2.1#log-filtering`.

If you configure your `host.json` as shown in the preceding snippet, then the logger provider used by the Azure Functions Runtime will send only the error and critical traces from your functions to Application Insights:

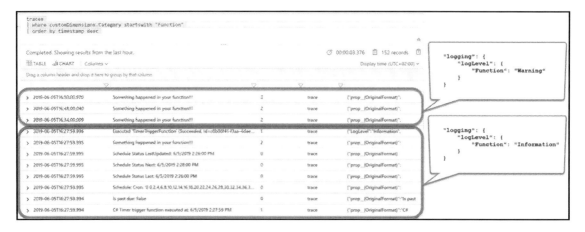

To complete the section, you need to know that Application Insights divides all the tracks it receives into the following categories:

- `traces`: The traces generated by the log of the runtime or the function code
- `requests`: One request for each function invocation
- `exceptions`: The exceptions thrown by the runtime
- `customMetrics`: The count of successful and failed invocations, the success rate, and duration
- `customEvents`: Events tracked by the runtime—for example, HTTP requests that trigger a function
- `performanceCounters`: Information about the performance of the servers that the functions are running on

You must choose the right category to do your analysis.

Summary

In this chapter, you learned how you can test your functions before you deploy them in Azure and how you can monitor them when they are running in a serverless environment.

Unit testing is one of the ways that you can use to empower your code and its quality. Designing your code with unit testing in mind may seem like a waste of time, but when you have to manage projects that evolve quickly or with a long lifetime, the time you spend on unit testing is well spent.

After reading this chapter, you will able to design your Azure Functions so that they are unit testable. You will also be able to implement a set of unit tests to check that the behavior of your functions is as expected.

In the next chapter, you will see how to deploy and run your functions in a container.

Questions

1. Which of the following are advantages of the unit test?
    - Your code is more beautiful.
    - The bugs found during the unit test are less expensive.
    - It increases your confidence when changing or maintaining code.
    - You can speed up development by parallelizing the tests.

2. How can you register your service instances to leverage the dependency injection pattern in your function?
    - You must implement the `IServiceCollection` interface to manage your services.
    - You can create a class that implements the `IWebJobsStartup` interface and set it as the `WebJobsStartup` class.
    - You can define a class derived from the `FunctionsStartup` class and set it as a startup class using the `FunctionsStartupAttribute` attribute.
    - You cannot register your own services; you must create them at runtime using reflection.

3. What is the value of the severity of inserting only warning-, error-, and critical-type traces in the `host.json` file to log?
    - Information
    - Warning
    - Error
    - Debug

Further reading

You can find more information about testing and monitoring Azure Functions by going to the following links:

- *Software Testing Fundamentals - Unit Testing*: http://softwaretestingfundamentals.com/unit-testing/
- *Get started with unit testing*: https://docs.microsoft.com/en-us/visualstudio/test/getting-started-with-unit-testing?view=vs-2019
- *Azure Monitor Documentation*: https://docs.microsoft.com/en-us/azure/azure-monitor/#5-minute-quickstarts
- *Monitor Azure Functions*: https://docs.microsoft.com/en-us/azure/azure-functions/functions-monitoring

Serverless and Containers

7

In previous chapters, you learned how to create, implement, and deploy Azure Functions based on Windows. Since the release of Azure Functions 2.0, Linux-based Azure Functions is now supported, using containers.

Containers are one of the best ways to ship code using immutable images, and are central in most IT organizations' strategies. Apart from Azure Functions, there are other ways to host containers on Azure, including **Azure Container Instances** (**ACI**) (a serverless way to host them) and Kubernetes (the leading container orchestrator, which can run on premises or on any cloud including **Azure Kubernetes Service** (**AKS**) on Azure).

This chapter will cover the following topics:

- Differences between hosting code and hosting a custom container on Azure Functions based on Linux
- Creating and hosting a custom container using Azure Functions
- Configuring and deploying your Azure Functions containers on Kubernetes, and how to scale them, both on premises and in the cloud
- Understanding and configuring ACI, a serverless way to host your containers

Technical requirements

This chapter requires basic knowledge of the following technologies:

- Containers and Docker
- Orchestrators and Kubernetes

To try the examples in this chapter, you should have Docker installed on your machine and have access to a container registry (such as **Azure Container Registry** (**ACR**) or Docker Hub). If you want to try **Kubernetes-based Event-Driven Autoscaling** (**KEDA**) and Kubernetes, you need to have a working Kubernetes cluster (Azure Kubernetes Service, either on premises or using other managed services).

Linux-based Azure Functions

Linux-based Azure Functions can run code or custom Docker images. If you decide to run code inside a Linux-based Azure Function, then everything will seem very similar to a Windows-based one. You can decide the hosting plan (the Consumption or App Service plan) and you can choose the runtime stack (at the moment, the choice is between .NET Core, Node.js, and Python):

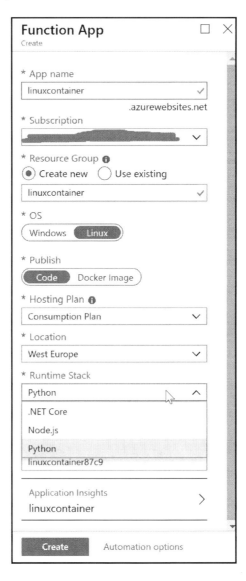

What happens under the hood is that the function will be deployed inside a container (maintained by Microsoft) that contains the Azure Functions runtime and the runtime stack selected by the user. Everything is similar to Windows-based Azure Functions. For more information about deploying code to a Linux-based Azure Function, go to `https://docs.microsoft.com/en-us/azure/azure-functions/functions-create-first-azure-function-azure-cli-linux`.

If you choose to deploy a custom Docker image inside your Linux-based Azure Function, you should create an App Service plan (custom images cannot run in a Consumption plan), and then you should tell the Azure Functions infrastructure in which container registry (ACR, Docker Hub, or a private registry) it will find the image.

Before talking about container registries, let's take a step back and see how to create a custom Docker image by following the steps in the following subsections.

You can run all the examples of this chapter on Linux, Windows, or macOS with Docker installed. On Windows and macOS, Docker will install a Linux VM behind the scenes, but everything will be transparent to the developer. In the future, Docker on Windows 10 will support the native Windows subsystem for Linux v2 (or WSL2), which was in preview at the time of writing. More information can be found at `https://docs.docker.com/docker-for-windows/wsl-tech-preview/`.

Creating an Azure Functions project with support to create a custom Docker image

There are two ways of creating a custom Docker image that contains an Azure Function:

- Create your custom Dockerfile and then use Docker tools to create the image
- Use the Azure Functions Core Tools to create the Dockerfile based on known images (.NET Core, Node.js, Python, PowerShell—preview) and then use Docker tools to create the image

You should use the first approach when you need to use language versions that are not currently supported in the official images, or when you need to work with your own language through extensibility.

You can go to `https://hub.docker.com/_/microsoft-azure-functions-base` to see all the Azure Functions base images, including the base image with only the Azure Functions runtime in it, which you can use to create new images. With every image, you can find the link to the Dockerfile used to create the image itself, which you can see and customize if needed.

The second approach relies on Azure Function Core Tools to create the project with the Dockerfile included:

```
func init MyCustomContainer --docker
```

You can choose one of the supported images, and then the project will be created, together with a Dockerfile. For example, the Dockerfile for a .NET Core Azure Functions will look like this:

```
FROM microsoft/dotnet:2.2-sdk AS installer-env
COPY . /src/dotnet-function-app
RUN cd /src/dotnet-function-app && \
    mkdir -p /home/site/wwwroot && \
    dotnet publish *.csproj --output /home/site/wwwroot
FROM mcr.microsoft.com/azure-functions/dotnet:2.0
ENV AzureWebJobsScriptRoot=/home/site/wwwroot \
    AzureFunctionsJobHost__Logging__Console__IsEnabled=true
COPY --from=installer-env ["/home/site/wwwroot", "/home/site/wwwroot"]
```

The Dockerfile instructs Docker to create the appropriate directory structure (based on the official .NET Core 2.2 Microsoft's image), then it compiles and publishes the C# project into `/home/site/wwwroot`, and then it creates a container based on the official Azure Functions .NET Core image. It sets some environment variables, and then it copies the `/home/site/wwwroot` folder into the container.

The command to execute the Azure Functions runtime is not in the newly created Dockerfile, but it's inside the base image. We'll skip the rest of the Dockerfile (which you can find at `https://github.com/Azure/azure-functions-docker/blob/master/host/2.0/stretch/amd64/base.Dockerfile`), and we will focus only on the last line, which starts the runtime:

```
CMD [ "/azure-functions-host/Microsoft.Azure.WebJobs.Script.WebHost" ]
```

If we build the container right now, there will be no functions at all, only the runtime.

To create a function, you can use Visual Studio, Visual Studio Code, or the command line:

```
func new --name MyHttpTrigger --template "HttpTrigger"
```

At this point, we have a project that includes a dummy Azure Function that responds to an HTTP trigger (it's the sample function that takes name as a parameter and responds with Hello, $name):

```
Administrator: Command Prompt

C:\MasteringServerless\MyCustomContainer>func new --name MyHttpTrigger --template "HttpTrigger"
Select a template: Function name: MyHttpTrigger

The function "MyHttpTrigger" was created successfully from the "HttpTrigger" template.

C:\MasteringServerless\MyCustomContainer>dir
 Volume in drive C is OSDisk
 Volume Serial Number is 6A1C-8903

 Directory of C:\MasteringServerless\MyCustomContainer

19/09/2019  15:49    <DIR>          .
19/09/2019  15:49    <DIR>          ..
19/09/2019  14:48                19 .dockerignore
19/09/2019  14:48             4.626 .gitignore
19/09/2019  14:48    <DIR>          .vscode
19/09/2019  14:51    <DIR>          bin
19/09/2019  14:48               451 Dockerfile
19/09/2019  14:48                26 host.json
19/09/2019  14:48               163 local.settings.json
19/09/2019  14:48               634 MyCustomContainer.csproj
19/09/2019  15:49             1.153 MyHttpTrigger.cs
19/09/2019  14:51    <DIR>          obj
               7 File(s)          7.072 bytes
               5 Dir(s)  289.013.796.864 bytes free

C:\MasteringServerless\MyCustomContainer>_
```

To test that everything works, we could start the local emulator if we want:

```
func start --build
```

When the Azure Function is ready, the following message will be displayed. At this point, you can navigate to the address that's displayed:

```
[19/09/2019 17:09:19] Host initialized (200ms)
[19/09/2019 17:09:19] Host started (219ms)
[19/09/2019 17:09:19] Job host started
Hosting environment: Production
Content root path: C:\MasteringServerless\MyCustomContainer\bin\output
Now listening on: http://0.0.0.0:7071
Application started. Press Ctrl+C to shut down.

Http Functions:

        MyHttpTrigger: [GET,POST] http://localhost:7071/api/MyHttpTrigger
```

 If you already have a working Azure Function, you can create the Dockerfile with the `func init --docker-only` command.

Creating a custom Docker image that contains an Azure Function

To create the container locally, we should use Docker tools. First, you have to build the container, and then you can run it locally. Then you can test it by launching the browser and pointing to `http://localhost:8080/api/MyHttpTrigger`:

```
docker build --tag mycustomimage:v1.0.0 .
docker run -p 8080:80 -it mycustomimage:v1.0.0
```

As you can see, we have tagged the container that we created with `mycustomimage` as the name of the repository, and with the tag `v.1.0.0`, so that we can easily identify it later. This container can be used locally, but we need to use a different syntax to tag it in a way that can be used with a container registry.

 If you receive an HTTP error 401 while testing the Azure Function locally inside the container, you should change the authorization key to anonymous, but only for local tests. This is not required when running on Azure, unless you really need anonymous access.

Publishing the custom Docker image to Docker Hub

Now we have the container running locally. We have created an image in the repository called `mycustomimage` with the tag `v1.0.0`, as you can see if you run the following:

```
docker images
```

The following screenshot shows the output of the preceding command:

To publish the image to Docker Hub, we can create another repository with our Docker ID or we can simply tag the current image with the new name, as shown in the following code:

> If you don't have a Docker ID, go to `https://docs.docker.com/docker-id/` to get one.

```
docker build --tag Docker-ID/mycustomimage:v1.0.0 .
```

We can also use the following:

```
docker tag mycustomimage:v1.0.0 Docker-ID/mycustomimage:v1.0.0
```

At this point, we can log into Docker Hub and push the image:

```
docker login --username Docker-ID
docker push Docker-ID/mycustomimage:v1.0.0
```

Publishing the custom Docker image to an ACR

If you prefer an ACR, you can use it to push your image.

> If you don't know how to create an ACR, you can set up the registry using the portal. For more information on how to do this, read the guide at `https://docs.microsoft.com/en-us/azure/container-registry/container-registry-get-started-portal`.

To connect to the ACR, you first need to authenticate it:

```
az acr login --name yourAcrName
```

At this point, you can create a new image with the `yourAcrName.azurecr.io` prefix (or you can tag an existing image), and then you can push it:

```
docker build --tag yourAcrName.azurecr.io/mycustomimage:v1.0.0 .
docker push yourAcrName.azurecr.io/mycustomimage:v1.0.0
```

Creating a function app based on a custom Docker image

At this point, we have our image published and we can use it to create our function app—in our case, through the Azure portal:

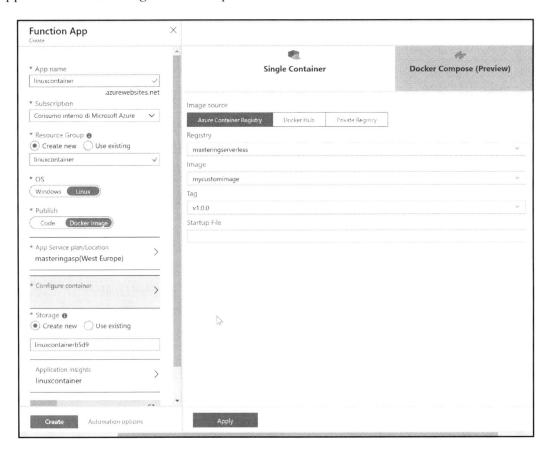

We created a new Linux-based function app with a custom Docker image, and then we can choose to configure an ACR (which we did in our example), a Docker Hub registry, or a private registry accessible by Azure.

 At the moment, the options to use Docker Compose and Kubernetes directly from the portal are disabled, and cannot be used.

When the deployment of the function app is completed, you can open it:

If you get the function URL from the portal and add the `name` parameter to the URL, you can see that the container is working:

If you want to create the function app using the command line instead of the Azure portal, you can go through the steps described at `https://docs.microsoft.com/en-us/azure/azure-functions/functions-create-function-linux-custom-image#create-a-resource-group`.

Updating the Docker image

Now that you have a function app with a custom Docker image up and running, you will want to update it.

There are many ways to do this when you've updated the source code:

- Manually create a new version of the image, tag it with a different tag (for example, v.1.1.0), push the new version to the registry, and manually update the tag in the Azure portal or by using the Azure CLI. This option is not recommended because it can lead to errors.
- Enable continuous integration on the function app and connect the function app to the container registry so that the function app knows when there is a new image. Now you can manually create a new version of the image, tag it with a different tag (for example v.1.1.0), and push the new version to the registry and it will be deployed automatically.
- Enable continuous integration on the function app, and connect the function app to the container registry so that the function app knows when there is a new image. Create an Azure pipeline that builds the custom Docker image and pushes it to the container registry. At that point, the image should be deployed automatically.
- Create an Azure pipeline that builds the custom Docker image and pushes it to the container registry and then create an Azure pipeline that deploys the image from the container registry to the function app.

You saw how to create Azure pipelines to build and deploy your code in `Chapter 6`, *Testing and Monitoring*. You can use Docker tasks to build and publish the container to the container registry and then you can decide to use a deployment pipeline or to enable continuous deployment directly from the registry, as explained in the next section.

Pointing the function app to a new tag and enabling continuous deployment

In the Azure portal, you can go to the underlying app service that runs the function app and then to **Container settings**. At this point, you can manually change the **Tag** to run a new version of the container:

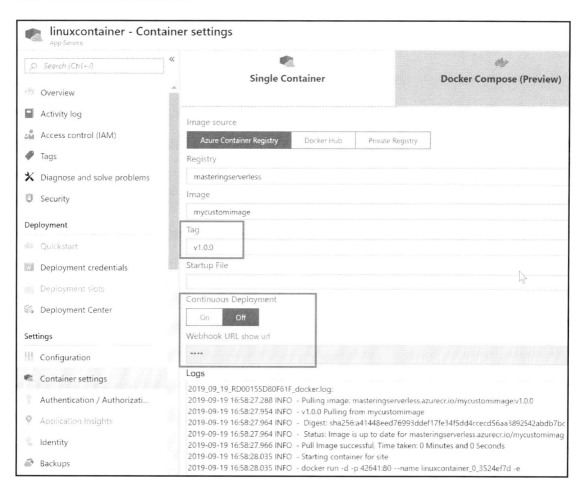

You can also enable **Continuous Deployment**. To do this correctly, you need to copy the **Webhook URL** and use it in your container registry.

At this point, you can go into your registry and create a webhook that calls the previous URL every time a new image is pushed:

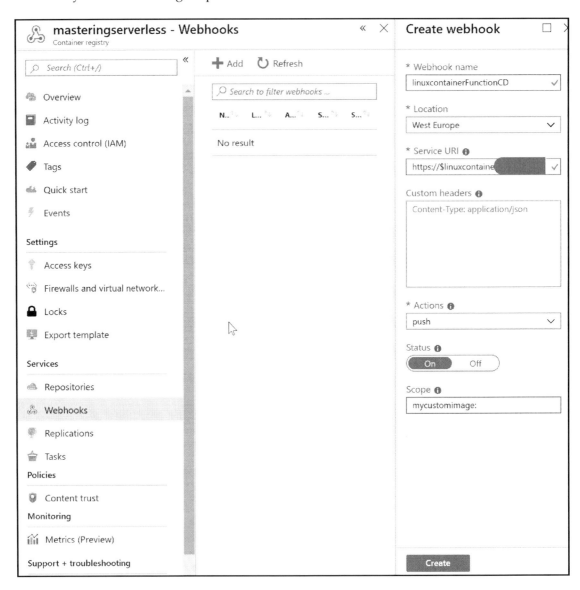

Pay attention to the **Scope** parameter—in our case, we used `mycustomimage:` to receive calls from the container every time a new version of the `mycustomimage` repository was updated, notifying us of the tag used.

If you want to create the webhook using the Azure CLI, or if you want to see instructions on how to do this with Docker Hub, you can refer to `https://docs.microsoft.com/en-us/azure/azure-functions/functions-create-function-linux-custom-image#enable-continuous-deployment`.

Hosting Azure Functions containers in Kubernetes with KEDA

Once you have Azure Functions packaged in a custom Docker image, you can also host the container directly in Kubernetes, without relying on the App Service plan.

Kubernetes is the leading container orchestrator, available as a managed service on the major cloud providers. It can be installed on premises or in the cloud, and can also run on small devices, such as a set of Raspberry Pis working as a single entity. More information about Kubernetes can be found at `https://azure.microsoft.com/en-us/resources/kubernetes-learning-path/`.

If you don't know anything about Kubernetes, then it's better to start by reading a book, such as *Mastering Kubernetes* (`https://www.packtpub.com/eu/virtualization-and-cloud/mastering-kubernetes`), because Kubernetes is a huge topic, and you need to be familiar with its core concepts before you install, configure, and administer it.

Kubernetes is highly modular and pluggable but was not created to handle event-based architectures that can scale from zero to n instances depending on the flow of events.

This is why Microsoft and Red Hat have created KEDA (`https://github.com/kedacore/keda`). With KEDA and Kubernetes, you can create an infrastructure similar to the one used to run Azure Functions containers in an App Service plan. This is an infrastructure that you can deploy everywhere and over which you have full control. KEDA is open source and free to use.

KEDA and Kubernetes are important for the following scenarios:

- Deploying and running functions on premises or on other cloud systems (there is no vendor lock-in)
- When you already have other Kubernetes apps that you're managing and you want to manage only one environment, or to integrate with them (maybe you have a restricted network, app mesh, custom environment, and so on)
- When you have a specific need for more control (GPU-enabled computing clusters, more knobs, and so on)
- When you want to scale to zero without the need for keeping your App Service plan running all the time with a minimum of one instance

Installing KEDA in the Kubernetes cluster

We won't cover how to install Kubernetes on the cluster and kubectl locally. Depending on where you're installing it or if you're using a managed service such as AKS, the setup instructions can be very different.

If you have Docker already installed on your machine, kubectl will already be installed, and so you won't need to do it manually.

If you want to authenticate kubectl to your AKS instance, you can execute the `az aks get-credentials -g yourResourceGroup -n yourAKSinstance --overwrite-existing` command.

Once you have your cluster up and running and you're logged into it using kubectl, you can use the Azure Functions Core Tools to install KEDA:

```
func kubernetes install --namespace keda
```

The default installation of KEDA will install two services: KEDA itself to autoscale all the different triggers (excluding the HTTP Trigger) to zero, and Osiris (`https://github.com/deislabs/osiris`) to autoscale HTTP workloads to zero.

KEDA is in active development, and will support many other external services in the future to support different scenarios. You can also run KEDA without Azure Functions. Look at the documentation found at `https://github.com/kedacore/keda` for more ways to install it.

Deploying and executing your functions in Kubernetes

Once KEDA is installed, you can deploy your container on it. When deploying a container on Kubernetes, you should set it up so that it will be able to access the container registry. If you're using AKS and want to authenticate to ACR, you can follow the guide found at `https://docs.microsoft.com/en-us/azure/container-registry/container-registry-auth-aks#grant-aks-access-to-acr`:

```
func kubernetes deploy --name nameOfTheFunctionAppInsideKubernetes --image-
name yourAcrName.azurecr.io/mycustomimage:v1.0.0
```

To see whether the container was deployed correctly, you can use the following command, with the optional `--watch` option to keep it running until you stop it:

```
kubectl get pods
```

The following screenshot shows the output of the preceding command:

```
C:\MasteringServerless\MyCustomContainer>kubectl get pods
NAME                                  READY    STATUS              RESTARTS    AGE
masteringkeda-http-75b8b455d7-bzp9n   0/2      PodInitializing     0           19s

C:\MasteringServerless\MyCustomContainer>kubectl get pods
NAME                                  READY    STATUS              RESTARTS    AGE
masteringkeda-http-75b8b455d7-bzp9n   0/2      PodInitializing     0           25s

C:\MasteringServerless\MyCustomContainer>kubectl get pods --watch
NAME                                  READY    STATUS              RESTARTS    AGE
masteringkeda-http-75b8b455d7-bzp9n   0/2      PodInitializing     0           32s
masteringkeda-http-75b8b455d7-bzp9n   1/2      Running             0           34s
masteringkeda-http-75b8b455d7-bzp9n   2/2      Running             0           38s

C:\MasteringServerless\MyCustomContainer>kubectl get pods
No resources found.
```

As you can see in the preceding screenshot, the container was loaded inside the pods. At some point, the pods were running, and after some minutes of inactivity, they were scaled to zero.

To test the function, you need the public IP of the load balancer associated with your deployments. You can use the following command until the external IP is displayed:

```
kubectl get services --watch
```

If you receive HTTP error 401, you should set the authentication of the function to anonymous, like in the local test under Docker. If you know Kubernetes and the YAML files associated with it, you can see the generated files without sending them to Kubernetes by adding the `--dry-run` option to the `func kubernetes` commands.

By default, KEDA takes all the secrets needed by Kubernetes from the `local.settings.json` file. You shouldn't store the file in Git, but consider using a pipeline task to generate it by reading the secrets from a secure source.

Always remember that KEDA has two phases: scale from zero to one pod and scale from one to the maximum number of pods inside the Kubernetes cluster. If you want real autoscaling, your cluster should support it. If you have an on-premises cluster with three nodes, it can scale to fill the capacity and nothing more, unless you manually add more nodes.

With AKS you can do the following:

- Manually scale the cluster by adding nodes, like every other Kubernetes installation
- Enable cluster autoscaling, as shown at https://docs.microsoft.com/en-us/azure/aks/cluster-autoscaler
- Use virtual nodes based on ACI, as shown at https://docs.microsoft.com/en-us/azure/aks/virtual-nodes-portal

Azure Container Instances

ACI is a serverless container engine that can be used when you want to run your containers for a limited amount of time during the day, when you need fast provisioning but don't need advanced orchestration capabilities, or when you need to handle peaks in your AKS infrastructure (using virtual nodes).

ACI provides all the scheduling and managing capabilities of a traditional orchestrator, but it's optimized to handle a single container, not a set of containers. You can run as many containers as you need, but each of them is independent of the others. With ACI, you don't need to think about the underlying VM infrastructure since all the resources are managed by Azure and are fully transparent.

With ACI, you only pay for the amount of time that your container is running, and you don't need to set up any infrastructure.

More information on ACI can be found at `https://docs.microsoft.com/en-us/azure/container-instances/container-instances-overview`.

 ACI is not limited to Azure Functions containers; it can run every workload.

ACI is more secure than traditional VMs to host your containers because it offers hypervisor-level security to isolate all the containers. This aspect is very important since your containers are running from a shared serverless infrastructure.

ACI supports Linux- and Windows-based containers. If you need to work with files that span multiple instances or multiple containers, you can mount an Azure file share inside your container.

Summary

In this chapter, you learned how to create a Linux-based function app to deploy code or a custom container that can run everywhere (on premises, on Azure, on AWS, on Google Cloud platform, and so on).

You also learned how to deploy the custom container on an App Service plan or on Kubernetes and especially on AKS.

At the end of this chapter, you learned about ACI, a serverless way to run containers on Azure, either alone or by creating virtual nodes for AKS.

In the next chapter, you will learn how to use durable functions to create code-based workflows.

Questions

1. Which of the following technologies are natively supported by Linux-based functions?
   - .NET Framework
   - .NET Core
   - Node.js
   - Python

2. Where can you deploy Azure Functions-based containers on Azure?
   - Consumption plan
   - App Service plan
   - AKS
   - ACI
   - Docker on a VM

Further reading

You can find more information about Linux-based Azure Functions, KEDA, and ACI at the following links:

- *Run Azure Functions App 2.0 in a Docker Container (on AWS, ZOMG)* (`https://blog.wille-zone.de/post/run-azure-functions-in-docker/`)
- *Run a Durable Azure Function in a Container* (`https://carlos.mendible.com/2018/01/14/run-a-durable-azure-function-in-a-container/`)
- *KEDA FAQ* (`https://github.com/kedacore/keda/wiki/FAQ`)
- *CI/CD for Containers* (`https://azure.microsoft.com/en-us/solutions/architecture/cicd-for-containers/`)
- *Azure Pipelines: build a container image* (`https://docs.microsoft.com/en-us/azure/devops/pipelines/ecosystems/containers/build-image?view=azure-devopstabs=dotnet-core`)
- *Create and configure an Azure Kubernetes Services (AKS) cluster to use virtual nodes in the Azure portal* (`https://docs.microsoft.com/en-us/azure/aks/virtual-nodes-portal`)
- *Find the right Azure service for your container needs* (`https://azure.microsoft.com/en-us/product-categories/containers/`)

3
Section 3: Serverless Orchestration, API Management, and Event Processing

This section shows how to add advanced features to serverless solutions, including orchestration (both using code and visual workflows), API Management (caching and security) and event processing (routing and filtering).

It comprises the following chapters:

- Chapter 8, *Orchestration as Code – Durable Functions*
- Chapter 9, *Orchestration as Design – Logic Apps*
- Chapter 10, *Empowering Your Serverless API with API Management*
- Chapter 11, *High-Scale Serverless Event Processing with Event Grid*

8
Orchestration as Code - Durable Functions

One of the limitations of Azure Functions is that they cannot call each other: you cannot call an Azure Function from inside another Azure Function. Every time you need to communicate between two different Azure Functions, you need to use an external service (for example, a storage queue or blob storage). In real-world scenarios, you need to orchestrate calls between Azure Functions, and one of the ways is to use Durable Functions.

In this chapter, we will look at Durable Functions and how you can use them to create complex orchestrations between Azure Functions.

The chapter will cover the following topics:

- What are Durable Functions?
- The kinds of problems they solve and the kinds of patterns they can implement
- The types of function in the Durable Functions framework and how Durable Functions manage the state
- How to manage Durable Functions versioning
- How to design and implement an order manager solution with Durable Functions

Technical requirements

Durable Functions are extensions of the Azure Functions you saw in the previous chapters, so it is important that you are familiar with topics such as triggers, bindings, and the function life cycle.

This chapter also contains a lot of C# code, so it is important that you are familiar with C# and object-oriented programming.

You can find the source code for this chapter here: `https://github.com/PacktPublishing/Mastering-Azure-Serverless-Computing/tree/master/Chapter08`.

What are Durable Functions?

In the previous chapters, you saw how Azure Functions work and what you can do with them. The first thing that comes to your mind when you think about what you cannot do with Azure Functions is that you cannot call a function from another function. In other words, you cannot orchestrate a sequence of function calls inside an Azure Function.

Fortunately, if you need to do something like this, you can use Durable Functions.

Durable Functions is an extension of Azure Functions that allows you to orchestrate functions and implement complex scenarios.

Some of the possible scenarios are as follows:

- **Chain**: In this scenario, you need to call a set of functions in an exact order and pass the result of one of them to the next one:

You can implement a similar scenario using an external service (for example, a storage queue), one for each call, to place the result of a function and trigger the next one. As you will understand, if you have a lot of functions, the scenario becomes more complicated.

- **Fan out/fan in**: In this scenario, you must call multiple functions in parallel and wait for all functions to finish to aggregate the results:

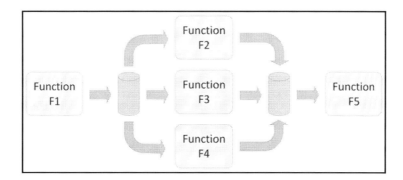

In this case, it's very difficult to implement the scenario using Azure Functions: you can try to use a single queue for each parallel call and a table to aggregate the results, but orchestrating all of this becomes very hard.

- **Async HTTP API**: In this scenario, you have an HTTP Trigger function that starts a long-time operation and another HTTP Trigger function you can call to know the state of the operation:

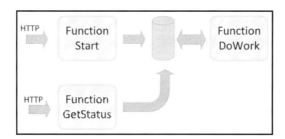

You can try to implement this scenario with Azure Functions, but you have to create an HTTP Trigger function to retrieve the status (and also write the status in the long operation function).

- **Monitor**: In this scenario, you have a flexible periodic process in a workflow. For example, you must poll a function that periodically retrieves the status of another function or the status of an external service:

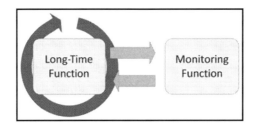

You can implement this scenario with Azure Functions using a time trigger function, but you cannot have, in a simple way, a flexible timer.

- **Human interaction**: In this scenario, you have an orchestration that depends on some human interaction. For example, imagine you have an order approval process such as the following:

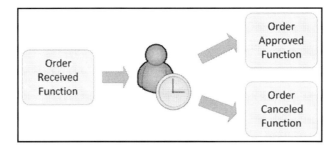

The orchestration calls the **Order Approved Function** if the back-office user signals that the order is paid or the **Order Canceled Function** if the user signals the order cancellation or the time frame for payment has expired. This kind of scenario is hard to implement using only an Azure Function.

- **Stateful entity**: In this scenario, you must collect a group of data in a single business entity (for example, for a time window or by a particular key), store the data in a state, and expose it to external clients:

Implementing this scenario using an Azure Function means that you have to implement a function to ingest data and a function to allow external clients to query the entity, and use an external service (for example, storage table) to store the data. Of course, you can do it, but you have to manage a lot of different functions and storage.

If you want to use Durable Functions in your function app, you must reference the `Microsoft.AzureWebJobs.Extensions.DurableTask` package, which contains the extensions (triggers and bindings) to support the previous scenarios.

This package contains the serverless version of the Durable Task Framework, an open source framework to implement long-running persistent workflows in C# using async/await capabilities. Later in this chapter, you will understand how the Durable Task Framework implements long-running persistent workflows.

Durable Functions currently supports only C#, F#, and JavaScript languages, but Microsoft and the community have the goal to support, in the future version, all the languages supported by Azure Functions.

 The Durable Task Framework GitHub project is located at `https://github.com/Azure/durabletask`.

Durable Functions is, in fact, an extension of Azure Functions that takes advantage of specific triggers and bindings to implement the orchestration patterns seen previously. In the next section, we will see the types of functions present in the Durable Functions ecosystem.

Function types

When you implement Durable Functions, you have three types of function you can use:

- Client functions
- Orchestrator functions
- Activity functions

The relationship between these types of functions is shown in the following diagram:

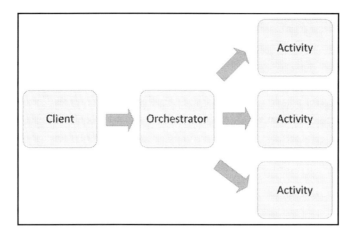

Let's look at client functions in the following section.

Client functions

The client function is a triggered function (like the standard Azure Function you saw earlier in this book) that can create or manage an orchestrator function.

When you implement a Durable Function, you have at least one client that allows you to start the orchestration.

The client can be triggered using one of the triggers you saw in the previous chapters (for example, HTTP, timer, or queue) and uses an orchestration client binding to manage the orchestration instance:

```
[FunctionName(FunctionNames.OrderReceiverFunction)]
public static async Task<HttpResponseMessage> Run(
    [HttpTrigger(AuthorizationLevel.Function, "post")] HttpRequestMessage
req,
    [OrchestrationClient] DurableOrchestrationClient starter,
    ILogger log)
{
    // Retrieves the order info from the request
    // .......

    // Starts a new orchestration
    var instanceId = await
starter.StartNewAsync(FunctionNames.OrderWorkflowFunction, order.Id,
```

```
order);

    // Returns the endpoints to manage the orchestration
    return starter.CreateCheckStatusResponse(req, instanceId);
}
```

`OrchestrationClientAttribute` in the client signature defines the function as a client and supports the `DurableOrchestrationClient` class as a binding payload.

The structure of `DurableOrchestrationClient` is shown in the following screenshot:

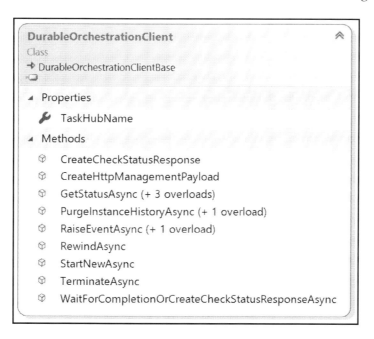

The most important methods exposed by this class are the following:

- `StartNewAsync`: Allows you to create a new orchestrator instance (a new instance of your workflow). Its signature is the following:

    ```
    public override Task<string> StartNewAsync(string
    orchestratorFunctionName, string instanceId, object input)
    ```

    `orchestratorFunctionName` is the name of the orchestrator function you want to start; `instanceId` is the ID of the new instance (if you pass `null`, the runtime creates a random ID), and `input` is the object you want to pass to the orchestrator. `input` can be JSON-serializable (you will understand the reason later in this chapter) and, of course, can be `null`.

If you try to start a function that doesn't exist or a function that isn't an orchestrator, you receive an exception.

If you try to start an orchestrator that is already started, the new one substitutes the old one.

- `CreateCheckStatusResponse`: Creates an HTTP response containing the API URLs used to manage the orchestrator (retrieve the status and terminate or send an event). The signature of the method is as follows:

```
public override HttpResponseMessage
CreateCheckStatusResponse(HttpRequestMessage request, string
instanceId)
```

You can use this method if you have an HTTP request, so the best place to use it is an HTTP triggered client function. The payload returned by the response has the following structure:

```
{
  "id": "90becab9-5da1-42ea-a1fd-62502eda5965",
  "statusQueryGetUri":
"http://ordermanager.azurewebsites.net/runtime/webhooks/durabletask
/instances/90becab9-5da1-42ea-a1fd-62502eda5965?....HusQ==",
  "sendEventPostUri":
"http://ordermanager.azurewebsites.net/runtime/webhooks/durabletask
/instances/90becab9-5da1-42ea-
a1fd-62502eda5965/raiseEvent/{eventName}?.....HusQ==",
  ....
}
```

You can use the URLs contained in the response to manage the orchestrator instance. For example, if you want to retrieve the status of the orchestrator, you can send a GET request to the URL contained in the `statusQueryGetUri` property. You can use those URLs even if your orchestration function was started by a client triggered by a trigger different from the HTTP.

If you look at the methods of the `DurableOrchestrationClient` class, they allow you to manage the orchestrator in the way you can do with the URLs of the previous response.

> You can find more information about `DurableOrchestrationClient` at `https://azure.github.io/azure-functions-durable-extension/api/ Microsoft.Azure.WebJobs.DurableOrchestrationClient.html`.

Orchestrator functions

The orchestrator function is the function responsible for the orchestration process: its code describes how the functions are executed and their order.

The orchestrator function is triggered by a special trigger called OrchestratorTrigger:

```
[FunctionName(FunctionNames.OrderWorkflowFunction)]
    public static async Task Run([OrchestrationTrigger]
DurableOrchestrationContext context,
    ILogger log)
{
    // Orchestration code
}
```

The DurableOrchestrationContext class allows you to call other functions or manage the payload passed from the client that calls the orchestrator function. Its structure is shown in the following screenshot:

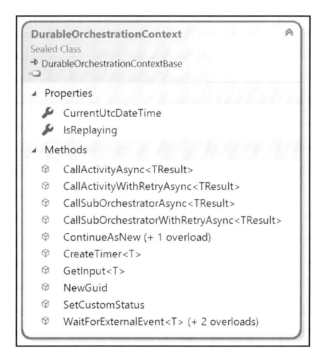

The most important methods exposed by this class are the following:

- `CallActivityAsync` and `CallActivityWithRetryAsync`: Allow you to call an activity function (see later in this section to understand what an activity function is). The second signature allows you to implement a retry policy calling the function:

```
var addResult = await
context.CallActivityWithRetryAsync<bool>("AddOrderFunction",
    new RetryOptions(TimeSpan.FromSeconds(1), 10), order);
```

In the previous snippet, you call the "`AddOrderFunction`" function with 10 retry attempts every second.

- `CallSubOrchestratorAsync` and `CallSubOrchestratorWithRetryeAsync`: Allow you to call another orchestrator function. You can use these methods to implement a sub-orchestrator pattern. The second signature allows you to call the sub-orchestrator function with a retry policy.
- `CreateTimer`: Allows you to suspend the orchestrator function for an amount of time. You cannot use the `Task.Delay()` method in the orchestrator (like you do in a standard class) because when the function is in pause and is waiting for the time to elapse, it isn't running (remember that you pay for the time for which the function runs). The durable timer created with this method is a special timer, based on the Durable Task Framework, that suspends the orchestrator and restarts it when the timer has elapsed.
- `WaitForExternalEvent`: These methods (you have three different signatures) allow you to suspend the orchestrator until some client function sends a particular event to the orchestrator (using `RaiseEventAsync` of the `DurableOrchestrationClient` class) or the runtime receives an HTTP POST to `sendEventPostUri` you saw earlier.
- `GetInput`: This method allows you to retrieve the parameter passed by the client function when it called your orchestrator function:

```
var order = context.GetInput<Order>();
```

If you try to get a type that isn't in the context, the runtime throws an exception.

An orchestrator instance is associated with an identifier. You can let the runtime generate it (autogenerate) or you can set your own identifier. Be sure that the identifier is unique: if you start two instances with the same identifier, the second overwrites the first.

You can find more information about `DurableOrchestrationContext` at `https://azure.github.io/azure-functions-durable-extension/api/Microsoft.Azure.WebJobs.DurableOrchestrationContext.html`.

`OrchestrationTrigger` uses a set of queues (stored in the default storage account of the function app) to manage the instance creation and the instance management. You don't care about the queues, but it is important that you know that the attribute uses them. The scalability of the orchestration depends on the scalability of the internal storage queues.

Another important thing you have to know when you implement a Durable Function is that the orchestrator function must contain only orchestration code (call activity functions, take decisions from a result of a function, execute a loop, and so on)—it shouldn't have business logic.

Another thing you keep in mind when you implement an orchestrator is that you shouldn't use random data or timestamp-based data. In fact, as you will read later in this chapter, the orchestrator uses a table to store its history and to replay the history every time it runs. If, for example, you use a random value, the past history may change, and it isn't a good idea to change the past!

Activity functions

The activity function is the unit work of a Durable Function. You can see an activity function as a standard Azure Function triggered by an orchestrator call.

An activity function is marked with the `ActivityTrigger` attribute:

```
[FunctionName(FunctionNames.AddOrderFunction)]
public static async Task<bool> Run([ActivityTrigger] Order order,
    [Table(SourceNames.OrdersTable, Connection = "StorageAccount")]
CloudTable giftTable,
    ILogger log)
{
    // Function code
}
```

The binding payload for the `ActivityTrigger` attribute is the entity that you use in the orchestrator function when you start it using `CallActivityAsync` or `CallActivityWithRetryAsync`.

If you want, you can use the `DurablaActivityContext` class as binding and retrieve the object sent by the orchestrator using the `GetInput` method:

```
[FunctionName(FunctionNames.AddOrderFunction)]
public static async Task<bool> Run([ActivityTrigger] DurableActivityContext
activityContext,
    [Table(SourceNames.OrdersTable, Connection = "StorageAccount")]
CloudTable giftTable,
    ILogger log)
{
    var order = activityContext.GetInput<Order>();
    // Function code
}
```

Inside an activity function, you can use all the binding you use in a standard Azure Function. It is an Azure Function that can have only `ActivityTrigger` as the trigger.

The Durable Functions execution state

In the previous sections, you learned about Durable Functions and the types of functions you can use when you create a solution using this technology.

In this section, you will see how Durable Functions manage the state and can orchestrate the activity functions (the execution state).

When you talk about the execution state, you keep in mind three pillars:

- Event sourcing
- Checkpoint
- Replay

The orchestrator functions manage their state using the event sourcing design pattern.

This pattern is based on registering all the events a single Durable Function receives. In this way, every moment a single instance of a Durable Function can rebuild its actual state simply replays the whole set of events received.

Every time a Durable Function calls an activity or an activity completes its work, the Durable Task Framework (transparently) saves the event inside a storage table (called the execution history). This operation is an append operation inside the execution history, and it's a much faster and more efficient than saving the entire state. When you save the state of something, in fact, you must do an update on a record in a table instead of a simple append using the Durable Task Framework.

The execution history also contains the payloads used by the orchestrator and the single activity. These payloads are stored in JSON format, and they are the reason why you must use only serializable objects between the orchestrator and activity.

When a Durable Function needs to proceed with its job, the Durable Task Framework replays all the events received and checks whether that event was completed and executed or not (for example, if an activity was called and it returned the result). In this way, the framework reconstructs the state of the orchestrator every time before continuing its job.

The Durable Task Framework saves the execution history in a storage table in a logical container called a Durable Functions task hub.

You can share the same task hub between different Durable Functions or use a single task hub for each function.

You can define which task hub your function must use by simply modifying the host.json file:

```
{
    "version": "2.0",
    "extensions": {
        "durableTask": {
            "hubName": "MyTaskHub"
        }
    }
}
```

If you like, the hub name can be retrieved from the app settings using the following format:

```
{
    "version": "2.0",
    "extensions": {
        "durableTask": {
        "hubName": "%MyTaskHub%"
        }
    }
}
```

Another way is to retrieve the hub name directly in the `OrchestrationClient` attribute:

```
[FunctionName("HttpStart")]
public static async Task<HttpResponseMessage> Run(
    [HttpTrigger(AuthorizationLevel.Function, methods: "post")]
HttpRequestMessage req,
    [OrchestrationClient(TaskHub = "%MyTaskHub%")]
DurableOrchestrationClientBase starter,
    string functionName,
```

```
        ILogger log)
    {
        // Function code
    }
```

By default, the task name is `DurableFunctionsHub`, and the history table is `DurableFunctionsHubHistory`:

PartitionKey	RowKey	Timestamp	EventId	IsPlayed	EventType	Name	Input
09631ec1-a631-497d-bfac-63f20893006a	0000000000000000	2019-06-15T08:10:56.387Z	-1	false	OrchestratorStarted	null	null
09631ec1-a631-497d-bfac-63f20893006a	0000000000000001	2019-06-15T08:10:56.387Z	-1	true	ExecutionStarted	OrderWorkflow	["$type":"OrderManager.Core.Entities.Order, Ord
09631ec1-a631-497d-bfac-63f20893006a	0000000000000002	2019-06-15T08:10:56.390Z	0	false	TaskScheduled	AckdOrder	null
09631ec1-a631-497d-bfac-63f20893006a	0000000000000003	2019-06-15T08:10:56.390Z	-1	false	OrchestratorCompleted	null	null
09631ec1-a631-497d-bfac-63f20893006a	0000000000000004	2019-06-15T08:10:57.583Z	-1	false	OrchestratorStarted	null	null
09631ec1-a631-497d-bfac-63f20893006a	0000000000000005	2019-06-15T08:10:57.587Z	-1	true	TaskCompleted	null	null
09631ec1-a631-497d-bfac-63f20893006a	0000000000000006	2019-06-15T08:10:57.587Z	-1	true	TaskCompleted	null	null
09631ec1-a631-497d-bfac-63f20893006a	0000000000000007	2019-06-15T08:10:57.587Z	1	false	TimerCreated	null	null
09631ec1-a631-497d-bfac-63f20893006a	0000000000000008	2019-06-15T08:10:57.590Z	-1	false	OrchestratorCompleted	null	null
09631ec1-a631-497d-bfac-63f20893006a	0000000000000009	2019-06-15T08:12:01.660Z	-1	false	OrchestratorStarted	null	null
09631ec1-a631-497d-bfac-63f20893006a	000000000000000A	2019-06-15T08:12:01.660Z	-1	true	TimerFired	null	null
09631ec1-a631-497d-bfac-63f20893006a	000000000000000B	2019-06-15T08:12:01.660Z	2	false	TaskScheduled	FinalizeOrder	null
09631ec1-a631-497d-bfac-63f20893006a	000000000000000C	2019-06-15T08:12:01.660Z	-1	false	OrchestratorCompleted	null	null
09631ec1-a631-497d-bfac-63f20893006a	000000000000000D	2019-06-15T08:12:02.263Z	-1	false	OrchestratorStarted	null	null
09631ec1-a631-497d-bfac-63f20893006a	000000000000000E	2019-06-15T08:12:02.263Z	-1	true	TaskCompleted	null	null
09631ec1-a631-497d-bfac-63f20893006a	000000000000000F	2019-06-15T08:12:02.263Z	3	false	TaskScheduled	SendMail	null
09631ec1-a631-497d-bfac-63f20893006a	0000000000000010	2019-06-15T08:12:02.267Z	-1	false	OrchestratorCompleted	null	null
09631ec1-a631-497d-bfac-63f20893006a	0000000000000011	2019-06-15T08:12:04.633Z	-1	false	OrchestratorStarted	null	null
09631ec1-a631-497d-bfac-63f20893006a	0000000000000012	2019-06-15T08:12:04.633Z	-1	true	TaskCompleted	null	null
09631ec1-a631-497d-bfac-63f20893006a	0000000000000013	2019-06-15T08:12:04.637Z	4	false	ExecutionCompleted	null	null
09631ec1-a631-497d-bfac-63f20893006a	0000000000000014	2019-06-15T08:12:04.637Z	-1	false	OrchestratorCompleted	null	null
09631ec1-a631-497d-bfac-63f20893006a	sentinel	2019-06-15T08:12:04.637Z	null	null	null	null	null

If you look at the storage account that store the history table, you will find another table called `DurableFunctionsHubInstances` that contains the list of the orchestrator instances executed or in execution in your solution. Here you can find the state of the single instance without the need to reconstruct the state from the event sourcing storage:

PartitionKey	RowKey	Timestamp	ExecutionId	LastUpdatedTime	RuntimeStatus	Output
05386918-7da3-4d0d-8c29-065d641155e2		2019-06-12T16:28:14.220Z	de1a3f02b2e24dd693e01b3fc819a2a9	2019-06-12T16:28:14.101Z	Failed	Orchestrator function 'OrderWorkflow' failed: The activ
09631ec1-a631-497d-bfac-63f20893006a		2019-06-15T08:12:04.700Z	a8f47eca18604671995688Za17eb8f40	2019-06-15T08:12:04.605Z	Completed	null
46682903-5259-4811-9b1f-14854711ce1f		2019-06-08T18:03:47.020Z	a21e2b417c5043T4871377e7fdf72aac	2019-06-08T18:03:46.612Z	Completed	null
78dc1f57-007d-4dd8-9e3b-dcfafac6f62d0		2019-06-12T16:28:18.427Z	dfc00e70bd844ce7b102e4f2c3e63d82	2019-06-12T16:28:18.336Z	Completed	null
90beab9-5da1-42aa-a1fd-62502eda5965		2019-06-12T16:30:26.753Z	de96aba640d84653811412492ada5ea5	2019-06-12T16:30:26.660Z	Completed	null
92310117-350b-479d-b4af-3f5229f6d5f6		2019-06-08T18:03:47.030Z	566dfa06be954045f8456647e18c563d	2019-06-08T18:03:46.612Z	Completed	null
bb1a071f-225d-4778-8314-61e9b995e3c1		2019-06-15T08:12:59.023Z	eb5efaba0a364ec9bf119fc8a6f9437d	2019-06-15T08:12:58.934Z	Completed	null
c0ce89ce-e5d0-41bb-8084-1869237cec2a		2019-06-13T16:52:49.480Z	58df0ac97adc4f45bc3845d1a71937c4	2019-06-13T16:52:49.237Z	Failed	Orchestrator function 'OrderWorkflow' failed: Unexpec
d1a7fa3ae4ae45eee19f1a7e47dd7d4e		2019-05-24T15:13:17.280Z	abb96152f6x4f6bf6a04525f664c287	2019-05-24T15:13:17.147Z	Completed	null

The status of a Durable Function is reconstructed, therefore, directly from the list of events that it has received, and these events are closely related to the code of the orchestration function. What could happen if the code changes? In the next section, we will see the problems that may arise if the code changes and how to manage the versioning.

Managing Durable Functions versioning

In the real world, we know that code is constantly changing. This is also the case for the solutions developed with Durable Functions.

Every time a Durable Function restarts, it uses its history to reconstruct its state, and there are several breaking changes you keep in mind every time you change your code:

- Changing activity functions
- Changing orchestrator functions

If you simply change the internal implementation of an activity function, you won't have an issue with the orchestration (the contract exposed by the activity function hasn't a breaking change so the running orchestrator function can continue to work correctly).

If you change the signature of the activity function, you may have issues with the running orchestrator instances.

Imagine you have the first version of your activity that accepts an `Order` instance and returns `int`:

```
[FunctionName(FunctionNames.OrderWorkflowFunction)]
public static async Task Run([OrchestrationTrigger]
DurableOrchestrationContext context,
    ILogger log)
{
    log.LogInformation($"[START ORCHESTRATOR] -->
{FunctionNames.OrderWorkflowFunction}");
    var order = context.GetInput<Order>();
    log.LogTrace($"Adding Order {order}");
    var addResult = await
context.CallActivityAsync<int>(FunctionNames.AddOrderFunction, order);
    // Other code to elaborate order
}
```

Now, suppose that you must change the signature of the activity and return `bool`:

```
[FunctionName(FunctionNames.OrderWorkflowFunction)]
public static async Task Run([OrchestrationTrigger]
DurableOrchestrationContext context,
    ILogger log)
{
    log.LogInformation($"[START ORCHESTRATOR] -->
{FunctionNames.OrderWorkflowFunction}");
    var order = context.GetInput<Order>();
    log.LogTrace($"Adding Order {order}");
```

```
    var addResult = await
context.CallActivityAsync<bool>(FunctionNames.AddOrderFunction, order);
    // Other code to elaborate order
}
```

The new instances of the orchestrator will have no issues, but the running instances when reconstructing their state will have an `int` value in the execution history and try to use it as Boolean (because the code requires the return of the function to be a Boolean). Therefore, the running instances will be in error.

In general, when you change the signature of an activity, you have issues with the running orchestrator instances.

You use the following strategies when you need to change an activity function:

1. Let the running instances of the orchestrators go in error, and if necessary restart them with the RESTful API.
2. Stop all the running instances before the change, and restart them with the API.
3. Create a new orchestrator that uses the new activity, switch to the new version, and remove the old one when all the running instances complete their jobs.

You can have the same kind of problem (reconstructing the state of a running orchestrator instance) when you change the orchestrator implementation itself.

Suppose you have the following orchestrator:

```
[FunctionName(FunctionNames.OrderWorkflowFunction)]
public static async Task Run([OrchestrationTrigger]
DurableOrchestrationContext context,
 ILogger log)
{
 log.LogInformation($"[START ORCHESTRATOR] -->
{FunctionNames.OrderWorkflowFunction}");
 var order = context.GetInput<Order>();
 var addResult = await
context.CallActivityAsync<bool>(FunctionNames.AddOrderFunction, order);
 await context.CallActivityAsync(FunctionNames.DoSomethingWithResult,
addResult);
 // other code
}
```

Suppose you must modify it in the following way:

```
[FunctionName(FunctionNames.OrderWorkflowFunction)]
public static async Task Run([OrchestrationTrigger]
DurableOrchestrationContext context,
    ILogger log)
{
    log.LogInformation($"[START ORCHESTRATOR] -->
{FunctionNames.OrderWorkflowFunction}");
    var order = context.GetInput<Order>();
    var addResult = await
context.CallActivityAsync<bool>(FunctionNames.AddOrderFunction, order);
    if (addResult)
    {
        // new code
    }
    await context.CallActivityAsync(FunctionNames.DoSomethingWithResult,
addResult);
    // other code
}
```

The issue occurs when a running instance is resumed because
the `DoSomethingWithResult` function completed its job. During a replay, if the call (the
original one that is in the execution history) to the `AddOrderFunction` returned true, the
instance tries to run the new code, but this code isn't in its execution history and it goes in
error (with a `NonDeterministicOrchestrationException` exception).

Also for this type of breaking change, you can use one of the strategies mentioned earlier.

Order manager sample

In this section, we'll look at a simple order manager application implemented using
Durable Functions.

You can find the code at `https://github.com/PacktPublishing/Mastering-Azure-Serverless-Computing/tree/master/Chapter08`.

The application has these requirements:

- A customer can place his or her order using an HTTP POST request.
- The following apply to every single order:
    - Can be approved by a third-party system using an HTTP PUT request.
    - Can be canceled by a third-party system using an HTTP PUT request.
    - Can be automatically canceled after an interval of time if it isn't approved.
- If the order has been approved, the application creates the invoice.
- The application sends an email to the customer with the status of the order whether it has been approved or canceled. If the order has been approved, the mail has the invoice as an attachment.

The following diagram shows the architecture of the solutions in terms of the functions involved:

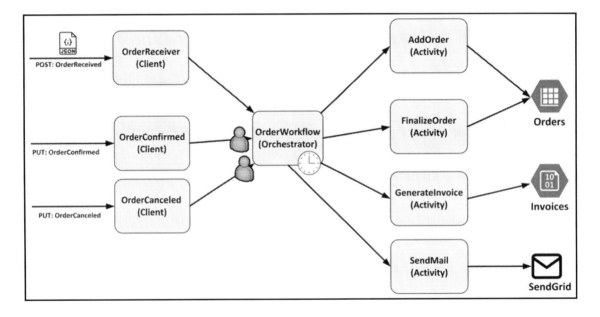

In the following sections, you will understand how to implement every single scenario.

OrderReceiver

The scenario is explained in the following diagram:

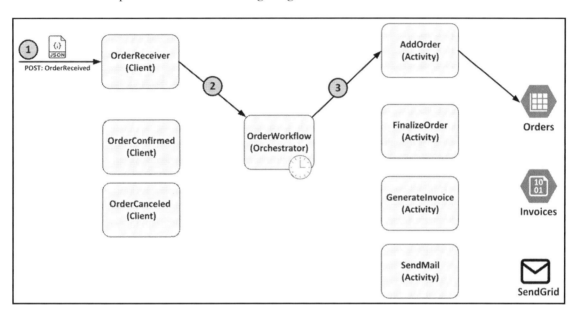

1. The `OrderReceiver` client function is triggered by an HTTP Trigger with a POST request:

```
[FunctionName(FunctionNames.OrderReceiverFunction)]
public static async Task<HttpResponseMessage>
Run([HttpTrigger(AuthorizationLevel.Function, "post")]
HttpRequestMessage req, [OrchestrationClient]
DurableOrchestrationClient starter, ILogger log)
{
    string instanceId = null;
    var orderDto = await ReadOrderFromRequestAsync(req);
    if (orderDto != null && orderDto.IsValid())
    {
        var order = orderDto.ToOrder();
        instanceId = await
starter.StartNewAsync(FunctionNames.OrderWorkflowFunction,
order.Id, order);
        return starter.CreateCheckStatusResponse(req, instanceId);
    }
```

```
    return new
HttpResponseMessage(System.Net.HttpStatusCode.BadRequest) {
ReasonPhrase = "Order not valid" };
}
```

The function deserializes the order from the JSON payload of the POST request:

```
{
  "Customer" : "Massimo Bonanni",
  "CustomerMail" : "massimo.bonanni@microsoft.com",
  "Amount" : 1234.56,
  "CreationTimestamp" : "6/7/2019 12:31:42 PM +02:00"
}
```

2. If the order is not null and it is valid, the client function creates the order from the payload (setting the order ID with a GUID) and starts a new orchestrator with an instance ID equal to the order ID.

3. The orchestrator retrieves the order (calling the `GetInput` method of `DurableOrchestratorContext`) and starts the `AddOrder` function:

```
[FunctionName(FunctionNames.OrderWorkflowFunction)]
public static async Task Run([OrchestrationTrigger]
DurableOrchestrationContext context,
    ILogger log)
{
    var order = context.GetInput<Order>();

    var addResult = await
context.CallActivityWithRetryAsync<bool>(FunctionNames.AddOrderFunc
tion,
    new RetryOptions(TimeSpan.FromSeconds(1), 10), order);

    if (addResult)
    {
        // code for other scenarios
    }
}
```

Finally, the `AddOrder` function saves the order in table storage:

```
[FunctionName(FunctionNames.AddOrderFunction)]
public static async Task<bool> Run([ActivityTrigger] Order order,
    [Table(SourceNames.OrdersTable, Connection = "StorageAccount")]
CloudTable giftTable,
    ILogger log)
{
    bool retVal = false;
```

```
try
{
    retVal = await giftTable.InsertAsync(order);
}
catch (Exception ex)
{
    log.LogError(ex, $"Error during adding order {order}");
}
return retVal;
}
```

In the next section, you will see the implementation of the OrderConfirmed function, used by an external system to confirm a particular order.

OrderConfirmed

The following diagram shows the **OrderConfirmed** scenario:

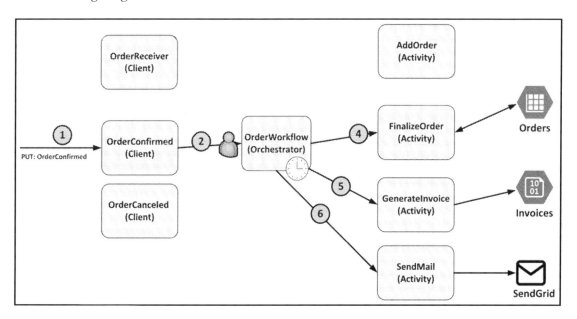

1. The OrderConfirmed function is triggered by HttpTrigger with a PUT request:

   ```
   [FunctionName(FunctionNames.OrderConfirmedFunction)]
   public static async Task<HttpResponseMessage> OrderConfirmed(
     [HttpTrigger(AuthorizationLevel.Function, "put")]
   ```

```
HttpRequestMessage req,
 [OrchestrationClient] DurableOrchestrationClient starter,
 ILogger log)
{
 return await SendEventToOrderAsync(req, starter, Events.OrderPaid,
log);
}
```

The payload accepted by the function looks like this:

```
{
 "OrderId" : "78dc1f57-007d-4dd8-9e3b-dcbfbc6f62d0"
}
```

2. The `OrderConfirmed` function calls an
   internal `SendEventToOrderAsync` method to send the `Events.OrderPaid`
   events to the orchestrator. Implementing the internal method means that you can
   use it also for the `OrderCancelled` scenario:

```
private static async Task<HttpResponseMessage>
SendEventToOrderAsync(HttpRequestMessage req,
 DurableOrchestrationClient starter,
 string orderEvent,
 ILogger log)
{
    var jsonContent = await req.Content.ReadAsStringAsync();
    OrderEventDto orderEventDto =
JsonConvert.DeserializeObject<OrderEventDto>(jsonContent);
    if (orderEventDto != null &&
!string.IsNullOrWhiteSpace(orderEventDto.OrderId))
    {
        await starter.RaiseEventAsync(orderEventDto.OrderId,
orderEvent, null);
        return starter.CreateCheckStatusResponse(req,
orderEventDto.OrderId);
    }
    return new
HttpResponseMessage(System.Net.HttpStatusCode.BadRequest) {
ReasonPhrase = "Order not valid" };
}
```

The orchestrator function is waiting for the event (or for the `OrderCancelled`
event or for the timeout):

```
[FunctionName(FunctionNames.OrderWorkflowFunction)]
public static async Task Run([OrchestrationTrigger]
DurableOrchestrationContext context,
    ILogger log)
```

```
{
    // Add order code
    if (addResult)
    {
        DateTime orderDeadline =
context.CurrentUtcDateTime.AddMinutes(1);
        var orderPaidEvent =
context.WaitForExternalEvent(Events.OrderPaid);
        var orderCancelledEvent =
context.WaitForExternalEvent(Events.OrderCancelled);
        var cancelTimer = context.CreateTimer(orderDeadline,
CancellationToken.None);
        var taskCompleted = await Task.WhenAny(orderPaidEvent,
orderCancelledEvent, cancelTimer);
        // Manage different scenarios based on what task is
completed

    }
}
```

As you can see in the orchestrator function, it creates three tasks: one for the external event `Event.OrderPaid` and one for the `Events.OrderCancelled` event and one task for the order canceled timer calling `CreateTimer`. Then, it waits for the completion of one of the tasks and performs the corresponding scenarios.

3. When the orchestrator receives `Events.OrderConfirmed`, it calls the `FinalizeOrder` function activity to change the state of the order to `Paid` inside the storage table.

4. After calling the `FinalizeOrder` function, the orchestrator calls the `GenerateInvoice` function to write the invoice file inside the storage blob.

5. Finally, it calls the `SendMail` function to send an email to the customer (using the SendGrid service):

```
if (taskCompleted == orderCancelledEvent || taskCompleted ==
cancelTimer)
{
    // Order Cancelled
}
else if (taskCompleted == orderPaidEvent)
{
    order = await
context.CallActivityAsync<Order>(FunctionNames.FinalizeOrderFunctio
n,
        new OrderStateChange()
            { NewOrderState = OrderStatus.Paid,
```

```
                          OrderId = order.Id });
        await
context.CallActivityAsync<string>(FunctionNames.GenerateInvoiceFunc
tion, order);
    }

    if (order != null)
        await
context.CallActivityAsync<bool>(FunctionNames.SendMailFunction,
order);
```

You can see the full code for the `FinalizeOrder`, `GenerateInvoice`, and `SendMail` functions in the GitHub repository containing the complete solution.

OrderCancelled

This scenario is similar to the **OrderConfirmed** scenario:

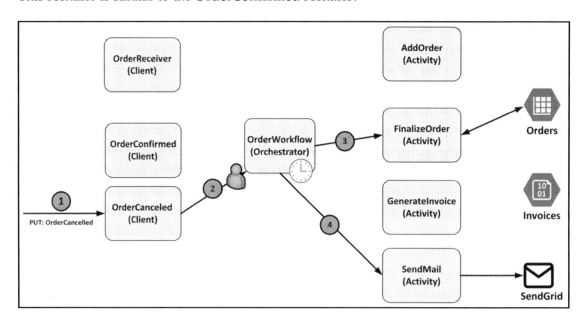

1. The `OrderCancelled` client function receives the same payload you saw previously for the `OrderConfirmed` function:

   ```
   [FunctionName(FunctionNames.OrderCancelledFunction)]
   public static async Task<HttpResponseMessage> OrderCancelled(
       [HttpTrigger(AuthorizationLevel.Function, "put")]
   ```

```
HttpRequestMessage req,
    [OrchestrationClient] DurableOrchestrationClient starter,
    ILogger log)
{
    return await SendEventToOrderAsync(req, starter,
Events.OrderCancelled, log);
}
```

2. `SendEventToOrderAsync` sends the `Events.OrderCancelled` event to the orchestrator (in the same way you saw in the **OrderConfirmed** scenario).

3. The orchestrator is waiting for one of the three tasks you saw in the `OrderConfirmed` scenario, but here it calls `FinalizeOrder` to change the status to canceled.

4. Finally, it calls the `SendMail` function to send a mail to the customer (using the SendGrid service):

```
if (taskCompleted == orderCancelledEvent || taskCompleted ==
cancelTimer)
{
    order = await
context.CallActivityAsync<Order>(FunctionNames.FinalizeOrderFunctio
n,
        new OrderStateChange()
            { NewOrderState = OrderStatus.Cancelled,
              OrderId = order.Id });
}
else if (taskCompleted == orderPaidEvent)
{
    // Order confirmed
}

if (order != null)
    await
context.CallActivityAsync<bool>(FunctionNames.SendMailFunction,
order);
```

Finally, the next section shows the scenario in which an order is canceled because too much time has passed since it was created and no one has explicitly confirmed or canceled it.

OrderCancelled time expired

This scenario is shown in the following diagram:

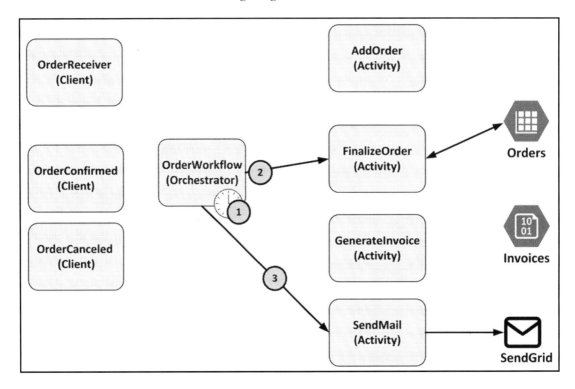

In this scenario, there isn't a client function that replays the orchestrator, but the orchestrator is woken up by a timer.

When the timer expires, the orchestrator executes the same code that it executes when it receives the `OrderCancelled` event.

Summary

In this chapter, you learned about Durable Functions and how you can use them to implement orchestration scenarios and workflows based on Azure Functions.

Durable Functions allow you to write orchestrations and workflows simply writing code; they don't have designer or JSON script. They are designed for developers with a knowledge of a programming language (that is, C #) and the Azure Functions framework. Durable Functions is a powerful tool to implement your orchestration, but you need to take care when you change the orchestrator function to implement a new version of your code. Therefore, before starting to implement your solution using Durable Functions, evaluate well all the pros and cons in relation to your requirements and those of your team.

In the next chapter, you will see another way to implement orchestration and workflow in the serverless world: logic apps.

Questions

1. Which of the following are function types of Durable Functions?
    * Orchestrator
    * Client
    * Activity
    * Proxy
    * Rest API

2. What kind of object can be used as a payload when creating a new orchestrator instance and passed as an argument to the `StartNewAsync` method?
    * No argument can be passed.
    * JSON-serializable.
    * DataContract-serializable.
    * Any.

3. What is the execution history?
    * A storage table containing all the instances of Durable Functions that have been started
    * A queue containing the payload used by the orchestrator to start the activities
    * A table containing all the HTTP requests received by the client functions
    * A storage table containing all the events that occur to Durable Functions instances

4. What is a Durable Functions task hub?
    - An Azure service that orchestrates multi-instance Durable Functions
    - A logical container in a table storage account that contains the tables used by the Durable Task Framework
    - A logical container in a blob storage account that contains the blobs used by the Durable Task Framework
    - The dashboard you can use to monitor all your Durable Functions instances

Further reading

You can find out more information about Durable Functions at the following links:

- *What are Durable Functions?*: `https://docs.microsoft.com/en-us/azure/azure-functions/durable/durable-functions-overview`
- *Durable Functions GitHub repository*: `https://github.com/Azure/azure-functions-durable-extension`
- *Durable Task Framework GitHub repository*: `https://github.com/Azure/durabletask`

Orchestration as Design - Logic Apps

9

In the previous chapter, you learned about one of the Azure serverless technologies that you can use to implement a workflow or to integrate external systems into your workflow. Durable Functions are a powerful tool that can be used to do this, but they are code-based functions, and their integration with external systems is poor. Durable Functions have only a dozen of the bindings that are needed to interact with enterprise systems, for example, they do not have native integration with Dynamic 365, SharePoint, or Office 365 Outlook. In enterprise scenarios, these types of integrations are very important and useful, and using Durable Functions to implement them, even if it is possible, is very hard.

In these scenarios, you can use Logic Apps that allow you to design and implement workflows and integrations with hundreds of connectors through different external systems.

In this chapter, you will learn about what Logic Apps are, and how you can use them to integrate data between different systems in Azure and on-premises.

This chapter will cover the following topics:

- What are Logic Apps?
- Logic App service components
- Versioning, monitoring, and API connections
- Why use Logic Apps?

Technical requirements

As you can see in the continuation of this chapter, Logic Apps are implemented through a graphic designer, so no programming knowledge is needed to understand what they are and how they work.

Understanding Logic Apps

Azure Logic Apps is a cloud service, hosted in Azure, that provides you with tools to design, schedule, orchestrate, and manage workflows and business processes.

A Logic App is designed using a web browser designer tool that is provided by Azure, or with a plugin for Visual Studio (or Visual Studio Code). You can choose and compose your tasks in a flow (such as a graphical programming language). You draw a sort of pipeline, in which your data passes, and is locally transformed or interacts with external systems.

If you want to use Visual Studio to develop your Logic App, you need Visual Studio 2015, 2017, or 2019, starting with the Community Edition. You also need the following:

- Microsoft Azure SDK for .NET (2.9.1 or later)
- Azure PowerShell
- Azure Logic Apps Tools for Visual Studio

You can install Azure Logic Apps Tools using the **Manage Extensions** view inside Visual Studio, as shown in the following screenshot:

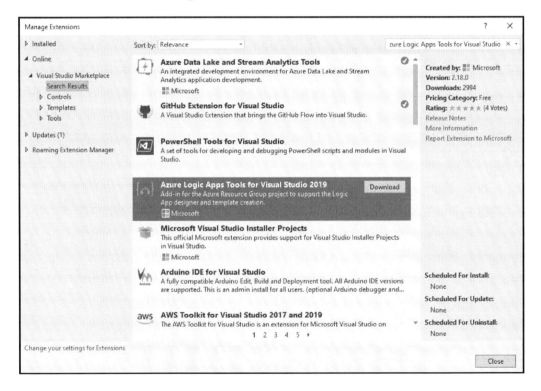

You can also download it and install it directly from the following URL: `https://marketplace.visualstudio.com/items?itemName=VinaySinghMSFT.AzureLogicAppsToolsForVS2019`.

Even after you implement your Logic App using Visual Studio, you need an internet connection. This is because the Visual Studio plugin needs to connect in order to create resources in Azure and to read properties and data from the tasks in your Logic App.

In this chapter, we use the web designer tool because, at the time of writing this book, the user experience that you have with the Visual Studio plugin is similar to the user experience that you have with the web-based designer. What we will say for the web-based designer, can also be applied to the plugin designer.

In the following screenshot, you can see how a Logic App appears in the web designer tool:

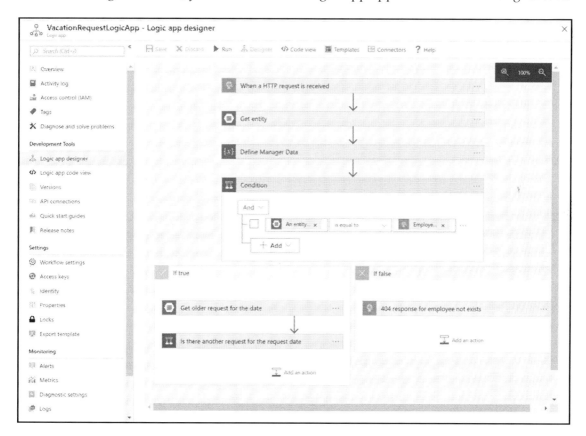

As you can see, a Logic App is a pipeline that is constructed using different building blocks that you can compose in order to design your own workflow. You can consider a Logic App as a logical container for the pipeline.

There are four types of building blocks:

- **Trigger**: The triggers in a Logic App have the same function that they have in the Azure Functions. They allow the flow to start. Every Logic App has a trigger, and it is the first step of the app. When the trigger fires its event, the Logic App service starts a new app instance and provides it with all the payload (that is, the object used by the trigger to contain the source data). There are two types of triggers:
    - **Polling triggers**: This type of trigger checks the external source continuously (using a polling approach), and when the criteria for creating Logic App occurs, the runtime starts the new instance. An example of this type of trigger is the recurrence trigger, or the storage queue trigger.
    - **Push triggers**: The trigger is fired when an external client sends a request to an endpoint that is exposed by the Logic App. An example of these types of triggers is the HTTP request that you can see in the Logic App shown in the previous screenshot.
- **Actions**: The actions are the building blocks that allow you to do things to the data flow in your app. For example, you can convert JSON into an object, or define and manage variables.
- **Connectors**: The connectors allow you to interact with external services or systems, and they are responsible for the connection and communication between your app and the external endpoint. For example, you can send an email using the Office 365 Outlook connector, or get data from Dynamics 365. The connectors are shared between the Logic App, Microsoft Flow, and PowerApps. A connector can expose also a trigger. There are two types of connectors:
    - **Standard**: Allow you to interact with Azure services such as SQL Azure
    - **Enterprise**: Provide access to enterprise systems such as SAP, IBM 3270, and generally have an additional cost
- **Control workflow**: The control workflow building blocks provide actions to control the flow of your Logic App. With these blocks, you can implement `if` conditions, loops, switches, and more.

You can find the complete list of available connectors at `https://docs.microsoft.com/en-us/connectors/`.

Behind the scenes, when you design a Logic App, the tool generates a JSON file that describes the Logic App. The schema that is used by the JSON is called **Workflow Definition Language**.

You can see the JSON file that is generated by the tool by using the **Logic app code view** menu in the Logic App blade, as shown in the following screenshot:

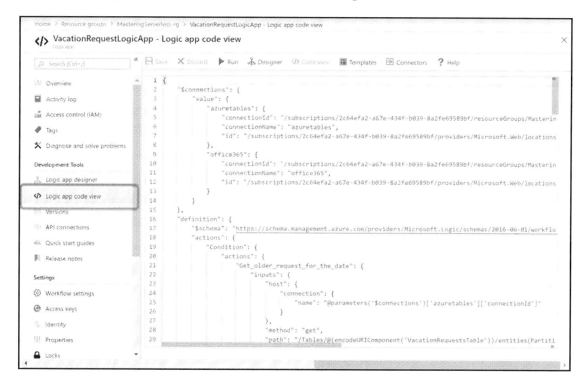

 You can find the complete schema for the Workflow Definition Language at `https://docs.microsoft.com/en-us/azure/logic-apps/logic-apps-workflow-definition-language`.

In the next section, we will learn about the different components of a Logic App.

Logic App service components

The Logic App service is the Azure service that hosts and manages your Logic App instances.

Even if the Logic App belongs to the serverless world, a Logic App runs on an infrastructure of an Azure region (a VM in a data center). Of course, you must not worry about the infrastructure behind your Logic App, and you cannot manage the VM in which the Logic App runs.

The Logic App service has the following components:

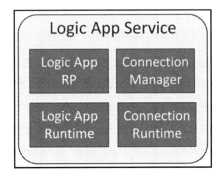

The components can be explained as follows:

- **Logic App RP**: This component reads and parses the workflow definition file, and creates the tasks to execute, including their composition and dependencies.
- **Logic App Runtime**: This component is responsible for the execution of the workflow tasks. It distributes and orchestrates all the tasks that are created by the Logic App RP. It also manages the execution of the flow.
- **Connection Manager**: This component manages all the connection configurations, credentials, and token refreshments for every connector that uses the Logic App.
- **Connector Runtime**: This component provides the OpenAPI description for the connectors that are used in the Logic App. The Logic App service, in fact, provides a set of RESTful APIs that you can use to query the infrastructure, and scaffold the configured connectors.

Next, let's look at versioning, monitoring, and API connections.

Versioning, monitoring, and API connections

The following screenshot shows the options that you have in the Logic App blade in order to manage versioning, monitoring, and API connections in your Logic App:

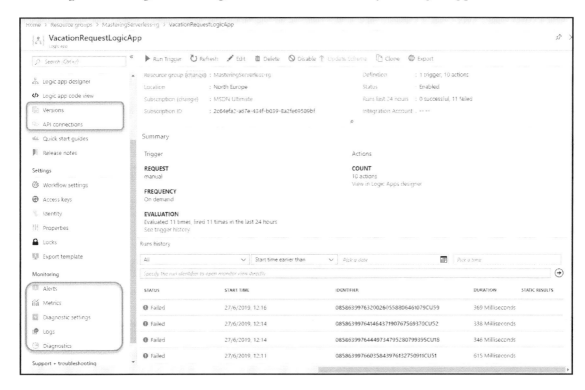

In the next sections, you will learn how you can use versioning, monitoring, and API connections in your Logic App.

Versioning

The Logic App service has a versioning system that it uses transparently when you change your Logic App using the web designer tool.

Every time you change something in your Logic App and then save it, the service adds a new version in the versions that are available to the Logic App:

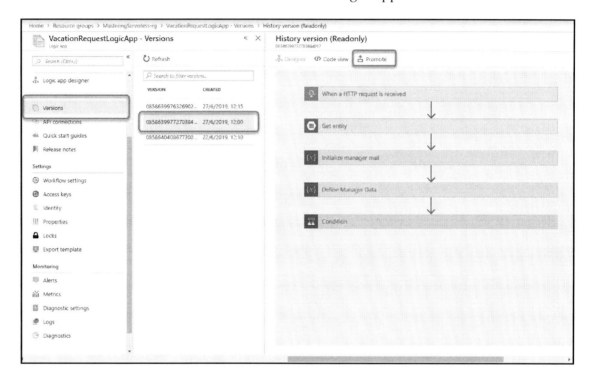

Using the **Versions** option in the left-hand side of the Logic App blade, you can see all the history versions for the Logic App. Every entry is a different version, and the top one is the current one.

In this view, the workflow is, of course, in read-only mode, and you cannot modify or delete it.

You can select one of the older versions and promote it to the current version by simply clicking the button on top of the designer. When you do this, the selected version becomes a new version, and it is promoted as the current. The old current version becomes the previous version on the list.

Versioning is important for Logic App for the following reasons:

- Every time a Logic App is triggered, the service creates a new instance of the Logic App, and it needs to know which is the current version to execute. It also needs to have a link between every instance and its corresponding version (in case of the Logic App will be paused and resuming later, or something similar).
- You can experiment with the Logic App without a problem because if you miss something or make a mistake, you can easily come back to a previous version.

API connections

Actually, a connector in a Logic App is a wrapper to an external system that uses a particular Azure resource (called the API connection). The API connection is an external resource with respect to the Logic App, but the Logic App is linked to it, because it needs it to call the external systems through the connector.

So, you can find the API connection resources in the resource group list of your Azure subscription, but in the Logic App blade, you will find an option to show all the API connections that are used by the Logic App:

Using this list, you can change the properties of every single connection that you are using in your Logic App.

Monitoring

The Logic App provides you with a set of tools to monitor its operation.

The first tools that you can use (and the simplest) are the runs history and the trigger history.

The **Runs history** section gives you an ordered list of the latest execution of your Logic App. You can find it in the **Overview** panel, as shown in the following screenshot:

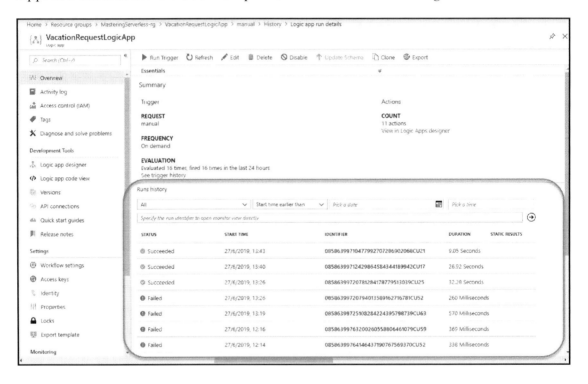

If you click on a log record in the **Runs history** section, you can see the complete overview of what's happened in the run:

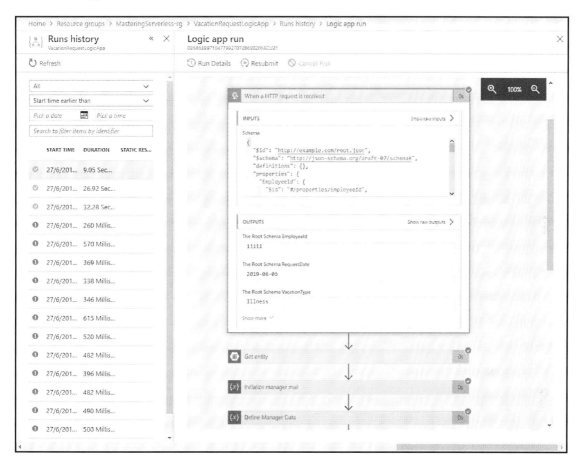

For each action of your Logic App, you can see the input and output, and if the step failed, what the reason for the failure was.

In this view, you can resubmit the instance of the Logic App (with the **Resubmit** button on top of the view), or show the run details. The run details view allows you to display the list of steps of the Logic App, and for each step, its duration and execution status:

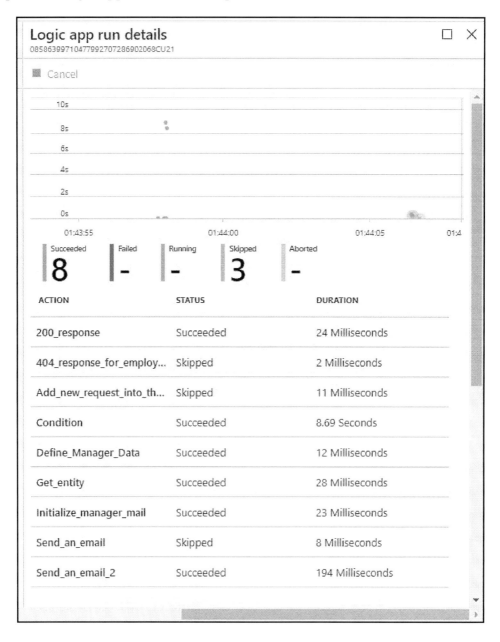

Logic app run details
0858639971047799270728690206800U21

■ Cancel

ACTION	STATUS	DURATION
200_response	Succeeded	24 Milliseconds
404_response_for_employ...	Skipped	2 Milliseconds
Add_new_request_into_th...	Skipped	11 Milliseconds
Condition	Succeeded	8.69 Seconds
Define_Manager_Data	Succeeded	12 Milliseconds
Get_entity	Succeeded	28 Milliseconds
Initialize_manager_mail	Succeeded	23 Milliseconds
Send_an_email	Skipped	8 Milliseconds
Send_an_email_2	Succeeded	194 Milliseconds

The trigger history, instead, allows you to have a list of trigger invocation. The trigger invocation is the step before starting the Logic App instance: a trigger can be fired properly, but the instance of the Logic App can have an error during the execution.

You can show the trigger history by using the link on the **Overview** page:

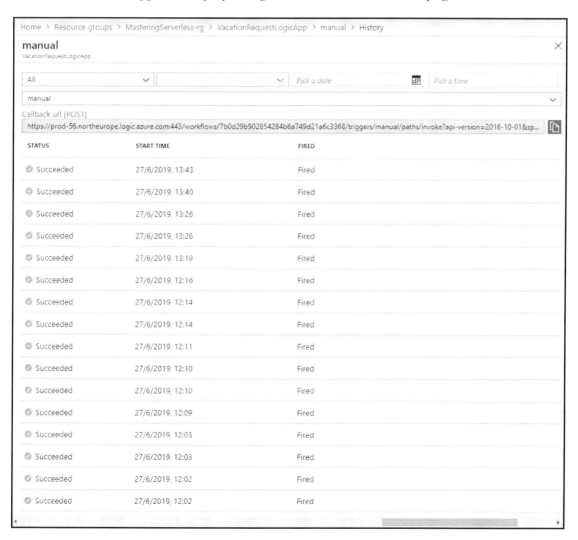

For every record in the trigger history, you have the complete information about the trigger, and you can also display the information about the run history for the specific trigger execution.

Finally, you can enable the diagnostic settings in order to store the diagnostic information of your Logic App in a storage account, stream it to an Event Hub, or send it to a Log Analytics instance. This can be achieved using the following instructions:

1. To enable the diagnostic, simply click on **Diagnostic settings** in the left panel of the Logic App blade.
2. Then, configure the diagnostic destination with the **Add diagnostic settings** link:

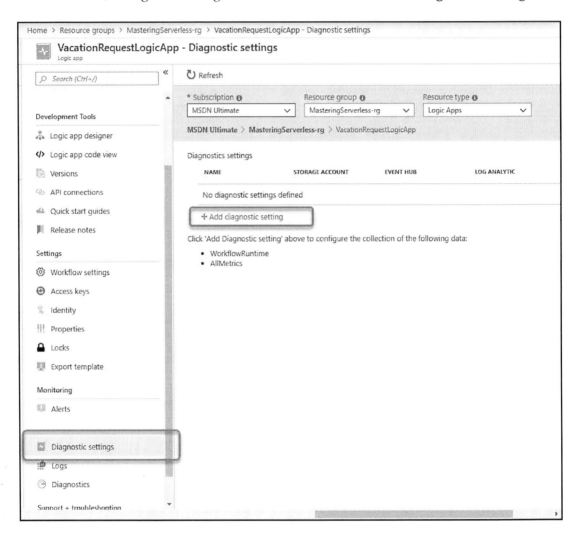

3. You can choose one or more destinations for the same configuration, and you can also set the retention duration (in days) for the log and for the metric:

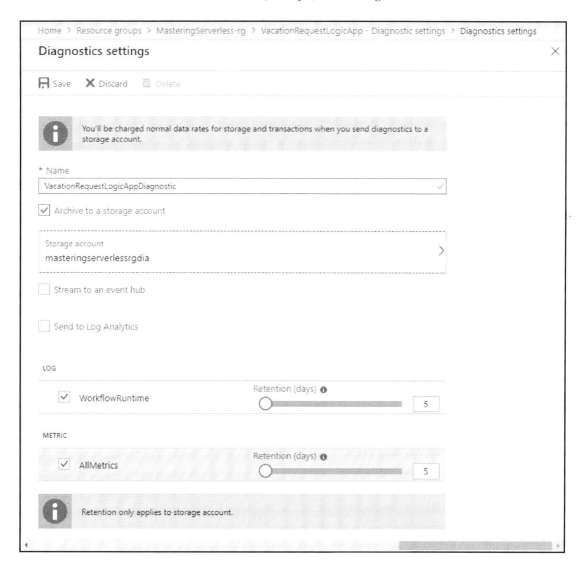

Once you have configured the diagnostic settings, you can use, for example, Log Analytics to query the log data and retrieve all the information you need to understand how your Logic App works.

Advantages of using Logic Apps

One of the most important requirements in the enterprise world is to integrate different systems that can be both on-premises and cloud-based (also in different cloud providers).

In this scenario, Logic Apps provide a great variety of connectors that can integrate with different systems, and, therefore, they are a powerful tool to achieve the target.

Therefore, Logic Apps are a serverless technology, so you don't need to worry about infrastructure, and the management of them is simpler than in other technologies.

The most important benefits of using Logic Apps are as follows:

- **Visual designer**: You can be more productive by using the designer tool. Designing a Logic App, instead of writing code, allows you to create the app quickly.
- **App templates**: You can create an app starting with a template. This approach allows you to be more productive, and also allows you to reuse your app by simply creating a custom template.
- **Over 200 connectors**: You can connect disparate systems across different environments (on-premises, hybrid cloud, and multi-provider cloud).
- **First-class support for enterprise integration and B2B**: Logic Apps allow you to adapt the different message protocols that are used in the enterprise and B2B world by different systems. Enterprises and organizations communicate with each other using industry-standard messaging protocols, but these protocols are often not the same, so you need to convert and adapt these protocols in order to enable communication.
- **Built-in extensibility**: If you don't find your connector, or you need to write code in order to complete a special task, the Logic App extensibility allows you to do this, while also extending your app with your custom connector or code.
- **Pay as you go**: The Logic App infrastructure monitors your instance executions and counts what actions, triggers, and connectors you use. You pay for each execution of the building blocks in your app. If you prefer, you can choose to pay a fixed cap monthly by using an **integration service environment (ISE)**.

Summary

In this chapter, you learned about Logic Apps, how you can use them to integrate external systems in an enterprise environment, and how you can reuse them using templates.

Logic Apps are a powerful tool that can be used to orchestrate workflow and exchange data between different systems. The designer approach allows you to quickly create your workflow, and the extensibility provides you with great flexibility. Over 200 connectors give you a set of building blocks that are ready to implement the most frequently used scenarios. Finally, using the template you can reuse your app when required.

In the next chapter, you will learn more about API management; a method that you can use to empower your API (REST or SOAP), while also adding security, caching, monitoring, and some enterprise-grade features, without modifying the code of your API.

Questions

1. What is the Workflow Definition Language file?
    - A JSON file that completely describes a Logic App
    - A Node.js file that defines a Logic App
    - A JSON file that enumerates the connectors that are available on Azure
    - An XML file that completely describes a Logic App
2. How many triggers can a Logic App have?
    - At least one
    - Only one
    - More than one
    - None

Further reading

You can find out more information about Logic Apps by looking at the following links:

- *Overview - What is Azure Logic Apps?*: `https://docs.microsoft.com/en-us/azure/logic-apps/logic-apps-overview`
- *Limits and configuration information for Azure Logic Apps*: `https://docs.microsoft.com/en-us/azure/logic-apps/logic-apps-limits-and-config`
- *Logic App GitHub*: `https://github.com/Azure/logicapps`

10
Empowering Your Serverless API with API Management

In the previous sections, you learned how to implement HTTP-triggered functions and expose them to your customers. These functions are basically awoken by an HTTP call and return information to the caller or change the status of a business entity. But what would happen if your business were to provide information via the API? How could you count the use of the API by a customer with a certain agreement or guarantee a specific SLA?

Implementing these kinds of functionalities within an Azure function (and, in general, in an API written with any technology) is not easy. One of the solutions is to put API Management in front of your API.

API Management is an Azure service that allows you to implement enterprise patterns such as authentication, throttling, and usage quotas for your API (both REStful than SOAP) without changing your API code.

This chapter will cover the following topics:

- Understanding Azure API Management
- Creating an API Management service
- How to expose your APIs
- How to implement API policies (caching, security, throttling, and so on)
- How to create a new product (an API that a developer can use)
- Managing API Management with the REST API
- The advantages of API Management

Technical requirements

As you will see in this chapter, API Management is an Azure service configurable through the Azure portal, so no programming knowledge is needed to understand what it is and how it works.

Understanding Azure API Management

Azure API Management is an Azure service that allows you to implement a consistent and secure access layer to your APIs. Thanks to API Management, you can easily add authentication, throttling, and caching features without changing the API code.

Furthermore, API Management allows you to make protocol changes to your APIs. You can easily publish a SOAP API with a REST protocol without modifying the code.

API Management is the ideal service if your business makes provision for the sale of online services through an API because it allows you to keep track of the uses that customers make of your APIs and thereby enable you to carry out precise billing.

Azure API Management comprises three components:

- **API Gateway**: This is the endpoint to which you expose your APIs. It accepts external calls from your customers and routes them to the actual API in the backend. It can enforce quotas, rate limits, transform API protocols, add security, and so on. It can also log call metadata for analytics purposes.
- **Administrative portal**: This is the administrative interface for your exposed APIs. You can use it to define APIs, configure them, create products, and configure subscriptions for your customers. All the administrative portal features are located in the left-hand menu of the API Management blade (in the Azure portal).
- **Developer portal**: This is the portal that a developer can use to get information about the APIs you expose. The developer portal allows developers to create accounts and to generate the API key to use them, provides an interactive console to test the APIs, and gives them the API documentation:

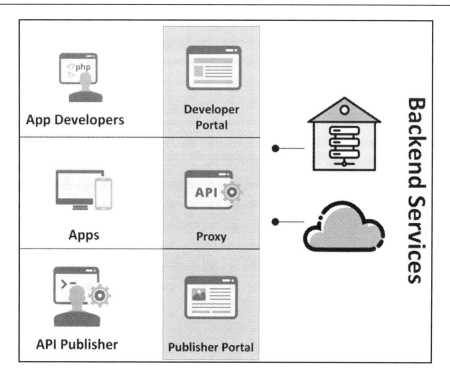

Before showing how to create an API Management instance, we need to clarify the terminology we will use:

- **APIs and operations**: APIs represent the fundamental entities managed by Azure API Management. An API is a group of operations available for developers. Each operation can map one or more APIs implemented on backend services. The operations in API Management are highly configurable, and it is possible to add policies concerning URL mapping, caching, security, rate limits, and so on.

- **Products**: A product is a grouping of APIs and is a way to package a set of APIs to which a developer can subscribe. A product is characterized by a title, a description, and terms of use. A product can be open or protected. An open product can be used by a developer without a subscription, while protected products can only be used following a subscription by the developer. Groups are used to manage product visibility for developers. Developers can view and subscribe to the products visible to the groups they belong to.

- **Groups**: Groups are used to manage the visibility of products to developers. API Management has three immutable groups:
    - **Administrators**: The users in this group are able to manage the API Management service instance. They can add products, remove products, configure APIs, and so on.
    - **Developers**: The users in this group can log in to the developer portal and call the API using API Gateway.
    - **Guests**: The users in this group can visit the developer portal and can use the open product (without portal registration and subscription), but cannot use the protected products.

Administrators can create custom groups (for example, to identify the developers of a particular customer) and a user can belong to more than one group.

- **Developers**: Developers are the users that use your API through API Gateway. A developer can sign up from the developer portal or can be invited by an administrator. A developer can subscribe to one or more products (depending on their subscription) and when they subscribe to a product, API Management generates a primary and a secondary key for the developer. The developer must use the keys to call the APIs contained in the specific product.
- **Policies**: Using policies, you can change the behavior of the APIs exposed by API Management. Policies are a declarative way to add features to all APIs, to a single API, or to a single operation. For example, you can implement a format conversion from XML to JSON, or add a caching policy to an operation or implement throttling.
- **Subscriptions**: A subscription is a way in which you can secure access to a set of APIs in API Management. When developers need to consume published APIs, they must have a subscription key and they must provide it in the API call. API Management rejects a request from the developer if the key is not valid without routing the request to the backend services. API Management supports OAuth 2.0, client certificates, or IP whitelisting as secure mechanisms.

Creating an API Management instance

Creating an instance of API Management is very simple: you just have to define the name of the instance (that becomes the root URL of API Gateway), the organization name (your company), the email of the admin user (to receive notifications from the API Management), the Azure location (in terms of subscription, resource group, and region) and, of course, the pricing tier:

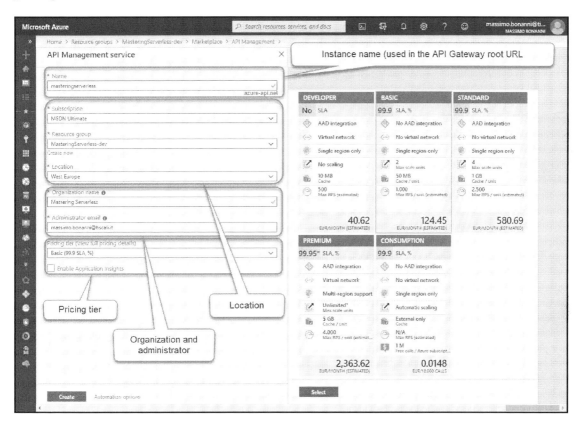

As you can see in the preceding screenshot, there are five pricing tiers for API Management:

- **Developer**: This is the tier for developer and test purposes. You should only use it for test and evaluation purposes, and not in production.
- **Basic, Standard, and Premium**: These are the production tiers with a fixed monthly price. Every tier has a different capacity (scale units, caching, and number of calls per second) and, of course, a different price.
- **Consumption**: This is the serverless version of API Management. You pay for what you use, but you have only the gateway component, and not the portals.

Once you fill in all the API Management information and press the **Create** button, Azure creates a new API Management instance (it can take some time to create this instance because it needs to create the API Management service and the portals).

At the end of the creation process, you can open the API Management blade and start using it (as you can see in the following screenshot):

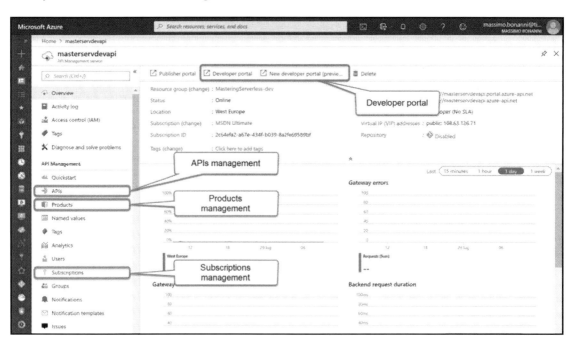

Using the API Management blade, you can configure APIs, define products, and manage subscriptions (and, of course, users and developers).

The developer portal

The developer portal allows your customer's developers to test your API, read the API documentation, and manage their subscriptions.

The developer portal supports logins for groups you define in API Management and allows new developers to sign up and create an account to use your API.

When you create a new API Management service, Azure creates the portal automatically.

If you log in as an administrator, you can personalize the portal by changing the layout, styles, and colors, as demonstrated in the following screenshot:

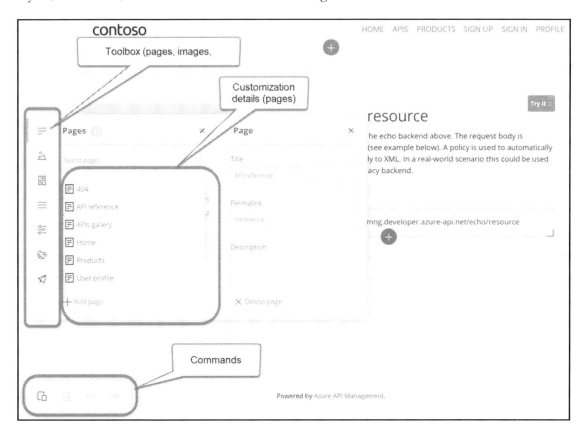

When a developer lands on your developer portal, they can log in (provided they are a registered user), but they can also create a new account:

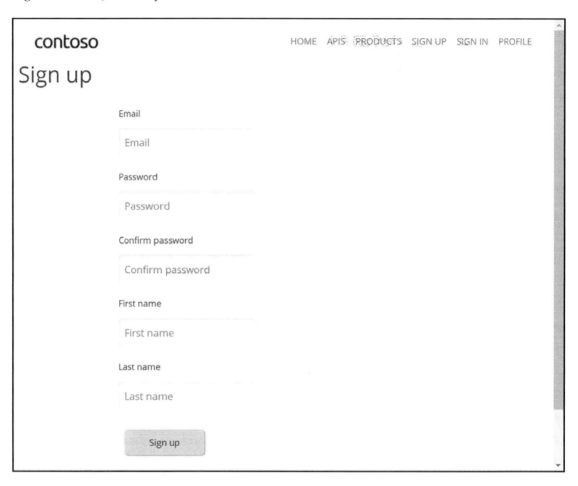

The developer portal provides you with the login and sign-up form and, of course, you can personalize them. The sign-up process provides you with CAPTCHA and email verification out of the box.

Once a developer signs up for your API Management service, they can manage their subscription and products. Initially, they are not entitled to have any products, but can use the portal features to add one of the products you exposed in your API Management service.

The developer can use the **PRODUCTS** menu to see the list of available products:

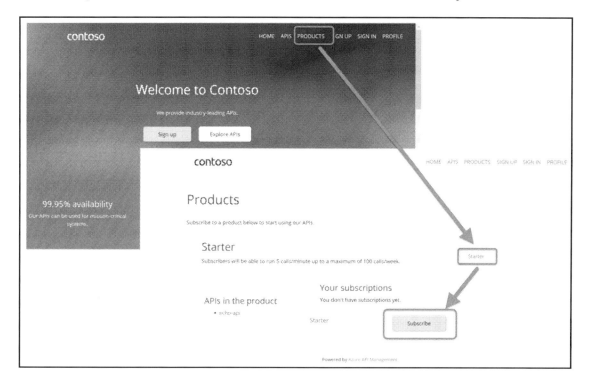

Then, they can choose one of them and subscribe to it. The following screenshot shows the subscription details:

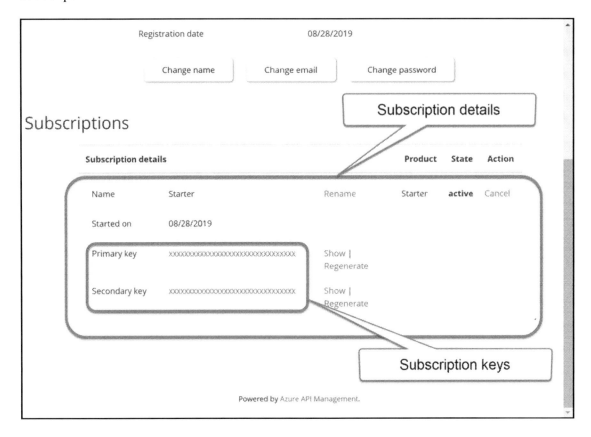

When a developer subscribes to a product, API Management creates a subscription associated with the developer for that product. The developer receives two subscription keys that they must use when calling the API of the product. The subscription keys allow you to control the utilization of the API and add policies to them.

The API menu allows developers to have a complete list of the available APIs and to read the API documentation for the API to which they are subscribed:

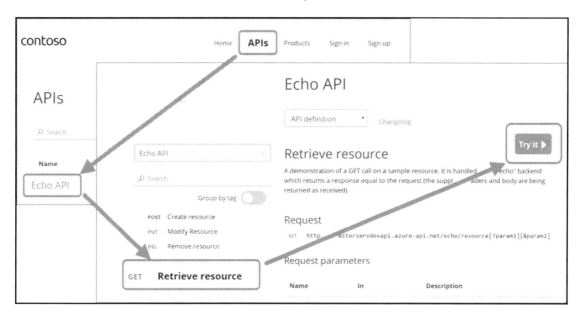

And, finally, developers can test every single API using the API console:

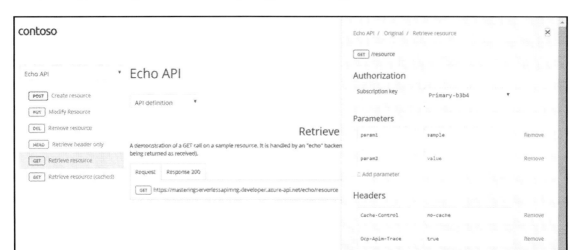

All the API information is defined in the API definition you see later in the following sections and it is updated every time you change the definitions. Developers always have up-to-date documentation and can test the latest version of your APIs.

Exposing a new API

In this section, you will learn how to add a REST API to your API Management products and how to expose the API to the developers who are using your API Management service.

We'll use an HTTP-triggered Azure function and, in particular, the Azure function created in Chapter 5, *Leveraging the Power of DevOps with Azure Functions*.

Just to recap, the Azure function mentioned before is an HTTP-triggered function that can be called using a GET verb and return its version number:

```
C:\>curl --get
https://masterservdevsite.azurewebsites.net/api/GetVersion?code=g5EKQzTFgdX
xWXGzH2t...Q==

Your awesome function version 1.1.0.0
```

You want to add this REST API to your API Management products and, in the next section, you want to add policies to the API (for example, caching or a limit quota):

1. On the API Management blade, you must choose the **APIs** option and, on the right-hand side, you will find various options to add a new API:

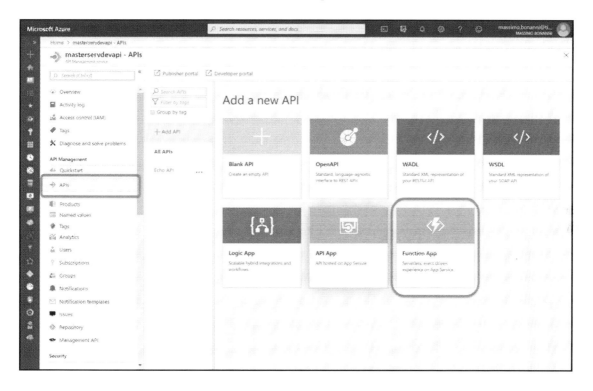

2. Once you select **Function App** as the API source, you must select the existing function app:

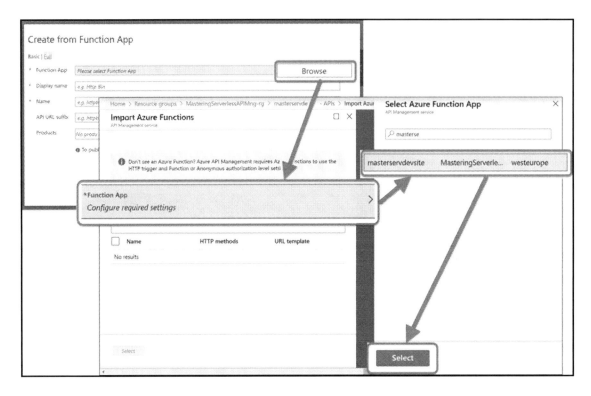

3. Now, you can configure it as follows:

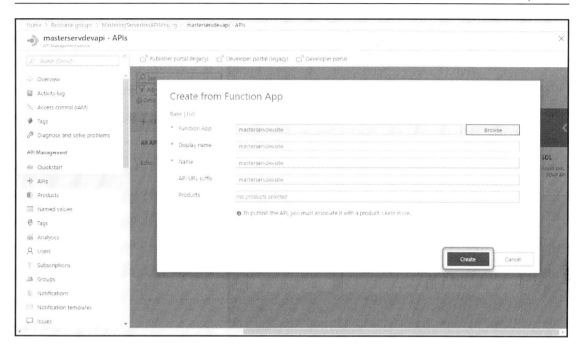

To complete the configuration, you must insert the following:

- **Display name**: This is the name that will appear in the API documentation. It is mandatory.
- **Name**: This is the internal name for the API. Again, it is mandatory.
- **API URL suffix**: This is the suffix that API Management adds to the URL for the API. API Management distinguishes every API by its suffix, so it must be unique for every API you publish.
- **Products**: This is the list of products the API is linked to. An API can belong to no products (in this case, the API is not visible to developers), or to one or more products.

An API can have more than one REST endpoint. In the previous sample, `GetVersionAPI` has only the GET verb endpoint.

As soon as you have added the new API to your products, all the developers subscribed to those products will see the new API and will be able to use it.

The new API will also appear in the API list available on the API blade, and you can call it using the `curl` command:

```
C:\>curl --get -H "Ocp-Apim-Subscription-Key:e707a6d2b....f86064"
https://masterservdevapi.azure-api.net/getversion/GetVersion

Your awesome function version 1.1.0.0
```

Here, the `Ocp-Apim-Subscription-Key` header is one of the two subscription keys for the registered user.

You can manage your API by creating a new version directly inside the Azure portal. API Management provides you with a sort of version control system that allows you to expose different versions of the same API (or the same operation inside an API) at the same time.

Creating a new policy

Policies are an API Management capability that allows you to change the behavior of your exposed API using a configuration file and without changing your application code.

Policies can be defined on all the APIs of your API Management instance, on a single API, or on a single operation in an API, and finally, you can also add policies to a single product. Policies are a set of statements you can apply to an API request (before the request is routed to the backend services) or to the response (before the response is returned to the caller).

Using policies, you can authenticate the request, implement restriction policies (for example, set a usage quota for a subscription or limit the number of calls for a product), implement caching, rewrite the URL, transform a request or response payload from JSON to XML, and so on.

You can display the policies applied to a single API operation simply by selecting the APIs option in the API Management blade and the single API in the corresponding list, as shown in the following screenshot:

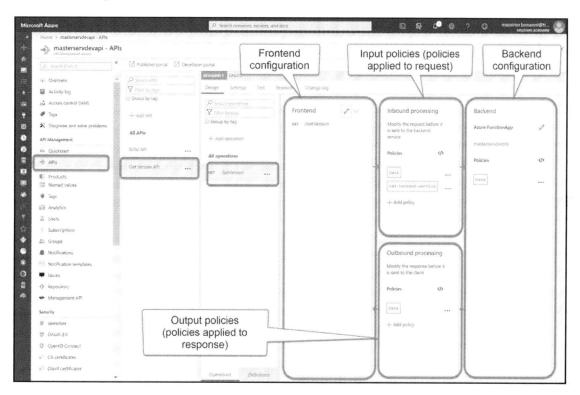

As you can see in the preceding screenshot, in the design area, you have four sections that you can configure:

- **Frontend**: In this section, you can configure how the API is exposed to developers. You can change the HTTP verb, the URL, the description, and so on. Here, you can also modify the OpenAPI specification for the API:

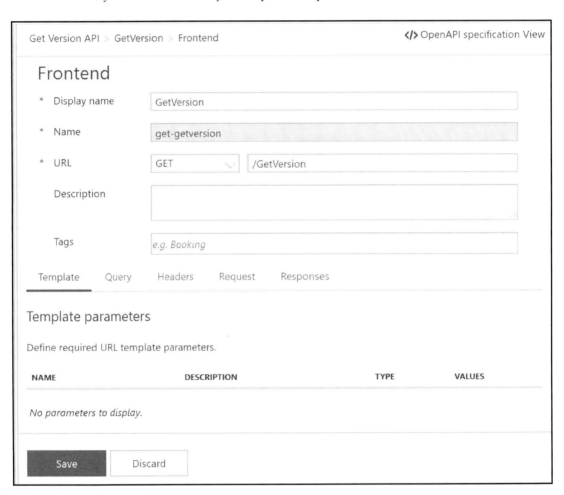

- **Inbound processing**: Here, you can configure the policies applied to the request.
- **Backend**: Here, you can add policies that are executed immediately before API Management calls the backend service and configures the backend service itself (for example, the Azure resource you are using, or the HTTP URL of your on-premises web service).

- **Outbound processing**: Here, you can configure the policies applied to the response before it is sent to the caller.

Behind the scenes, the policies are described in an XML file:

```
<policies>
    <inbound>
        <base />
        <set-backend-service id="apim-generated-policy" backend-
id="masterservdevsite" />
    </inbound>
    <backend>
        <base />
    </backend>
    <outbound>
        <base />
    </outbound>
    <on-error>
        <base />
    </on-error>
</policies>
```

As you can see in the previous XML snippet, you have an `on-error` section you can use to manage what happened if there is an error during an API call.

You can define the order in which the policies are evaluated simply by moving the policy XML tags that define them. The API Management policies engine will evaluate the policies starting from the top ones.

You can define policies in relation to products: all API; single API; or single operation level; and the `<base />` tag tells the API Management policy engine to apply the policies present in the level that is immediately higher.

The order in which API Management evaluates policies is as follows:

- Global (all the APIs of your API Management instance)
- Product
- Single API
- Single operation

In the previous snippet, for example, when the API Management policies engine evaluates the inbound policies, it first applies the `Get Version API` policies, and then applies the `<set-backend-service />` policy.

To add a new policy, for example, at a single operation level, you can modify the XML file manually, or you can use the **+ Add policy** button you can find in the **Inbound processing** and **Outbound processing** sections.

For example, you can add a caching feature to your API simply by choosing the `cache-lookup/store` policy:

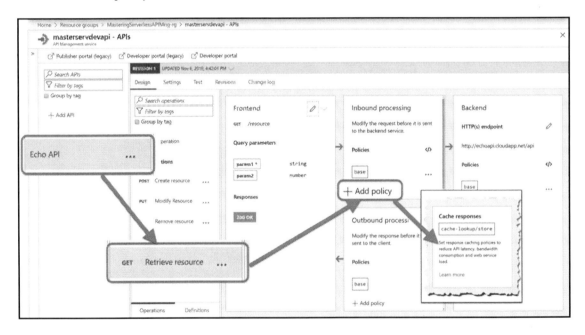

Every policy has its configuration form with different parameters that you can set. In the previous sample, you set a cache timeout at 60 seconds and set a cache for each developer (identified by its subscription keys):

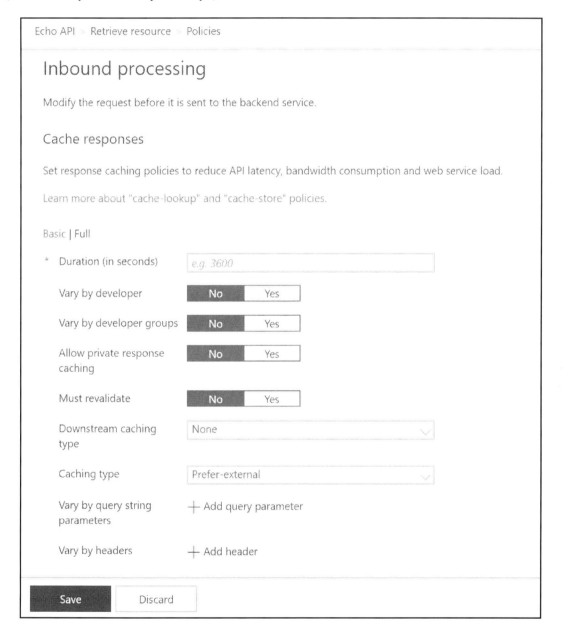

When you save the policy, the Azure portal modifies the XML file:

```
<policies>
    <inbound>
        <base />
        <set-backend-service id="apim-generated-policy" backend-
id="masterservdevsite" />
        <cache-lookup vary-by-developer="true" vary-by-developer-
groups="false" downstream-caching-type="none" />
    </inbound>
    ...
    <outbound>
        <base />
        <cache-store duration="60" />
    </outbound>
    ...
</policies>
```

As you can see in the previous code snippet, the caching policy is composed of two single entries in the XML file:

- **Cache lookup**: This policy works on the request and looks for the response stored in the cache (for every developer using their subscription keys).
- **Cache store**: This policy works on the response and stores the response itself for the developer.

> You can find the complete list of policies at `https://docs.microsoft.com/en-us/azure/api-management/api-management-policies`.

Defining a new product

A product contains one or more APIs, as well as defining a usage quota and terms of use.

If you want to create a new product, you can use the **Products** option in the API Management blade:

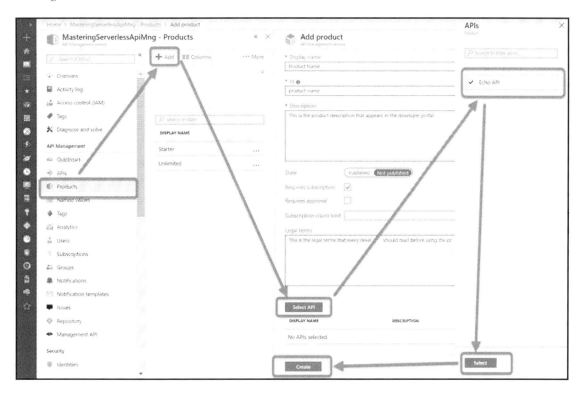

When you create a new product, you must add some information pertaining to it:

- **Display name**: This is the full name that appears in the developer portal.
- **Id**: This is the internal name for the product.
- **Description**: This is the description of the product (it also appears in the developer portal).
- **State**: If you select **Published**, the product will be available as soon as it has been created.
- **Requires subscription**: If you select this option, a developer needs to subscribe to the product (create a new subscription) in order to use it.

- **Requires approval**: If you select this option, an administrator needs to approve a developer subscription when they want to use the product.
- **Subscription count limit**: This option allows you to set a limit on the number of simultaneous subscription for the product.
- **Legal terms**: This is the legal terms disclaimer that appears in the developer portal.
- **APIs**: This is a list of APIs contained in the product.

Once you publish the product, it appears in the developer portal and developers can choose to subscribe to use it:

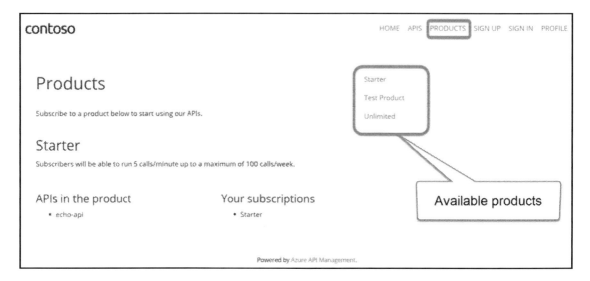

You can modify an existing product by entering the product blade (simply by clicking on the product record in the product list):

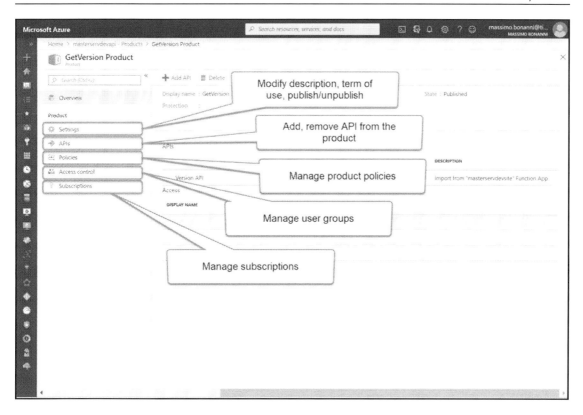

The Azure portal provides you with a complete UI to manage all the aspects of your APIs exposed by API Management but, in some cases, it may transpire that you cannot manage your API Management instance using the portal (for example, you need to generate periodic reports on products or active subscriptions). In those scenarios, you can leverage the REST API exposed by the API Management service.

The API Management REST API

The API Management service (like all services exposed by Azure) provides you with a set of APIs that allow you to do all the operations you can perform using the Azure portal.

You can use them when you are unable to use the web interface provided by the portal (for example, to automate product creation or generate periodical reports).

The base URL you can use to invoke the REST API for API Management has the following format:

```
https://management.azure.com/subscriptions/{subscriptionId}/resourceGroups/
{resourceGroupName}/providers/Microsoft.ApiManagement/service/{serviceName}
/
```

Here, the following applies:

- `subscriptionId`: This is the subscription ID of your Azure subscription. You can find it in the **Overview** option inside the API Management blade.
- `resourceGroupName`: This is the name of the resource group containing your API Management instance.
- `serviceName`: This is the name of your API Management instance.

A valid base URL is as follows:

```
https://management.azure.com/subscriptions/2c64efa2-a67e-434f-b039-8a2fe695
89ba/resourceGroups/MasteringServerless-
dev/providers/Microsoft.ApiManagement/service/masterservdevapi
```

You can find a complete list of APIs supported by API Management at `https://docs.microsoft.com/en-us/rest/api/apimanagement/`.

For example, if you want to retrieve all the products you have in your API Management service, you can use HTTP REST:

```
GET
https://management.azure.com/subscriptions/2c64efa2-a67e-434f-b039-8a2fe695
89ba/resourceGroups/MasteringServerless-
dev/providers/Microsoft.ApiManagement/service/masterservdevapi/products?api
-version=2019-01-01
Authorization: Bearer eyJ0eXAiOiJKV1QiLCJhbGciOiJS.....-aVw
```

The API returns a JSON result along the lines of the following:

```
{
    "value": [
    {
        "id": "/subscriptions/2c64efa2-a67e-434f-
b039-8a2fe69589bf/resourceGroups/MasteringServerless-
dev/providers/Microsoft.ApiManagement/service/masterservdevapi/products/get
version-product",
        "type": "Microsoft.ApiManagement/service/products",
        "name": "getversion-product",
        "properties": {
            "displayName": "GetVersion Product",
```

```
            "description": "This is the new product for GetVersion API",
            "terms": "This is the legal terms of the product",
            "subscriptionRequired": true,
            "approvalRequired": false,
            "subscriptionsLimit": null,
            "state": "published"
        }
    },
    ...
    ]
}
```

As you can imagine, using the API Management REST API, you simply automate product creation or generate reports for every single customer, or automate the subscription approval.

Advantages of API Management

The Azure API Management service doesn't have a free tier you can use to try and test it. Even the Developer tier has a monthly cost (you can use the Consumption tier, which allows you to have a number of free calls each month, but, with that tier, you don't have the developer portal).

So, the question may be: Why should you use it and pay?

One of the answers may be that it *depends*: it depends on what your business is, what kind of API you have to expose, how much chance you have of modifying your APIs, and so on.

Of course, API Management is not the answer to every scenario, so you should evaluate carefully whether you should use it.

In this section, we'll try to list all the advantages you can leverage if you use API Management, while the bigger disadvantage is, of course, the cost.

 You can find out more information about pricing and features at `https://azure.microsoft.com/en-us/pricing/details/api-management/`.

The main advantages of using API Management are summarized in the following bullet points:

- **It abstracts APIs from their implementation**: Using API Management, you can put a layer between your users (developers, applications, and so on) and your actual API, and this layer allows you, in the future, to change backend services with minimal impact on your clients.

- **It secures APIs without exposing them directly**: You can add authentication and authorization features to your APIs simply by adding rules to your API Management instance. The same API can have different kinds of authorization and authentication without modifying the API code.

- **It executes rules on API**: As with security, you can add rules to your APIs at the API Management layer without changing your code. Caching, throttling, and quota limits are hard to implement in API code, while it is so simple to add using an API Management rule. On the other hand, you can have different products with the same APIs but with different rules (for example, a free product for a particular API with a call quota limit, and the same API in a paid product without a call quota limit). Another useful scenario for using the API Management rules is to expose *old-style* APIs (for example, SOAP or the XML web service) in a modern way (REST).

- **It simplifies API development**: Your developers can develop APIs thinking just from the perspective of application features without having to implement infrastructure features (monitors, security, and so on). This simplifies development, maintenance, and, ultimately, minimizes the cost of development.

- **It simplifies API versioning**: Thanks to the versioning features provided by API Management, you can have multiple versions of the same API exposed simultaneously.

- **It affords developer, product, and subscription management out of the box**: API Management provides you with an infrastructure to manage developers, products, and subscriptions, both with a portal as well as with the REST API. You can integrate these features with OAuth2, Azure Active Directory, and so on. If you don't use API Management, you should consider the cost of implementing the management functions (API, portal, and suchlike) and maintenance.

- **It offers API monitoring**: If your business entails selling services, it is very important to be able to monitor the consumption of the same API by individual customers. API Management provides out-of-the-box monitoring without having to implement anything in your APIs.

- **API documentation**: The API Management developer portal allows you to give your customers the documentation, test consoles, and everything else they need to use your APIs in the right way, and you can do so without writing any lines of code.

To conclude, there are scenarios in which it makes sense to have a fixed monthly cost of managing API Management, such as, for example, companies that sell services, or companies that need to modernize *old-style* APIs but cannot do so on account of the fact that the cost of the modification is high.

Summary

In this chapter, you learned what API Management is and how it works.

API Management is an Azure service that allows you to expose your APIs to your customers, adding features such as security, throttling, and quota limits without modifying your code.

After reading this chapter, you should be able to understand whether you can use API Management to expose your APIs and how you can leverage the power of API Management.

In the next chapter, you will see what Event Grid is and how you can use it in your solutions.

Questions

1. What are the three main components of API Management?
    - API Gateway
    - Administrative portal
    - Analytics portal
    - Developer portal
    - Documentation portal

2. What is a product?
   - A product contains a set of APIs, a description, and terms of use, and can be published to be used by the developer
   - A product is a way in which you can secure access to a set of APIs in API Management
   - A product is a REST endpoint in backend services
   - A product is an XML definition applied to a request

3. Where can a policy be applied?
   - To a product
   - To all APIs in your API Management instance
   - To a subscription
   - To a developer
   - To an API

Further reading

You can find more information about API Management by referring to the following links:

- *API Management documentation*: `https://docs.microsoft.com/en-us/azure/api-management/`
- *GitHub samples*: `https://github.com/Azure/api-management-samples`
- *Channel 9 API Management series*: `https://channel9.msdn.com/Blogs/AzureApiMgmt`

High-Scale Serverless Event Processing with Event Grid

11

In this section, you will learn about an Azure service that allows you to implement high-scale event processing. Azure Event Grid allows you to manage and route a great number of events from different sources to several destinations by simply defining and designing routing rules.

Event Grid is an Azure service that allows you to manage events coming from different sources (generally, other services in Azure) and route them through other Azure services. In this chapter, you will learn what events are in Azure and how Event Grid manages them.

This chapter will cover the following topics:

- Understanding Event Grid and filtering your events
- Creating an Event Grid subscription
- Understanding how Event Grid manages event delivery and retries

Technical requirements

In this section, you will learn about Azure Event Grid and how you can use it to route and manage a great variety of cloud events and implement an event-driven architecture. Event Grid is based on configuration and no code is needed to configure it. You only need programming skills to understand the Azure function that we use to implement the event handler.

You can find the source code for this section on GitHub at `https://github.com/ PacktPublishing/Mastering-Azure-Serverless-Computing/tree/master/Chapter11`.

Understanding Event Grid

Event Grid is an Azure service that allows you to listen to and route events coming from a source (typically another Azure service) to one or more destinations (other Azure services). Using Event Grid you can easily implement an event-driven architecture, which means your system can react and perform operations when something happens in one of the services of your solution.

The following diagram shows the logical diagram for Event Grid:

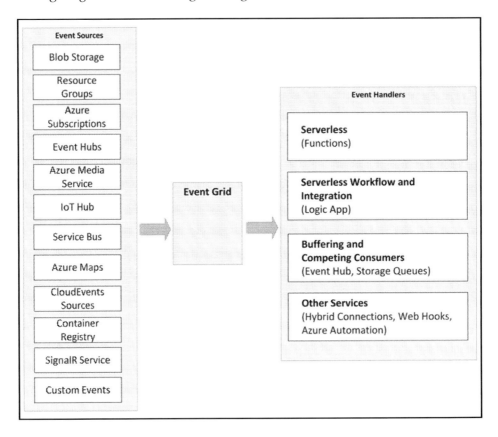

Before analyzing how to create and configure an Event Grid instance in depth, it's important to define some topics related to it.

Events

An event represents something that happens inside an Azure service (called the **source**) that communicates the event externally and that can be intercepted and managed by another Azure service (called the **destination**).

An event is composed of a set of information coded in a JSON format with a well-defined schema.

Azure Event Grid supports two different schemas for the events it can manage:

- **Azure event schema**: This is a schema defined by Azure, and its format is like the following:

```
[
    {
        "topic": string,
        "subject": string,
        "id": string,
        "eventType": string,
        "eventTime": string,
        "data":{
            object-unique-to-each-publisher
        },
        "dataVersion": string,
        "metadataVersion": string
    }
]
```

Events have a common set of properties that identify each event and its source:

- `topic`: Identifies the source of the event (the full resource path)—for example, a blob storage event has the following topic:

```
/subscriptions/{subscription-
id}/resourceGroups/Storage/providers/Microsoft.Storage/stor
ageAccounts/{storageAccountName}
```

- subject: The full path of the event's subject is defined by the source publisher—for example, a blob storage event can publish a subject like the following:

```
/blobServices/default/containers/oc2d2817345i200097containe
r/blobs/oc2d2817345i20002296blob
```

- eventType: Describes the event type—for example, blob storage can publish an event with eventType Microsoft.Storage.BlobCreated.
- eventTime: The UTC time when the event was generated.
- id: The event's unique identifier.
- dataVersion: The schema version of the data object. This property allows sources to evolve and change their data schema in the future.
- metadataVersion: The schema version of the event metadata. Event Grid defines the schema of the top-level properties.
- data: Contains the data for the specific events—for example, a blob storage event looks like the following:

```
"data": {
    "api": "PutBlockList",
    "clientRequestId":
"6d79dbfb-0e37-4fc4-981f-442c9ca65760",
    "requestId": "831e1650-001e-001b-66ab-eeb76e000000",
    "eTag": "0x8D4BCC2E4835CD0",
    "contentType": "application/octet-stream",
    "contentLength": 524288,
    "blobType": "BlockBlob",
    "url":
"https://oc2d2817345i60006.blob.core.windows.net/oc2d2817345i20
0097container/oc2d2817345i20002296blob",
    }
```

- **CloudEvents schema**: An open specification for describing events in a generic cloud provider. Azure Event Grid supports both Azure event schemas and CloudEvent schemas. An event serialized on CloudEvents schemas looks like the following:

```
{
    "specversion" : "0.3",
    "type" : "Microsoft.Storage.BlobCreated",
    "source" : "/subscriptions/{subscription-
```

```
id}/resourceGroups/{resource-
group}/providers/Microsoft.Storage/storageAccounts/{storage-
account}",
    "subject" :
"/blobServices/default/containers/oc2d2817345i200097container/blobs
/oc2d2817345i20002296blob",
    "id" : "173d9985-401e-0075-2497-de268c06ff25",
    "time" : "2018-04-05T17:31:00Z",
    "comexampleextension1" : "value",
    "comexampleextension2" : {
        "othervalue": 5
    },
    "datacontenttype" : "text/json",
    "data" : "{ 'api': 'PutBlockList',..., 'blobType': 'BlockBlob',
'url':
'https://oc2d2817345i60006.blob.core.windows.net/oc2d2817345i200097
container/oc2d2817345i20002296blob' }"
}
```

 You can find more information about the CloudEvents open specification at `https://cloudevents.io/`. The official GitHub repository for the specification is `https://github.com/cloudevents/spec`.

You can use both Azure events schemas (also known as Event Grid schemas) and CloudEvents for your input and output in Azure Event Grid.

Event sources always send events to Azure Event Grid as an array, even if there is only one event and the maximum size for the array is 1 MB. Each event in the array may have a size of up to 64 KB. If the size of the array is over the limits, you will receive an HTTP error 413 (payload too large) when you try to send the array.

Event sources

An event source is a cloud service where an event happened. Azure provides a set of services that are automatically configured to throw events when particular scenarios occur.

At the time of writing this book, the available event sources are as follows:

- **Blob storage**: This source throws events when a blob is created or deleted. You can find the event schema for this kind of event at `https://docs.microsoft.com/en-us/azure/event-grid/event-schema-blob-storage`.

- **Resource groups and Azure subscriptions (management operations)**: This source throws events when something changes in a resource inside a resource group or inside an Azure subscription—for example, you can manage the event of a resource deletion. You can find more information about event schemas and the list of supported events at `https://docs.microsoft.com/en-us/azure/event-grid/event-schema-resource-groups` and `https://docs.microsoft.com/en-us/azure/event-grid/event-schema-subscriptions`.

- **Container registry**: This source throws events when an image contained in a container service changes—for example, you can manage the creation of a new image inside a container registry. You find more information about event schemas and the list of supported events at `https://docs.microsoft.com/en-us/azure/event-grid/event-schema-container-registry`.

- **Event Hubs**: This source throws events when a capture file is created inside an Azure Event Hub. You can find more information about event schemas and the list of supported events at `https://docs.microsoft.com/en-us/azure/event-grid/event-schema-event-hubs`.

- **Media Services**: This source throws events when a media service job state changes—for example, you can manage the completion of a media service job. You can find more information about event schema and the list of supported events at `https://docs.microsoft.com/en-us/azure/media-services/latest/media-services-event-schemas`.

- **IoT Hub**: This source throws an event when you add, remove, connect, or disconnect a device from an IoT hub or when telemetry information is sent to IoT Hub. You can find more information about event schemas and the list of supported events at `https://docs.microsoft.com/en-us/azure/event-grid/event-schema-iot-hub`.

- **Service bus**: This source throws events when someone pushes a message in a queue or subscription for a service bus without an active listener. You can find more information about event schemas and the list of supported events at `https://docs.microsoft.com/en-us/azure/event-grid/event-schema-service-bus`.

- **Azure Maps**: This source throws events to respond to geofence events—for example, you can do something when a device enters a specific geofence area. You can find more information about event schemas and the list of supported events at `https://docs.microsoft.com/en-us/azure/event-grid/event-schema-azure-maps`.

- **Azure SignalR**: This source throws events when something happens in a SignalR client connection—for example, you can manage a new client connection. You can find more information about event schema and the list of supported events at `https://docs.microsoft.com/en-us/azure/event-grid/event-schema-azure-signalr`.
- **Custom**: Using this source, you can manage your own custom events thrown by an application. Your application can send events to an Event Grid endpoint. Your application becomes an event source and you can define what kind of data the event should bring in its data property.

Topics

Topics are the Event Grid endpoints where every event source sends its events.

Every event publisher (for example, blob storage or a service bus) knows if it needs one or more topics to manage and create its events.

The subscribers (event handlers) can choose which topics they need to respond to particular events and subscribe to them.

Azure services provide built-in topics that you don't see in your subscription because the single service owns the topics and you can only subscribe to them. If you can access a resource that publishes events, you can subscribe to its topics.

Custom topics are the third-party endpoints you can use to receive custom events from different applications. For this kind of topic, if you can access them, you will see them in your Azure subscription and you can subscribe to them.

In a large solution, the best pattern is to create a topic for each event category. For example, if you are designing a solution to manage orders and products, you can choose to create a topic for the event related to the orders (for example, order creation, order payments, and so on) and a topic for the products (for example, new products, product quantity changes in the warehouse, and so on).

In a small solution, you can choose to have only a topic and let the event handler filter the received events.

Event subscriptions

When you want to receive events from an Azure service, you need to subscribe to a topic. The subscription is the connection between a topic and your event handler.

You can create a subscription using the Azure portal, PowerShell cmdlet, or the CLI interface, but behind the scenes, the creation of a subscription is a PUT HTTP REST call to an address with the following form:

```
PUT /subscriptions/{subscription-id}/resourceGroups/{group-
name}/providers/{resource-provider}/{resource-type}/{subscription-
name}/Microsoft.EventGrid/eventSubscriptions/{event-type-definitions}?api-
version=2018-01-01
```

The subscription name must be a string with a length of 3-64 characters and can only contain a-z, A-Z, 0-9, and -. The payload of the PUT call looks like the following:

```
{
    "properties": {
        "destination": {
            "endpointType": "webhook",
            "properties": {
                "endpointUrl":
"https://example.azurewebsites.net/api/HttpTriggerCSharp1?code=VXbGWce53148
Mt8wuotr0GPmyJ/nDT4hgdFj9DpBiRt38qqnnm5OFg=="
            }
        },
        "filter": {
            "includedEventTypes": [ "Microsoft.Storage.BlobCreated",
"Microsoft.Storage.BlobDeleted" ],
            "subjectBeginsWith":
"blobServices/default/containers/mycontainer/log",
            "subjectEndsWith": ".jpg"
        }
    }
}
```

Every subscription has `destination` and `filter` sections:

- `destination`: Identifies the object that defines the endpoint that will receive the events.
    - `endpointtype`: The type of the endpoint (for example, webhook, queue, and so on).
    - `endpointurl`: The destination URL for the endpoint.

- `filter`: Any filters to apply to topic events before sending them to the event handler. This object is optional.
  - `includedEventTypes`: An array of event types that will be sent to the event handler. The events in this array must exactly match the event names registered in the event source. If you use an incorrect name here, you will receive an error.
  - `subjectBeginsWith`: A prefix match for the subject of the events thrown by the source. If you use it, only the events with a subject that starts with the string you use will be sent to the event handler.
  - `subjectEndsWith`: A suffix match for the subject of the events thrown by the source. If you use it, only the events with a subject that ends with the string you use will be sent to the event handler.
  - `isSubjectCaseSensitive`: Chooses whether or not the filter is case sensitive.

You can also implement advanced filtering based on values contained in the data fields of the event payload. The filter section of the JSON payload also accepts a property called `"advancedFilters"`, which allows you to define filtering such as the following:

```json
"filter": {
    "advancedFilters": [
        {
            "operatorType": "NumberGreaterThanOrEquals",
            "key": "Data.Key1",
            "value": 5
        },
        {
            "operatorType": "StringContains",
            "key": "Subject",
            "values": ["container1", "container2"]
        }
    ]
}
```

In the previous snippet, the subscription sends to the event handler only the events that have a property called `Key1` in the `data` section with a value greater or equal to 5 and a subject that contains `"container1"` or `"container2"`.

 You can find more information about filtering at `https://docs.microsoft.com/en-us/azure/event-grid/event-filtering` and `https://docs.microsoft.com/en-us/azure/event-grid/how-to-filter-events`.

Event handlers

An event handler is the place where an event is sent if it meets any of the filters of the subscription.

Azure provides you with a set of event handlers:

- **Azure automation**: You can use an event generated by an Azure service to start an Azure runbook—for example, you can manage a VM creation event to start a runbook that automatically adds tags to the new VM.
- **Azure function**: You can start an Azure function when some kind of events occurs. Azure functions have a special trigger called an **Event Grid trigger**, which you can use in this scenario (instead of using an HTTP-triggered function).
- **Event hubs**: You can use this handler to ingest events as quickly as possible inside an event hub.
- **Hybrid connections**: You can use this event handler to send events to applications inside an enterprise network that haven't got a public endpoint.
- **Logic apps**: You can use events to start workflows inside a logic app.
- **Service bus queue**: This event handler is in preview at the time of writing. It allows you to buffer your events into a service bus queue in enterprise applications.
- **Queue storage**: You can use this handler to push events into a storage queue and use them for long process operations (for example).
- **Webhooks**: This is the custom event handler. You can use your REST HTTP endpoint to manage events in the way you prefer and with the technologies you know.

In the next section, we will learn how to create and manage events using Event Grid.

Creating an Event Grid subscription

In this section, you will learn how to manage events using Event Grid.

Suppose you have a storage account and you want to log what happens inside it (the creation or deletion of blobs, containers, and so on) using an Azure function. To do this, you should go through the following steps:

1. First of all, you must write your Azure function that implements the event handler:

```
[FunctionName("EventHandlerFunction")]
public static void
EventGridHandler([EventGridTrigger]EventGridEvent eventGridEvent,
ILogger log)
{
    log.LogInformation(eventGridEvent.EventType);
    log.LogInformation(eventGridEvent.Data.ToString());
}
```

The Azure function uses the `EventGrid` trigger to receive the event payload when it is called by Event Grid.

2. You must reference the `Microsoft.Azure.WebJobs.Extensions.EventGrid` package to use the `EventGridTrigger` attribute.

When you complete the function implementation and you have deployed it into a function app, you can create the subscription for the storage account event and link it to your Azure function:

1. First of all, you must go to the storage account blade on the Azure portal and select the **Events** option:

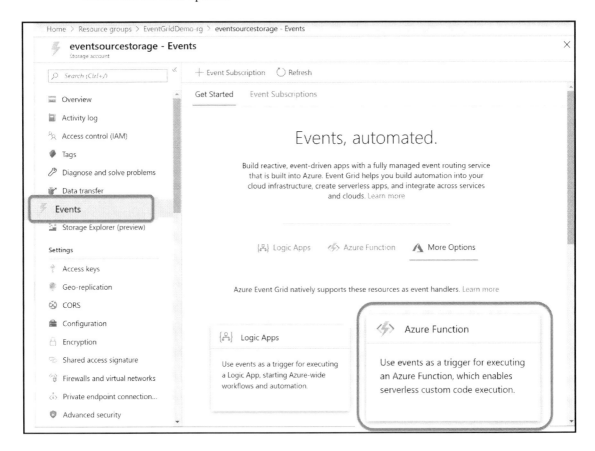

2. Then, you choose **Functions** as the event handler.
3. The next step is to select the Azure function:

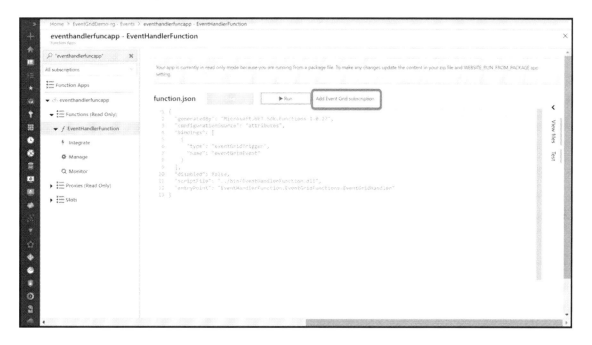

Then, you should configure the Event Grid integration (the event subscription):

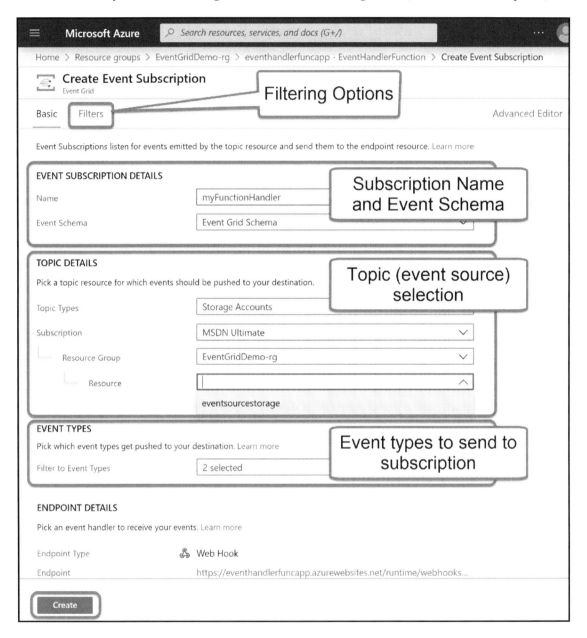

4. Once you have created the subscription, you can see it in the **Events** option of the storage account:

5. If you try to upload a file inside the storage account, you will see that your Azure function will be called. Its log will look like the following:

```
2019-08-12T10:49:12.059 [Information] Microsoft.Storage.BlobCreated
2019-08-12T10:49:12.059 [Information] {
 "api": "PutBlob",
 "clientRequestId": "c36e12c0-bcee-11e9-901b-410ce3d31e2a",
 "requestId": "80cd0d9e-c01e-010a-29fb-5016c1000000",
 "eTag": "0x8D71F12B5BEEE27",
 "contentType": "image/png",
 "contentLength": 3638,
 "blobType": "BlockBlob",
 "url":
"https://eventsourcestorage.blob.core.windows.net/test/717556_man_5
12x512.png",
 "sequencer": "00000000000000000000000000000F8D0000000002b786d5",
 "storageDiagnostics": {
 "batchId": "0b931f81-3006-002e-00fb-501e6c000000"
 }
}
```

As you can see, the `EventGridEvent` object provided by `EventGridTrigger` contains all the information of the event generated by the storage account.

Understanding event delivery and retries

One of the key features that Event Grid provides is the durable delivery of the events that it manages. Event Grid assures you that every message it manages will be delivered, at least once, for each subscription.

Every time an event is received on one of its topics from Event Grid, it will be sent immediately to the corresponding registered endpoint and then to the subscription registered for that endpoint.

If the endpoint doesn't return the acknowledgment for the event (that is, if the event isn't delivered correctly to the subscription), Event Grid will try to deliver the event again.

By default, Event Grid waits for 30 seconds for a timeout after sending an event to an endpoint; then, if the endpoint doesn't respond or responds with an error, Event Grid puts the event in the retry queue.

The retry policy is, as usual for Azure services, an exponential back-off retry policy, and the scheduling is as follows:

- 10 seconds
- 30 seconds
- 1 minute
- 5 minutes
- 10 minutes
- 30 minutes
- 1 hour
- Hourly, for up to 24 hours

Event Grid tries to use this schedule on best effort: it may happen that scheduling is not respected if Event Grid is engaged in other operations with higher priority. and adds small randomization to every retry, and it can skip one or more retries if the endpoint is unhealthy or down for a long period.

If Event Grid receives a 400 (Bad Request) or 413 (Request Entity Too Large) response code when it tries to deliver an event, it sends the event to the dead letter queue (if this has been configured) or retries the delivery operation based on the retry scheduling if you don't configure the dead letter queue.

The retry schedule also depends on the result code Event Grid receives when it tries to deliver the event to the endpoint. The following table shows the different retry timings for each possible HTTP status code that Event Grid considers an error:

HTTP status code	Retry behavior
400 Bad Request	Retry after 5 minutes or more (dead letter immediately if the dead letter is set up)
401 Unauthorized	Retry after 5 minutes or more
403 Forbidden	Retry after 5 minutes or more
404 Not Found	Retry after 5 minutes or more
408 Request Timeout	Retry after 2 minutes or more
413 Request Entity Too Large	Retry after 10 seconds or more (dead letter immediately if the dead letter is set up)
503 Service Unavailable	Retry after 30 seconds or more
All others	Follow the scheduling

You can configure some parameters of the retry process for a single subscription using the subscription properties you can find in the **Events** option in the source event blade, as shown in the following screenshot:

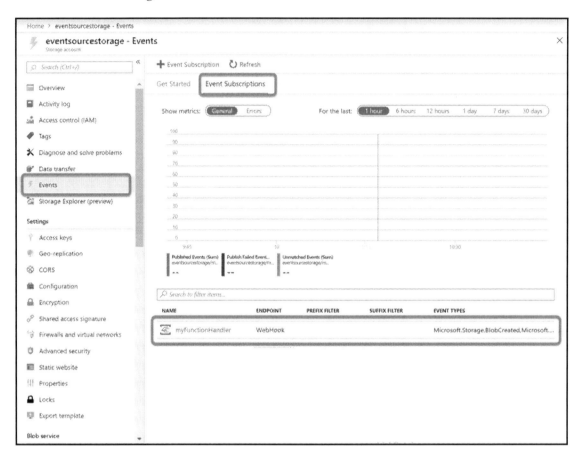

The subscription form has a tab dedicated to the advanced parameter (called **Features**) for the subscription itself. In this tab, you can find the configuration for the retry process, as shown in the following screenshot:

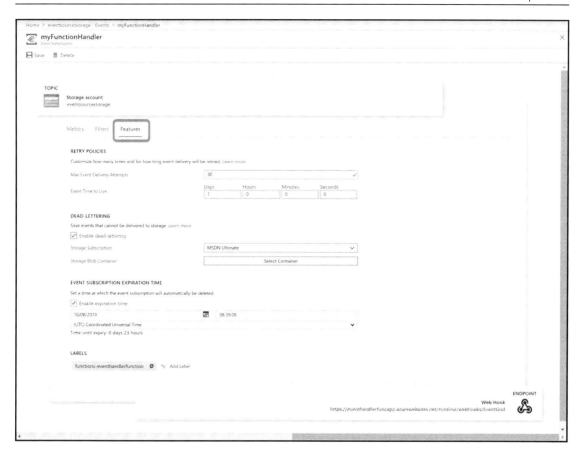

In the **RETRY POLICIES** section, you can configure the maximum number of attempts (the default is 30) and the maximum time to live (the default is 1 day) for each message. If the maximum number of attempts is reached or the time to live expires, Event Grid deletes the event or saves it in a dead letter queue (depending on whether you configured a dead letter queue).

You can configure a dead letter queue using the **DEAD-LETTERING** section by simply choosing the storage and the container inside the storage you want to use as the queue.

Finally, you can configure, using the **EVENT SUBSCRIPTION EXPIRATION TIME** section, the duration of the subscription: after the date that has been set in this section, the subscription will be automatically deleted and, of course, will no longer receive events.

Summary

In this chapter, you learned what Event Grid is and how it works.

Event Grid is a serverless Azure service that allows you to listen to and route a great variety of cloud events from other services to one or more destinations (typically, other Azure services). Using Event Grid, you can easily implement an event-driven architecture, and your system can react and perform operations when something happens in one of the services of your solution.

After reading this chapter, you will be able to understand whether Event Grid is the right choice for your solution and if it is, how you can use it in the right way.

In the next section, you will learn some of the best practices you must use when you implement a serverless solution, as well as a set of possible scenarios for using serverless architecture.

Questions

1. Which of the following event schemas are supported by Event Grid?
   - Azure event schema
   - AWS event schema
   - OAuth schema
   - CloudEvents schema

2. What type of retry policy is used by Event Grid?
   - Event Grid hasn't got a retry policy.
   - Fixed-time retry policy.
   - Fixed-time retry policy for Azure event schema and an exponential back-off retry policy for other types of schema.
   - Exponential back-off retry policy.

Further reading

You can find more information about Event Grid by going to the following links:

- *What is Azure Event Grid?*: `https://docs.microsoft.com/en-us/azure/event-grid/overview`
- *Event Grid message delivery and retry*: `https://docs.microsoft.com/en-us/azure/event-grid/delivery-and-retry`
- *Event handlers in Azure Event Grid*: `https://docs.microsoft.com/en-us/azure/event-grid/event-handlers`
- *GitHub specifications*: `https://github.com/Azure/azure-rest-api-specs/tree/master/specification/eventgrid`
- *An overview of Azure Event Grid*: `https://www.youtube.com/watch?v=p8ia7J4Y7tI`

Section 4: Real-World Serverless Use Cases

This section shows some real-world serverless use cases and best practices.

It comprises the following chapter:

- Chapter 12, *Best Practices and Use Cases for Azure Serverless Computing*

12
Best Practices and Use Cases for Azure Serverless Computing

In the previous chapters, you learned how to create, implement, and deploy Azure functions, durable functions, logic apps, containers, API Management, and more.

This chapter is different because it will not introduce new technologies, but we will explore some best practices and use cases for Azure serverless computing, such as the following:

- Choosing between consumption plans and traditional ones for Azure Functions and API Management
- Azure Functions best practices for scalability and performance
- Integrating different external SaaS services
- Integrating **Internet of Things (IoT)** devices and processing their data
- Backend for single-page web apps or mobile apps

Azure serverless best practices

In this section, we'll discuss some Azure serverless best practices:

- Choosing between consumption plans (serverless) and traditional ones (**platform-as-a-service (PaaS)**-based)
- Scalability and performance best practices for Azure Functions

Choosing the right plan can lead to significant savings, but different plans also have different features: if you need some of the advanced features, you have to choose the right plan.

If your Azure functions are not optimized, you can spend more money than you need to, both on the consumption plan and traditional ones.

Choosing between consumption plans and traditional ones

Azure Functions and Azure API Management are two examples of Azure services that can be run in a pure serverless way (using the consumption plan) or in a traditional PaaS way (using traditional plans).

With consumption plans, you don't pay for dedicated or provisioned resources, but you use resources from a pool managed by Azure, and you only pay for the number of times you use the resources, or for other metrics (for example, in Azure Functions, you also pay for the memory allocated by every function app over time). If you don't use a resource, you won't pay anything.

With traditional plans, you have dedicated resources (for example, virtual machines) that run your workloads, and you pay even when you're not using those resources.

Other Azure services are now starting to offer consumption plans that are serverless—for example, Azure SQL Database has a serverless compute tier in preview (for more information, go to `https://docs.microsoft.com/en-us/azure/sql-database/sql-database-serverless`).

The ability to choose between serverless and traditional PaaS plans is crucial in many scenarios because it allows us to design a solution using serverless services and principles, but run them in a traditional way if needed, without changing the code (in most cases).

Serverless scenarios

Serverless plans are normally chosen in the following scenarios:

- You have intermittent and unpredictable usage patterns, with a lot of periods of inactivity.
- You don't know the usage patterns in advance.
- You don't know whether your solution will need to scale really quickly or if nobody will use it.
- You don't know the pricing model of your solution yet.

Serverless plans are useful in these scenarios because you're not forced to allocate resources in advance. You shouldn't monitor your resources to find out whether they need to be scaled up or down.

If you don't yet know the pricing model of your solution, with a serverless plan, you will know how much it will cost for a *single transaction*, and you can start with a *preview pricing* model that allows you to cover your costs, and then you can move to the final pricing plan without losing money on dedicated resources that, perhaps, nobody will use.

Traditional PaaS scenarios

Traditional plans are normally chosen in the following scenarios:

- Regular and predictable usage patterns, with higher utilization over time
- Solutions that are consolidated and that have a consistent pricing model
- Solutions that require features that aren't available with Consumption plans (see the next section)

Azure Functions – differences between consumption plans and app service plans

With a consumption plan, you don't have a dedicated set of resources, but your Azure functions are hosted on a pool of resources based on the number of incoming events.

Here are the main things to consider when choosing a consumption plan:

- You pay only when your functions are running and you pay based on the execution time, memory used, and the number of executions. After a certain period of inactivity, your function times out and will be removed, and you stop paying for the execution time and memory used.
- Functions scale out automatically; you don't have to configure anything.
- Function apps in the same region can share the same consumption plan.
- Since you don't have a dedicated resource, some advanced features, such as Visual Studio Live Debugging and VNet connectivity, are not available when using a consumption plan.

With the app service plan (dedicated plan), you have a fixed set of resources (virtual machines) allocated to run your Azure functions.

Here are the main things to consider when choosing an app service plan:

- You pay for the virtual machines that are included in your app service plan, regarding the usage.
- You can scale your app service plan up and down, based on time and other metrics, and you'll pay accordingly. Scaling occurs every five minutes with an app service plan.
- You can share the same app service plan for Azure Functions and other web apps. If you already have other web apps in your subscription, with spare capacity, you can use that capacity to run your Azure functions (if it's enough).
- Since you have dedicated resources, you can use advanced features, such as Visual Studio Live Debugging and VNet connectivity.
- Since you have dedicated resources, you must keep your Azure functions alive and never time out, by choosing the **Always on** setting .

 If you're using an HTTP triggered function, please remember that there is a timeout of 230 seconds to respond to a request. This timeout is set by Azure Load Balancer. You should consider using Durable Functions if you need more time.

Azure Functions – premium plan

The Azure Functions premium plan was created to overcome the limits of the consumption plan and app service plan.

With the Azure Functions premium plan, you pay per core seconds, execution time, and memory used across various instances. Premium plans have reserved instances that are *warmed* before use to avoid cold starts, and you will also pay for these.

Here are the main features of the premium plan:

- VNet connectivity and Visual Studio Live Debugging
- Unlimited execution duration
- Faster scale up and scale down than the app service plan
- No cold start time

 Since plan features and limitations change over time, it's better to refer to the official documentation to see the actual values and current differences between various plans. This documentation can be found at `https:// docs.microsoft.com/en-us/azure/azure-functions/functions-scale.`

API Management – difference between consumption plans and traditional plans

API Management was created with developer, basic, standard, and premium plans. Every plan had a fixed monthly price (depending on how many hours the service was active), that users should pay regardless of whether the service was used or not.

Different plans had different features—for example, the developer plan was not supported in production, the basic plan had no Azure Active Directory integration, and the standard plan had no VNet support and was not intended to be used in multi-region deployments.

Every plan had its maximum throughput per unit, with a maximum number of units that depended on the plan, and every plan also had a fixed amount of space to be used for caching.

A consumption plan was later introduced because, in many small projects, using API Management wasn't cost effective. The consumption plan has a fee for every 1 million calls (with 1 million free calls per Azure subscription), so it can also be used for small projects because you only pay for the number of calls needed.

The API Management consumption plan doesn't include caching (you need to configure an external Redis cache for that), and doesn't have a maximum throughput because it can automatically scale.

More information on different plans for API Management and their associated costs can be found at `https://azure.microsoft.com/en-us/pricing/details/api-management/`.

Azure Functions best practices for scalability and performance

Here are some best practices for better scalability and performance of Azure Functions:

- Reuse connections to external resources—for example, by using a static HTTPClient instead of creating one for every request. Resources can be exhausted very quickly if they are not reused.
- Don't deploy unused code in production: since Azure functions in the consumption plans are also billed based on memory usage, if you deploy code or assets that are not needed, you end up paying more money.

- Use durable functions or logic apps to handle long-running operations and cross-function communication instead of traditional functions.
- Functions should be stateless and idempotent because it's not guaranteed that they're called exactly in the same order or at the same time.

Some Azure serverless use cases

In the next sections, we'll see some of the most common use cases for serverless computing. Serverless computing is not restricted to these scenarios, and every day a new scenario is created that needs these powerful technologies.

IoT and Edge devices

IoT devices can be used to gather and process data from various sources and use directly in the field. One important use case can be using IoT to feed data into Stream Analytics, which can work with it. Stream Analytics can call Azure Functions when it needs to perform custom processing of the data using algorithms that are not included in the product.

Another use case could be using an Azure function running inside a container deployed on an Edge device to process data before transmitting it to the cloud, to filter out data that is not important (or not in scope) to reduce the number of calls and bandwidth usage. The same Azure function can then run in the cloud to check the data using the same code.

Backend for single-page web apps or mobile apps

Single-page web apps or mobile apps often need to call server-side APIs to store data, process it, call external services, and more.

Azure functions are the perfect companion since they can scale up and down very quickly depending on application usage patterns, which can be difficult to predict, especially for web and mobile apps.

Integrate different SaaS services

You can use Azure Functions or Azure Logic Apps to integrate different SaaS services—for example, you can read a file stored in OneDrive, analyze it, and create an Excel sheet with data and charts extracted from the file. Logic Apps offers hundreds of connectors already working to integrate with many SaaS apps. For Azure Functions, you need to connect using the appropriate SDKs.

To connect with many Microsoft SaaS services, you can use Microsoft Graph, a unified endpoint to query and work with Azure Active Directory, OneDrive, Excel, SharePoint, Outlook, Teams, and so on. You can connect with Microsoft Graph from Azure Functions using the bindings found at `https://docs.microsoft.com/en-us/azure/azure-functions/functions-bindings-microsoft-graph`.

Backend for Amazon Alexa skills

Amazon Alexa is the virtual assistant that powers Amazon Echo, Amazon Fire TV, and other devices.

Alexa can be extended with custom skills that can provide features to query custom data, activate or deactivate components, and more. Alexa skills can be built in many languages and using many technologies, but if you're proficient with .NET and Azure Functions, you can use those. More information can be found at `https://blogs.msdn.microsoft.com/appconsult/2018/11/02/build-your-first-alexa-skill-with-alexa-net-and-azure-functions-the-basics/`.

Summary

In this chapter, you've seen how to choose the best plan for serverless services that could also be used as PaaS services. You now know about Azure Functions and its best practices. You also saw which use cases are better suited to be implemented with a serverless approach, including IoT, backend apps (mobile, single-page web apps, or Alexa skills), and integrating different SaaS services.

Since this is the last chapter of the book, we hope that you've enjoyed reading it and found it useful. Happy coding in the serverless world!

Questions

1. When should you choose a premium plan or an app service plan with Azure Functions?
    - When you need VNet connectivity
    - When your usage pattern is predictable and always in use
    - When you need longer function timeouts
    - All of the above

2. What should you use when you need to implement a long-running serverless task?
    - Azure Functions
    - Durable Functions
    - Logic Apps
    - None of the above

3. Can Azure functions run both in the cloud and on Edge devices?
    - Only if they are written in C#
    - Only if they run inside a container
    - Only when using Durable Functions
    - Never

Further reading

You can find other information about best practices and use cases at the following links:

- *Optimize the performance and reliability of Azure Functions*: https://docs.microsoft.com/en-us/azure/azure-functions/functions-best-practices
- *Estimating Consumption plan costs*: https://docs.microsoft.com/en-us/azure/azure-functions/functions-consumption-costs
- *Azure Functions Premium Plan (preview)*: https://docs.microsoft.com/en-us/azure/azure-functions/functions-premium-plan
- *Tutorial: Deploy Azure functions as IoT Edge modules*: https://docs.microsoft.com/en-us/azure/iot-edge/tutorial-deploy-function
- *Microsoft Graph Home*: https://developer.microsoft.com/en-us/graph/

Assessments

Chapter 1, Developing and Running Azure Functions

1. C#, JavaScript, Java
2. Visual Studio, Azure Function Core Tool
3. Yes, only in V1.x
4. Using the Cloud Explorer extension on Visual Studio and the remote debugger.

Chapter 2, Customizing Your Azure Functions

1. They must always have only one trigger.
2. As many bindings as you want.
3. Manages custom events and executes Azure Functions when they occur.
4. You can use the `AddExtension` method of the `IWebJobsBuilder` interface in the configuration phase of the startup phase.

Chapter 3, Programming Languages Supported in Azure Functions

1. Host, Language worker
2. C#, PowerShell, Python
3. gRPC

Chapter 4, Deploying and Configuring Your Azure Functions

1. A JSON file
2. An Azure storage, A function app
3. `dependsOn`
4. Add the right line in the `.gitignore` file.
5. Yes, but the function app needs to have the right permission.

Chapter 5, Leverage the Power of DevOps with Azure Functions

1. Azure Pipelines, Azure Repos
2. YAML pipeline
3. Pull Request Validation, Scheduled
4. At least one

Chapter 6, Testing and Monitoring

1. The bugs found during the unit test are less expensive.

   It increases your confidence when changing or maintaining code.

2. You can create a class that implements the `IWebJobsStartup` interface and set it as the `WebJobsStartup` class.

   You can define a class derived from the `FunctionsStartup` class and set it as a startup class using the `FunctionsStartupAttribute` attribute.

3. Warning

Chapter 7, Serverless and Containers

1. .NET Core, Node.js, Python
2. App Service plan, AKS, ACI, Docker on a VM

Chapter 8, Orchestration as Code – Durable Functions

1. Orchestrator, Client, Activity
2. JSON-serializable.
3. A storage table containing all the events that occur to Durable Functions instances
4. A logical container in a table storage account that contains the tables used by the Durable Task Framework

Chapter 9, Orchestration as Design – Logic App

1. A JSON file that completely describes a Logic App
2. Only one

Chapter 10, Empower Your Serverless API with API Management

1. API Gateway, Administrative portal, Developer portal
2. A product contains a set of APIs, a description, and terms of use, and can be published to be used by the developer
3. To all APIs in your API Management instance.

   To an API

Chapter 11, High Scale Serverless Event Processing with Event Grid

1. Azure event schema, CloudEvents schema
2. Exponential back-off retry policy.

Chapter 12, Best Practices and Use Cases for Azure Serverless Computing

1. All of the above
2. Durable Functions, Logic Apps
3. Only if they run inside a container

Another Book You May Enjoy

If you enjoyed this book, you may be interested in another book by Packt:

Azure Serverless Computing Cookbook - Second Edition
Praveen Kumar Sreeram

ISBN: 978-1-78961-526-5

- Integrate Azure Functions with other Azure services
- Understand cloud application development using Azure Functions
- Employ durable functions for developing reliable and durable serverless applications
- Use SendGrid and Twilio services
- Explore code reusability and refactoring in Azure Functions
- Configure serverless applications in a production environment

Leave a review - let other readers know what you think

Please share your thoughts on this book with others by leaving a review on the site that you bought it from. If you purchased the book from Amazon, please leave us an honest review on this book's Amazon page. This is vital so that other potential readers can see and use your unbiased opinion to make purchasing decisions, we can understand what our customers think about our products, and our authors can see your feedback on the title that they have worked with Packt to create. It will only take a few minutes of your time, but is valuable to other potential customers, our authors, and Packt. Thank you!

Index

B

BindAsync method 63
binding pipeline
  classes 67, 68
Blob storage
  reference link 309
build pipeline
  creating 149, 150, 151, 152, 153, 154
  History tab 159
  Options tab 157, 158
  Tasks tab 160, 161, 162, 163, 164, 165, 166,
    167, 168, 169, 170, 171, 172, 173, 174, 175,
    176
  Triggers tab 156
  Variables tab 154
  YAML definition 178, 180, 181
  YAML definition, using 177, 179

C

caching policy
  cache lookup 296
  cache store 296
client functions 234, 235
CloudEvent
  reference link 308
CloudEvents open specification
  reference link 309
cmdlets, Az.Accounts module
  reference link 118
Command-Line Interface (CLI) 15
connectors, types
  enterprise 260
  standard 260
connectors
  about 260
  reference link 260
container registry
  reference link 310
continuous deployment (CD)
  about 141, 187
  reference link 221
continuous integration (CI) 141, 187
custom binding
  creating 67, 68, 71, 73, 74

custom Docker image
  creating 211, 212, 214
  function app, creating 216, 217
  publishing, to ACR 215, 216
  publishing, to Docker Hub 215
  updating 218
custom trigger
  creating 54, 55, 56, 57, 62, 64, 65

D

dependencies, Azure Function signature
  bindings 193
  logger 193
  trigger 193
dependency injection
  in Azure Functions 195, 196, 197
deployment slots
  using 121, 122
destination 307
developer portal 281, 282, 283, 285, 286
Docker Desktop WSL 2
  reference link 211
Docker Hub
  custom Docker image, publishing 215
Docker ID
  reference link 215
dotnet command
  reference link 162
Durable Functions, scenarios
  async HTTP API 231
  chain 230
  fan out/fan in 231
  human interaction 232
  monitor 232
  stateful entity 232
Durable Functions
  about 230, 233
  execution state 240, 241
  version, managing 243, 245
Durable Task Framework
  reference link 233
DurableOrchestrationClient, methods
  CreateCheckStatusResponse 236
  StartNewAsync 235
DurableOrchestrationClient

Triggers tab 156
triggers, configuring
    build completion 157
    continuous integration 156
    pull request validation 157
    scheduled 157

U

unit tests, implementation
    benefits 192
unit tests
    disadvantages 192

V

Variables tab 154
version control, Azure DevOps
    Git 143
    Team Foundation Version Control (TFVC) 143
versioning 263, 264, 265
Visual Studio Code
    about 27, 28, 29, 30, 31, 32
    reference link 28
    used, for debugging Azure Function 46, 47, 48

Visual Studio debugger
    used, for debugging Azure Function 43, 44, 45, 46
Visual Studio
    Azure Functions, developing with 23, 24, 25, 26

W

Web Services Description Language (WSDL) 32
Workflow Definition Language
    about 261
    reference link 261

X

xUnit.net
    URL 194

Y

YAML definition
    using 177, 178, 179, 180, 181
YAML, in Azure DevOps
    reference link 181
YAML
    URL 177

Made in United States
Troutdale, OR
10/20/2023

13890583R00201